China Income Distribution Research

China has experienced radical societal change since the initiation of the reform and openness programme in 1978. These changes have brought about significant income discrepancy between regions, social classes and generations; rendering the fair distribution of income an ever more important socio-economic question.

This book is a collection of eleven papers on the income distribution problem in Chinese society from 1978 to the early 21st century authored by Zhao Renwei, the former director of the Institute of Economics of the Chinese Academy of Social Sciences. The author examines the imbalance in income distribution in Chinese society from a socio-economic perspective and uses a myriad of examples to support his arguments while drawing conclusions as to ways forward for policy makers.

The book is an essential reference for students and scholars interested in social and economic reform in Chinese society. It will appeal additionally to policy makers concerned with the question of income distribution.

Zhao Renwei is a member of the Chinese Academy of Social Sciences (CASS), president of the Cairncross Economic Research Foundation, former director of the Institute of Economics CASS and former chief editor of the *Economic Research Journal*. He has been a visiting scholar at St. Antony's College of Oxford University, Columbia University, University of California, Riverside (UCR), University of Duisburg and All Souls College, Oxford, since the 1980s. He has won the 1st, 2nd and 6th Sun Yefang Fiscal Science Award.

China Perspectives

The *China Perspectives* series focuses on translating and publishing works by leading Chinese scholars, writing about both global topics and China-related themes. It covers Humanities & Social Sciences, Education, Media and Psychology, as well as many interdisciplinary themes.

This is the first time any of these books have been published in English for international readers. The series aims to put forward a Chinese perspective, give insights into cutting-edge academic thinking in China, and inspire researchers globally.

Titles in sociology currently include

**Living Conditions and Targeted Aiding Mechanisms
of the Urban Underclass in China**
Zhu Li, Mao Feifei

The Way to a Great Country
A Macroscopic View on Chinese Population in the 21st Century
Tian Xueyuan

Social Structure and Social Stratification in Contemporary China
Lu Xueyi

Social Construction and Social Development in Contemporary China
Lu Xueyi

Economic Transition and People's Livelihood
China Income Distribution Research
Zhao Renwei

Economic Transition and People's Livelihood
China Economic Transition Research
Zhao Renwei

For more information, please visit www.routledge.com/series/CPH

China Income Distribution Research

Zhao Renwei

This book is published with financial support from the Chinese Fund for the Humanities and Social Sciences.

First published in English 2020
by Routledge
2 Park Square, Milton Park, Abingdon, Oxon OX14 4RN

and by Routledge
52 Vanderbilt Avenue, New York, NY 10017

Routledge is an imprint of the Taylor & Francis Group, an informa business

© 2020 Zhao Renwei
Translated by Zhang Xiaotong

The right of Zhao Renwei to be identified as author of this work has been asserted by him in accordance with sections 77 and 78 of the Copyright, Designs and Patents Act 1988.

All rights reserved. No part of this book may be reprinted or reproduced or utilised in any form or by any electronic, mechanical, or other means, now known or hereafter invented, including photocopying and recording, or in any information storage or retrieval system, without permission in writing from the publishers.

Trademark notice: Product or corporate names may be trademarks or registered trademarks, and are used only for identification and explanation without intent to infringe.

English Version by permission of China Social Sciences Press.

British Library Cataloguing-in-Publication Data
A catalogue record for this book is available from the British Library

Library of Congress Cataloging-in-Publication Data
A catalog record for this book has been requested

ISBN: 978-0-367-41584-6 (hbk)
ISBN: 978-0-367-81535-6 (ebk)

Typeset in Times New Roman
by Apex CoVantage, LLC

Contents

List of figures	vii
List of tables	viii
Author's preface and personal statement	xi

1 Some trends of change of personal income distribution
of laborers   1

2 Two contrasting phenomena in current income distribution   17

3 Some special phenomena of income distribution in
China's transformation period   24

4 Residents' income distribution in China: in cities, rural
areas and regions   41

5 Widening of Chinese residents' income gap and cause   67

6 Context of the income gap among Chinese residents   90

7 Building the taxation concept of "no progress means
retrogression"   99

8 Study of property distribution of Chinese residents   104

9 Income distribution, property distribution and gradual
reform – in commemoration of the 20th anniversary
of the publication *Comparative Economic & Social
Systems*   133

vi *Contents*

10 Significance of attaching importance to residents'
property and their income   141

11 Focusing on vertical imbalance in income distribution   146

Index   154

Figures

1.1	The Absoluteness and Relativity of Distribution According to Work and their Relationship	2
1.2	The Curve of a Laborer's Labor Contributions in his/her Lifetime	9
1.3	The Impact of Salary Freezing on Employees of Different Ages	10
3.1	Comparison of Income of Urban and Rural Residents	31
3.2	Distribution of Urban and Rural Households by Income Level	34
5.1	Gini Coefficients of Income of Rural and Urban Residents from 1978 to 1995	72
5.2	Ratio of Income of Urban and Rural Residents from 1978 to 1995	73
5.3	Distribution of Urban and Rural Residents by Income Level	74
8.1	Changes of Income Distribution and Property Distribution in Rural Areas (1988, 1995 and 2002)	109
8.2	Distribution of Urban and Rural Residents by Income Level and Property Level	123

Tables

1.1	Effects of Distribution Methods for Families in Socialist Economy	14
3.1	Monetary Income Level Per Capita Per Year of Staff Members in State Sector and Private Sector Based on Ten Equant Groups in Cities in 1988 (Yuan)	26
3.2	Income Gap in the Planned System and Income Gap in the Unplanned System in 1988	27
3.3	Salary Income Ratio of Senior and Junior Personnel before and after Salary Reform	27
3.4	Salary Income Comparison between Self-Employed Entrepreneurs and Employees under Ownership by the Whole People in 1988	28
3.5	Comparison of Annual Per Capital Income of Urban and Rural Households	29
3.6	International Comparison of Income Inequality between Rural Areas and Cities	30
3.7	Respective Proportion of Urban and Rural Households in Ten Equant Groups of National Households	33
3.8	Salary Income and Extra-Salary Income of Urban Employees (1)	36
3.9	Salary Income and Extra-Salary Income of Urban Employees (2)	36
3.10	Income in Kind of Urban Residents in Zhejiang Province in 1988	37
3.11	Proportion of Housing Rent Expenditure Per Capita Per Year in Gross Living Expenses Per Capita Per Year for Urban Residents	38
4.1	Income Gap of Urban Residents and Its Sources	44
4.2	Income Distribution Effects of Subsidies	48
4.3	Distribution of Gross Income and Subitem Income of Rural Residents	52
4.4	Property Distribution of Rural Resident Households (1988)	56
4.5	Percentage of Urban and Rural Resident Households in Ten Equant Groups of National Resident Households	59
5.1	Various Kinds of Estimation of Degree of Income Inequality before the Reform (Gini Coefficient)	68
5.2	Degree of Income Distribution Inequality in Some Asian Countries	68
5.3	International Comparison of Income Inequality between Rural Residents and Urban Residents	69

Tables ix

5.4	Gini Coefficients of Income of Rural and Urban Residents from 1978 to 1995	71
5.5	Gini Coefficients in 1988 and 1995	72
5.6	Income of Urban and Rural Residents and Gap from 1978 to 1995	73
5.7	Percentage of Urban and Rural Residents in Ten Equant Groups by Income	74
5.8	Per Capita Income in Three Major Regions in Rural Areas and Its Changes (in 1988 and 1995, Based on the Prices in 1988)	75
5.9	Rural Per Capita Income in Jiangsu and Gansu and Its Changes (in 1988 and 1995, Based on the Prices in 1988)	76
5.10	Per Capita Income in Coastal Areas and Mainland China Cities and Its Changes (in 1988 and 1995, Based on the Prices in 1988)	77
5.11	Urban Per Capita Income in Jiangsu and Yunnan and Its Changes (in 1988 and 1995, Based on the Prices in 1988)	77
5.12	Property Income, Subsidy and Rental Valuation of Owner-Occupied Housing of Urban Residents	78
5.13	Financial Assets of Urban Residents and Their Changes	79
5.14	Distribution of Financial Assets of Urban Residents (in Five Equant Groups, June 30, 1996)	79
5.15	Distribution of Salary Income Per Capita in Cities and Ratio Change (Yuan) in 1988 and 1995	80
5.16	Impact of Growth, Reform and Policy on Income Distribution	82
5.17	Gini Coefficients of Salary Income of Staff Members in State-Owned Sectors and Non-State-Owned Sectors in Cities	82
5.18	Gini Coefficients of Agricultural Income and Non-Agricultural Income in Rural Areas	83
8.1	Per Capita Property Level and Composition in Rural Areas in 2002	105
8.2	Proportion of Property Held by Each of Ten Equant Groups of Rural Population in 2002	107
8.3	Income Distribution and Property Distribution in Chinese Rural Areas (1988, 1995 and 2002)	108
8.4	Inequality of Per Capita Property Distribution in Rural Areas in 2002	109
8.5	Level and Composition of Per Capita Property in Cities and Towns in 2002	111
8.6	Proportion of Property Held by Each of Ten Equant Groups of Urban Population in 2002	112
8.7	Differences between Market Prices of Commodity Houses and Selling Prices of State-Owned Houses in 1995	114
8.8	Inequality of Per Capita Property Distribution in Cities and Towns in 2002	115
8.9	Composition and Distribution of Per Capita Financial Assets (and Debts) in Cities and Towns in 2002	117
8.10	Level and Composition of National Per Capita Property in 2002	119

x *Tables*

8.11	Proportion of Property Held by Each of Ten Equant Groups of National Population in 2002	120
8.12	Inequality of Per Capita Property Distribution Nationwide in 2002	121
8.13	Percentage of Urban and Rural Residents in Ten Equant Groups by Income and Property	122

Author's preface and personal statement

I was born in an ordinary family of intellectuals in Chengdong District, Jinhua County, Zhejiang Province, on March 23, 1933. My father was a geography teacher of Jinhua Middle School (the present Jinhua No.1 Middle School). My childhood coincided with the War of Resistance against Japanese Aggression, so I could only flee from calamity with my parents while attending school. During my primary school, I spent more time dropping out of school than at school. I did not have the opportunity to carry out systematic learning.

After the end of the war, I was admitted to Junior High of Jinhua Middle School in 1946. I received systematic education during this period. After graduating from Jinhua Middle School in 1953, I was admitted to the Department of Economics of Peking University through the college entrance examination. Since then, I have begun my lifelong learning and studying of economics.

My study at university coincided with the First Five-Year Plan (1953–1957) period. During this stage, except for the Anti-Rightist Movement just before my graduation, there were relatively fewer political movements, so the education I received in my university years was systematic. However, under the "leaning to one side" policy in those years, the university education copied the model of the USSR. Especially in the field of social science, it was completely inculcated rather than heuristic. In a number of years, students were busy with taking notes in class while memorizing notes before exams. The professors' situation was rather unusual: after the adjustment of departments and colleges between universities in 1952, the professors of economics of many prestigious universities (including Tsinghua University, Peking University and Yanjing University) were gathered in Peking University, such as Ma Yinchu, Chen Daisun, Chen Zhenhan, Zhao Naituan, Zhou Binglin, Fan Hong, Xu Yunan, Yan Rengeng and others. Many of these professors were PhD graduates from Harvard, Cambridge, Columbia and other universities, but they could only teach in accordance with Soviet textbooks and syllabuses drawn up by Soviet experts. However, then again, the fine tradition of Peking University since the May Fourth Movement, especially the spirit of inclusiveness advocated when president Cai Yuanpei was in charge as well as the independent thinking spirit of the then president Ma Yinchu in his research of economics and demography, still had an invisible and profound influence on my philosophy of learning. In general, the education I

xii *Author's preface and personal statement*

received during my years at Peking University was doctrinal on the one hand and freethinking on the other hand.

After graduating from university in 1957, I was assigned to the Economic Research Institute of the Chinese Academy of Sciences. After the establishment of the Chinese Academy of Social Sciences in 1977, the Economic Research Institute became affiliated with the Chinese Academy of Social Sciences. I worked for a lifetime at the Economic Research Institute until retirement.

My life at the Economic Research Institute could be divided into the following stages.

First was the foundation-laying stage for the academic research in between political movements. From my first year at the Institute to the outbreak of the "Cultural Revolution", there were a lot of political movements, but I still managed to engage in the study and research on economics. Especially in the Great Chinese Famine (1959–1961), I actively participated in the discussion of some major economic issues (such as the issue of commodity production and law of value, the issue of economic accounting and economic effect and the issue of reproduction) presided over by Xue Muqiao, Sun Yefang and Yu Guangyuan. I often did some recording and data collation work, and a small amount of research as well. In general, the work of this stage could only be regarded as laying foundations.

Second was the stage of loss of the decade of the "Cultural Revolution" and the further foundation-laying stage during the intervals of the "Cultural Revolution". The ten-year "Cultural Revolution" was time lost. However, I did not want to give up my academic research and did some research during the intervals of the movement. For example, from 1972 to 1974, under the guidance of Gu Zhun, I studied economics and English. Between 1975 and 1976, I taught myself economics and English by using the collection of books of the library of the Economic Research Institute. This further laid the foundation for future research.

Third was the full-bloom stage of the first decade since the reform and opening-up. During this stage, I engaged in researches in many fields. First of all, I participated in the criticism of the economic theory of the "gang of four", which was followed by the exploration of the direction of economic reform in accordance with the guiding principle of the Third Plenary Session of the Eleventh Central Committee of the Chinese Communist Party, which included: studying the relationship between planning and market, introducing the economic theory by Eastern European reformists, studying the theory of economic reform under Professor Bruce of Oxford University at the recommendation of Sun Yefang, attending international conferences on China's economic reform (including the 1985 conference on the ship *Bashan*), studying comparative economics and participating in setting up China's Association for Comparative Economics, and so on. In this period my study focused on the transformation of the economic system.

Fourth was further study in the second decade since the reform and opening-up. After 1991, I no longer took any administrative work, so I had more time to engage in academic research. Moreover, toward the end of the last stage, I had launched a project – the Study of Chinese Residents' Income Distribution. Because this project needed to collect a large number of micro-data of urban and rural residents,

Author's preface and personal statement xiii

and it also needed to use some popular international economic theories and analysis methods, I spent a lot of time and energy on this project, organizing domestic young scholars and inviting foreign experts to engage in empirical researches. At the same time, I also went to many foreign universities as visiting scholars, communicating with foreign scholars, to promote the further development of this research project.

Fifth was moderate expansion and synthesis stage of the third decade since the reform and opening-up. In addition to continuing my study on the issue of income distribution, I further expanded my research into the field of property distribution and social security, and reviewed and summarized the issues on the economic reform and the transformation of the economic system in the past 30 years.

I was an assistant researcher in 1962, a deputy researcher in 1979, a researcher in 1985 and a doctoral tutor in 1990. I had been director of the Economic Research Institute, Chinese Academy of Social Sciences, editor of the magazine *Economic Research*; vice president of China's Research Association of Comparative Economics, and director of Beijing Kane Claus Economic Research Foundation. In August 2006, I was awarded honorary membership of the Chinese Academy of Social Sciences.

Since the 1980s, I have served as a visiting scholar at St. Antony's College of Oxford University, Colombia University and University of California of the United States, University of Duisburg of Germany, All Souls College of Oxford University of the UK, and Lingnan University of Hong Kong.

I think that my academic achievements over the years are reflected in my academic exploration. To sum up, my academic exploration can be divided into the following inter-related aspects.

I. Planning and market and the explorations for the related issues on the transformation of the economic system

In the late 1970s and 1980s, I mainly studied the relationship between planning and market in the transformation of the economic system and the comparison of economic system models, the choice of target models, the transition of the dual systems and so on. In 1979, Liu Guoguang and I coauthored and published the article "On the Relationship between Planning and Market in the Socialist Economy". The significance of this article was that it put forward the idea that the role of the market mechanism should be used in the allocation of material resources, financial resources and human resources. In other words, it advocated breaking up the dominance of the planned economy. This was to be achieved not only by adding a little market mechanism as a supplement on the outside or the edge of the planned economy, but by making the market mechanism an essential part of the planned economy. These research results, judged by the domestic standards at that time, were at the forefront. They played the role of promoting reform and exerted wide influence. Thanks to my study of this issue, in 1984, I won the first Sun Yefang Award for Papers of Economics. Of course, looking back now, I realize

xiv *Author's preface and personal statement*

that my study at that time had great limitations. At that time, advocating the role of the market mechanism carried some risks, so my research had not jumped out of the big frame of the planned economy fundamentally. Instead, it emphasized giving as much play as possible to the role of market mechanism within the framework of the planned economy. Since then, I have continued to explore along this direction, and logically, in the 1990s, a fundamental change to the market economy was achieved.

In the 20 years after that, I have paid close attention to the transformation of the economic system, mainly studying the difficult problems and challenges faced in the economic system transition. These issues can be divided roughly into the following aspects.

A. *Paying close attention to the materialization tendencies during the process of market-oriented reform*

I think that the dominant feature of the planned economy, in addition to the high concentration of decision-making, is the physical allocation of resources. Therefore, the market-oriented economic reform is bound to overcome the tendencies of bartering of resource allocation. However, China's market-oriented economic reform was often disrupted by the tendencies of bartering. I studied this issue with several young researchers and published the article "Tendencies of Bartering in the Process of Market-Oriented Reform" in *Economic Studies*, pointing out that the tendencies of bartering were a kind of inhibitory phenomenon during the marketization reform process. The article systematically analyzed the performance, the cause, the defects and the solution of the tendencies of bartering. The analysis of the tendencies of bartering was conducive not only to understanding the difficulties of market-oriented reform, but also to promoting the process of this reform.

B. *Summarizing and assessing the risk of rising costs brought about by the progressive approach of economic reform*

At the early stage of reform and opening-up, domestic and foreign economists had a lively discussion about whether China's economic reform should take a radical or a gradual way. In general, I favor the gradual approach, but I am always aware of the risk brought about by the friction of the dual system in the progressive reform. Given the complexity of China's economic situation, we could take only a gradual and two-track transitional approach, one that had achieved remarkable results both in price reform, where "the government first adjusted the price and then abandoned control over it", and in the ownership reform (the so-called "fighting the external war"), where the non-state economy was allowed to enter the sphere of the state-owned economy. These results showed that the original intention of gradual reform was to reduce the cost of reform; but the gradual approach of economic reform also has the risk of rising costs. The connotation of gradual reform is incremental reform. Specifically, it is that the increment or the new wealth enter the new system (the market track), while the stock or the original wealth remain in the old

Author's preface and personal statement   xv

system (the planning track). With the advancement of reform and development of the economy, the proportion of wealth remaining in the old system will continue to decline, and the proportion of wealth entering the new system will continue to rise, which will help the final replacement of the old system by the new one. However, in fact, many of China's new wealth had not entered the new system in accordance with the requirements of the incremental reform (for example, a large number of new cars to be used by civil servants in their official duties had entered the old system in the form of physical rationing), and the incremental entry into the old system was a manifestation of the rise in the reform cost.

C. Correctly leveraging the functions of the market and those of the government

I think that China's discussion of planning and market issues in the late 1970s and early 1980s had been further evolved into the issues of how to properly leverage the functions of the market and those of the government in the late 1990s and early 21st century. I stated clearly in the article of summing up the experience of China's three decades of economic reform that in the process of China's economic transformation, there appeared to be confusion between the market functions and the government functions, as well as the coexistence of inadequate marketization (the ones that should have been marketized were not marketized) and excessive marketization (the ones that should not have been marketized had been marketized).

I wrote,

in the field of personal products or private products, mainly in the field of food, clothing and other daily necessities, resources are allocated through the market mechanism, with individuals responsible for their distribution. In the field of public goods, mainly in the areas of national defense, environmental protection, basic public services and others, the resources are allocated by the government. The functions and responsibilities in these two areas are clearly differentiated. The problem lies in the field of quasi-public goods.

In the field of quasi-public goods, mainly including education, health care, housing for the low-income groups and others, the responsibilities should be taken respectively by the market and government, in other words, by individuals and the state. The difficulty in this area is how to distinguish between the functions of the market and those of the government. Because there is uncertainty in this field, it is easy for the government and individuals to shirk their responsibilities. In China's reform since the 1990s, we have seen the tendencies of shifting too many responsibilities to individuals and the market, which, we may as well call the tendencies of over marketization or over commercialization. Since the beginning of the 21st century, China has been making attempts to reverse this tendency. Of course, in the transition from a planned economy to a market economy, some sectors and areas (especially monopoly sectors and areas) still have the problem of insufficient marketization. How to

xvi   *Author's preface and personal statement*

solve the problem of the coexistence of insufficient and excessive marketization is still an important task for future reform.[1]

II.   Exploration in issues regarding income and property distribution

Income distribution is the field where my research work lasted the longest and which consumed most of my energy. The research in this field began in the middle and late 1980s and lasted for about two decades. The income distribution task group that I directed conducted two national investigations on the income of urban and rural residents in 1988 and 1995; at the beginning of the 21st century, Li Shi became the head of the task group after I retired, and I served as a consultant. In 2002 and 2007, two more national surveys were made. The research conducted on the basis of these surveys and the corresponding results had a wide impact both at home and abroad. The research and achievements I have made in the field of income distribution and in its extension – the distribution of wealth – can be summarized as the following.

A.   *The changes in research methods*

1.   *From bringing order out of chaos to theoretical analysis*

At the beginning of the reform and opening-up, the Chinese economic circles had a lively discussion on the issue of distribution according to work. The main topics of the discussion at that time were whether distribution according to work should be implemented, whether the distribution according to work was bourgeois right of law or proletarian right of law, whether the distribution according to work was the basis for the generation of bourgeois and so on. These discussions played a significant role in setting things right. I focused on the study of the transformation of the economic system, so I was not directly involved in the discussion, but I still paid close attention to it. In the study of the transformation of the economic system in the early 1980s, I gained from the literature of the reform of Eastern Europe some experience about the empirical analysis for the traditional system. So, I tried to apply this empirical approach to the study of income distribution. In the mid-1980s, I conducted empirical analysis of the different effects of basic double freezing of wages and prices in the traditional system on different generations of people, especially the negative effects on the young generation. In my article "A Number of Variation Trends in Personal Income Distribution of Laborers" in *Economic Research*, I pointed out, in the case of the long-term freezing of wages, it seems that everyone is equal before the freezing, but in fact inter-generational or vertical income distribution imbalance will be produced between the old, the middle-aged and the young generations. This analysis undoubtedly conducted a scientific summary of the freezing policy under the planned economy, and provided theoretical support for the necessity and direction of economic reform, which can be regarded as a further study on the basis of the previously mentioned practices of bringing

Author's preface and personal statement   xvii

order out of chaos. This exploration of the initial transition to empirical analysis was affirmed by my peers in the circle of economics, and hence in 1986 I won the second Sun Yefang Economic Science Paper Award. The *International Journal of Social Economics* in the UK translated and published this article in 1991.

2.   Development from theoretical analysis to empirical analysis

However, I soon discovered that this empirical study without data support had a lot of limitations. When some foreign economists criticized some empirical researches without data support in the literature on Eastern European reform as "non-empirical demonstration", I realized what they were talking about. Analysis with no data support can only be called theoretical analysis; analysis with data support, namely empirical evidence, can be called a real empirical analysis. There-fore, not until the end of the 1980s and early 1990s did I begin to use empirical evidence in the study of income distribution and to achieve a series of research results. For example, when analyzing the special phenomena of income distribu-tion in the transformation of the economic system, I pointed out that in the case of the coexistence of dual systems, there appeared in the field of income distribution a phenomenon that egalitarianism and large income gaps existed side by side. Under the prevailing conditions of China's economic transition and special policy back-ground, the income gap between urban and rural residents appeared to have been narrowed first and then widened; after the focus of the reform was turned to cities, the income gap among urban workers appeared to have been narrowed within the ranges of their wages but to have obviously widened outside the ranges of their wages. These data-supported research results had a great impact both at home and abroad. At the international level, the data provided by the research group under the charge of Li Shi and me even had a proper term: Chips (China Household Income Projects). Because of this, Li Shi and I won the sixth Sun Yefang Economic Science Paper Award in 1994.

B.   Analysis of the status of income distribution and its causes

Income Distribution: from prevalence of egalitarianism to large income gaps.

I argued that China before the reform was a society with a high degree of equal-ization (or a low degree of inequality). At the same time, there were some inequal-ity factors in income distribution. The status where there was inequality in equality, and where there was equality in inequality, explained the complexity of China's socio-economic situation. In general, prevalence of egalitarianism was still the starting point of China's income distribution reform.

After more than 30 years of reform, the general level of people's income had increased, but the income gap was growing wider and wider. I studied all aspects of the change in income gap, including overall income disparities, urban-rural income disparities, regional income disparities, income disparities in sectors (especially in monopolistic and competitive sectors), property income disparities and so on. In addition, I analyzed the changes in income distribution of various

xviii *Author's preface and personal statement*

stages since the reform and their main trends. I consider the first stage (from the late 1970s to the mid-1980s) to be a period dominated by egalitarianism. The second stage (from the middle and late 1980s to the early 1990s) was characterized by the coexistence of two phenomena: the egalitarianism within the planning system and the large income gap between the inside and the outside of the system. The period since the mid-1990s was the third stage, which was characterized by increasingly widening income gaps. According to the survey of the subject, by 1995 the country's Gini coefficient had reached 0.445. If we consider the abnormal widening of the income gap caused by the activities such as power-for-money deals, corruption, monopoly, rent-seeking and rent-making, rent-creating and others, the problem of income distribution was more serious. It had become a focus of social concern.

The reasons for the widening income gap:

In addition to analyzing the realities of the change in income disparities, I am unique in analyzing the reasons for the change in income disparity. At the international level, many economists have focused on the relationship between economic growth and income distribution. In China, the situation is much more complicated. China is not only in the transitional period from a planned economy to a market economy in respect of economic system, but it is also in the transitional period from the dual economy to the modern economy. In this context, the factors that affect the pattern of changes in income distribution are extremely complex. This complexity, on the one hand, increases the difficulty of the study; on the other hand, it provides more space and room for exploration. I divided the causes of the change in the income gap in China's economic transitional period into four categories and twenty or so factors, and analyzed how these factors affected the changes in income distribution. The four major categories refer to economic development (or economic growth), economic reform (or institutional change), economic policy and foreign economic relations. Analysis of the impact of these factors on income distribution is not only in line with China's actual situation, but also conducive to the depth of the study.

In analyzing the reasons for the change in the income gap, the relationship between the widening income gap and the economic reform is the most controversial issue and that has attracted the greatest attention. I think that in this analysis, there are two tendencies to prevent. One is to simply blame the economic reform itself for the widening of the income gap and the associated problems; the other is to simply regard the widening of the income gap as the price that we should pay to achieve economic reform. I believe that we should deal with the widening of the income gap from three different levels: the first level belongs to the incentives that are conducive to improving efficiency. This part is the reform results of overcoming egalitarianism, which should be affirmed. The second level is the price that economic reform must pay. For example, China's reform can take only a gradual approach of two-track transition, thus activities such as using the dual-track for "rent-seeking" and other undesirable practices are inevitable. To a certain extent, this can be called the price that the reform should pay. The third level is excessive prices that should be prevented and avoided.

Author's preface and personal statement   xix

I think that since we cannot simply look for reasons for the widening income gap in the market-oriented economic reform, we should turn our eyes to the institutions (and the policies associated with them). Therefore, the reasonable judgment can only be: deepening the reform, including economic reform and political reform, is the fundamental way to solve the problem of income distribution.

C.   Analysis of the distribution of wealth: from little personal wealth to rapid accumulation and significant differentiation of personal wealth

After entering the 21st century, I also discussed the issue of wealth distribution on the basis of the study of income distribution. I think that the study of wealth distribution in China is still in its infancy, but it is undoubtedly an important start. The importance of wealth distribution has begun to manifest as follows. First, at the beginning of reform and opening-up, Chinese residents had little personal wealth, but since the reform and opening-up, residents' wealth had experienced a period of rapid accumulation and significant differentiation. Second, China has established the goal of building a moderately prosperous and harmonious society. The achievement of this goal depends not only on the status of income distribution, but also on the distribution of wealth. Therefore, it is predictable that the issue of wealth distribution will become a new focus point for the public. Whether from the perspective of strategic decision-making or future-oriented study, we need to attach importance to the distribution of wealth. In terms of the general distinction between income and wealth, wealth is a stock at a point in time, and income is the flow per unit of time. There is an interaction between income and wealth: past flows certainly affect today's stock; and today's stock will inevitably affect future flows. With continuous expansion of the scale of wealth and the changes in the distribution pattern of wealth, the distribution of wealth not only has an important influence on the stability of the entire macro-economy, but also has important influence on the long-term change of income distribution in the future.

As for the distribution of wealth, the Gini coefficient of the total wealth distribution in China had reached 0.550 in 2002, which was higher than the Gini coefficient of the income distribution (0.454) in the same year. Among various assets, the Gini coefficient of housing was 0.6302, and that of the financial asset was 0.6291. In accordance with international standards, China's Gini coefficient of wealth distribution is not particularly high. However, if you consider the following two points, you will realize that we must pay particular attention to this issue. First, the accumulation of personal wealth in developed countries took place over several hundred years, and counted from the mid-1980s, China's accumulation of wealth has experienced only about 20 years. It can be said that this speed and momentum of China's personal wealth accumulation are extraordinary. Second, the Gini coefficient of China's income distribution has significantly exceeded that of the developed countries, and as mentioned earlier, today's differentiation of income distribution will inevitably affect the future differentiation of the distribution of

xx   *Author's preface and personal statement*

wealth, so it is predictable that for a considerable period of time in the future, further widening of the gap in wealth distribution will continue.

I think that the idea of "increasing the proportion of middle-income earners" proposed by the 16th National Congress of the Communist Party of China and the idea of "creating conditions for more people to have property income" put forward by the 17th National Congress of the Communist Party of China have important guiding significance. These ideas make specific the goal of building a moderately prosperous and harmonious society. In the language of economics, the growth of the middle class is the basis of social stability. I have argued in the relevant article that it is of great significance to pay attention to the inhabitants' wealth and their income. The significance can be summarized as follows: First, it embodies the idea of hoarding wealth in the people and reflects the spirit of building a moderately prosperous society in all respects as well. Second, in addition to labor income, residents can also have property income, which is conducive not only to improving the efficiency of the allocation of human, material and financial resources, but also to broadening the channels through which residents increase their income, reflecting the diversification of income sources for residents. Third, it points out the interaction between income and property. Fourth, too large a gap between property and its income should be prevented. In order to prevent such a gap between property and its income, I also proposed to study the issue about how to let the farmers obtain the rights and interests from the land (even if they have only the right to contracted management) and the issue about whether the property tax and inheritance tax should be levied.

III.   Thoughts from my academic pursuits and views about developing the science of economics

A.   *Thoughts from my academic pursuits*

In the 1980s, during my tenure as director of the Economic Research Institute, I had put forward the following views on the development of an excellent academic and working atmosphere.

First, create the atmosphere of inclusiveness and promote the spirit of diversification. An important condition for academic development is to have an environment and atmosphere of academic freedom. This is in line with Marxism. Marx himself wrote, "You admire the delightful variety, the inexhaustible riches of nature. You do not demand that the rose should smell like the violet, but must the greatest riches of all, the spirit, exist in only one variety?" This is in line with the CPC's policy of letting a hundred flowers bloom and a hundred schools of thought contend. The so-called "hundred" is to recognize the variety and diversity of the spiritual world. Adherence to such a spirit not only is not contradictory with the insistence of Marxism, but it is precisely in order to develop Marxism under the new conditions.

Second, is the atmosphere of unity and harmony. The unity of the Economic Research Institute is generally good, for there is an invisible cohesion. But in

Author's preface and personal statement xxi

some particular situations, interpersonal relationships seem tense, especially in the case of a certain mood. In fact, many problems, if not dealt impetuously but analyzed calmly and rationally, and making a dialogue about them in a harmonious atmosphere, will be easy to solve. Therefore, tolerance and dialogue should be promoted. Some comrades suggest that whether interpersonal relationships are loose and harmonious is the manifestation of whether we have the scholarly demeanor and is the expression of our own academic quality. This opinion is very pertinent, so the promotion of an atmosphere of unity and harmony should be taken as a task of improving academic quality and carrying forward scholarly demeanor.

Third is the spirit of equal and civilized competition. The atmosphere of unity and harmony does not exclude competition. Only the encouragement of competition can help form a mechanism where the diligent are rewarded and the lazy are punished, and can make the outstanding talents come to the fore. Of course, in the competition, the rules should be understood and complied with, just as we need to comply with the rules in a variety of games; in particular, we promote respect for the independent personality of others, because regardless of the level of ability, everyone is completely equal in personality. In other words, the competition we want is based on the recognition and respect for the independent personality of our competitors – this is the question of civilized competition.

Fourth is the spirit of preciseness, steadfastness and bench-warming. This atmosphere and spirit has always been a fine tradition of the Economic Research Institute. But we should note that in the era where eagerness for quick success, instant benefits and short-term behavior have become the scourge of the age, the fine tradition and style of study of the Institute have somewhat been damaged. The kind of behavior that pursues media hype, and the kind of self-touted behavior, are not in line with the scientific spirit, and are out of tune with the fine traditions of our institute. Of course, in an era of great change where stagnation is shifted to reform, and where isolation is changed into opening up, the generation of maladies, where people are indiscriminate in theory while anxious to achieve quick success and get instant benefits, can be said to have its complex social and historical causes. However, as an academic research institute, we must be keenly aware of this and correct and guide our people in a timely manner.

Our time needs academic masters. With regard to the generation of academic masters, in terms of individual efforts, ten years of studies in straitened circumstances only helps lay the foundation. Defeating others by a surprise move can only help one become a transient figure, and it is difficult to become an academic master with profound foundations.

Fifth is the spirit of exploration, innovation and pioneering. Scientific research itself is to explore, innovate and pioneer; otherwise, the life of science is over. Our institute has a spirit of pioneering in the climax of the reform. During the period when the reform encounters difficulties and the economy undergoes adjustment, we should still continue to maintain and carry forward this spirit. The adjustment is essential for better reform and development in future. In the

xxii *Author's preface and personal statement*

climax of the reform, we should prevent ourselves from getting hot-headed; and during the period of adjustment, we should prevent ourselves from getting dejected. We should overcome the short-term behavior during the climax of the reform and draw lessons from it, and prevent the short-term behavior during the adjustment period. The Economic Research Institute must not lose the banner of the reform.

B. Views about developing the science of economics

In the 1990s, I offered the following suggestions on how to develop the science of economics.

First, we must correctly handle the relationship between hot economic spots and cold ones. We have to have the bench-warming spirit, so that we can express our insights on hot issues. Moreover, the expert on one hot issue is not necessarily the expert on another. In this sense, where there is no cold spot, there is no hot one.

Second, we must have a scientific evaluation mechanism for research results. This is one of the important conditions to improving the level of economics. As for the evaluation of the results of an economic research, we should mainly see whether it has made analysis and anatomy of the laws of economic operation, instead of whether it has put forth some ideas or wordings.

Third, the study of economics should combine national character and internationalization. Academic learning has no borders. International exchanges, or internationalization in the academic field, are, in fact, beneficial for all countries and peoples; on the contrary, self-seclusion can only result in the restriction of our freedom of action. International exchanges of academic learning, including international exchanges in the field of economics, are always bidirectional and reciprocal. Since the reform and opening-up, we have learned and absorbed a lot more from abroad than we did in the past, and foreign countries have also learned and absorbed some useful things from China. In international exchanges, we can not only promote the internationalization and modernization of our economic research, but can also make greater international contributions with our own national characteristics to promote China's economic research so that it will progress along with the rest of the world.

Fourth, we should distinguish the functions between the academic departments and the government departments. The functions of the academic research department are different from those of the government administrative department, which should be common sense. When Sun Yefang served as director of the Economic Research Institute, he never considered himself to be a chief executive, and he completely trivialized the administrative rank of the Institute. Many foreign countries do not include the director of a research institute or the president of a university in the bureaucratic series. The function of the enterprise is different from that of the government. Therefore, it has long been proposed that the separation of government and enterprises be realized. Since the function of the academic department is different from that of the government department,

Author's preface and personal statement xxiii

it seems logical to propose the separation of government and academic learning. The distinction between the two different functions is conducive to overcoming the administrative tendency of academic research institutions, which in turn will prevent the bureaucratic tendencies of academic leaders, which is further beneficial to the making of achievements and bringing forth talents in the research institutions.

For more than 30 years since the launching of reform and opening-up, I have gradually formed such a view: the economy is in transition, economics is in transition, and economists are also in transition. Here, the economic transition refers to the transformation of the economic system and economic development. The transition of economics refers to the transformation of the study of economic problems from a closed and stagnant state to the open and developing direction where we strive to absorb advanced results of human civilization. The transition of economists refers to the practice that economic research workers adapt themselves to the first two transitions, so that their research work can keep up with the pace of the times.

After years of practice, I realize that a more in-depth study of an area of economic problems often requires researchers to have higher and more comprehensive attainments. These attainments include: having high theoretical attainment, that is, being able to master the theoretical results created by human civilization in the field so far; mastering more advanced analytic methods and tools, especially econometric tools; mastering the data related to research topics, as it is best to have firsthand data or information; having the real sense about the subject of the study, it is best to obtain and enhance this sense through field surveys, and the real sense and data should be combined in the analysis; having the ability to express oneself clearly, including the rationality of framework analysis, the logic of narration and reasoning, and the accuracy and clarity of wording (except for the expressive ability of Chinese, it is better to have presentation ability of one or more foreign languages); being able to conduct longitudinal (time) and horizontal (spatial) comparison under the theme. It seems difficult for one researcher to possess all these attainments. Therefore, many of today's research topics often require the collaborative efforts of a team of researchers. This kind of cooperative research should, in principle, take the form of a combination of the old, middle-aged and young researchers.

According to my own experience, this cooperation is not only static, but also dynamic. In other words, the elderly should gradually withdraw, and the young people should continue to enter. This is the issue of intergenerational cooperation and replacement in the research. Over the years, I have taken this form and mechanism in the research of the field of income distribution. In popular terms, it is several generations of joint operations, plus generations of continuous combat. Among them, if the joint operations are mainly a static state, then continuous combat is mainly a dynamic state. Because of the special situation of China in the past half century, the golden time of the research by the people of my age was disrupted, and we have many deficiencies as compared to the requirements of the aforementioned attainments. After recognizing my own limitations, I think

xxiv *Author's preface and personal statement*

I should consciously make the exit and help the younger generation of scientists to grow rapidly so that our economic research can catch up with the international advanced level and better serve China's economic reform and economic development.

Zhao Renwei
December 7, 2013

Note

1 Zhao Renwei (2008). Reflection on the Economic Reform of China in the Past Thirty Years. *Contemporary Finance & Economics*, 9, p. 10.

1 Some trends of change of personal income distribution of laborers

The issue of personal income distribution of laborers in the socialist economy is not only an important practical issue in the socialist economic construction, but also an important theoretical subject in socialist political economics. This paper tries to study some change trends of the personal income distribution of the laborers in China based on the practical experience of China in the past. Before we study these change trends respectively, let me express my views on the absoluteness and relativity of "distribution according to work".

I. Beginning with the absoluteness and relativity of distribution according to work

In past discussions, economic circles in China have been holding two views on how to understand distribution according to work. Some comrades hold that the so-called distribution according to work means that the amount of remuneration laborers receive is completely equal to the amount of labor they provide to society after social deduction, or the proportion of remuneration of labor that different laborers receive is identical to the proportion of the amount of labor they provide.[1] Some comrades hold that distribution according to work does not always strictly require a fixed ratio between laborers' quantity of work and the remuneration they get. Assume that the ratio of the amount of labor provided by four laborers is 1:2:3:4, which accords with the law of distribution according to work, whether the ratio of the remuneration they get is 1:2:3:4, 2:3:4:5, or 3:4:5:6.[2] Of the comrades who hold the first view, some also hold that strict distribution according to work and non-strict distribution according to work should not be differentiated at all. Admitting the existence of non-strict distribution according to work is theoretically unthorough.

In my opinion, the controversy over these two views is not an issue of whether they are theoretically thorough or not, and we cannot simply say which one is right and which one is wrong. Here, it actually concerns how we should fully understand the absoluteness and relativity of distribution according to work. The first view emphasizes the absoluteness of distribution according to work, while the latter emphasizes the relativity of distribution according to work. Only after we fully understand the absoluteness and relativity of this law can we better

2 Some trends of change

understand and apply this economic law. In an abstract sense, the law of distribution according to work has its absoluteness, just like the law of value. The former requires acquisition of an equivalent amount of remuneration from an equivalent amount of labor, while the latter requires the amount of socially necessary labor to determine the quantity of value and to exchange according to the quantity of value. However, in real economic life, economic laws are often manifested as relative laws. For example, in the laissez-faire capitalist economy, the law of value is implemented through the price's fluctuations around the value or even through the value's conversion into the production price. This is because in addition to the impact of the essential factor, namely that socially necessary labor determines the value, there are impacts of other factors, such as the supply-demand relationship and capitalist groups' carving up of profits. In the socialist economy, the law of distribution according to work also has its relativity. That is, while using this economic law consciously, people must not only consider the essential factor that an equivalent amount of labor leads to an equivalent amount of remuneration, but also consider such factors as how to facilitate unity among laborers with different labor capacity and labor contributions, and social stability. Therefore, in the actual economic life, the amount of remuneration laborers receive often deviates from the amount of labor they provide to society to some extent while being largely consistent with the latter.

The absoluteness and relativity of distribution according to work and their relationship may be expressed with figures of normal distribution and non-normal (deviated) distribution. The horizontal axis in Figure 1.1 represents the size of

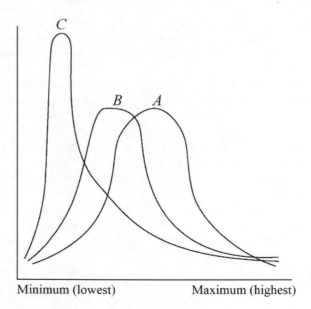

Figure 1.1 The Absoluteness and Relativity of Distribution According to Work and their Relationship

Some trends of change 3

laborers' labor contributions and amount of labor remuneration, and the vertical axis represents the number of laborers. Furthermore, we abstract the differences between laborers' labor capacity and labor contributions in order to analyze the relationship between labor contributions and labor remuneration in a centralized manner, or we abstract the three kinds of forms of labor as often discussed in the economic circles (potential form, flow form and coagulated form). Then, laborers' labor contributions are normally distributed, that is, the number of people with moderate contributions is the largest, other people are distributed on both sides relatively evenly and only a small number of people make the smallest and biggest contributions, as shown in the bell-shaped curve A. The so-called distribution according to work in the absolute sense means that laborers' income distribution matches the distribution of their contributions, that is, the labor remuneration curve overlaps the labor contribution curve, as shown in Curve A. The so-called distribution according to work in the relative sense means that the number of people with the middle and low income is the largest, as shown in the skew bell-shaped curve B.

It is not difficult to understand that in actual economic life, laborers' income is in the skew bell-shaped distribution. The point is how to control this skewness. Certainly, this skewness is restricted by many conditions, such as income distribution formed in history, productivity development level, national income level, proportional relation between accumulation and consumption in national income, proportion of individual consumption and social consumption in the consumption fund. Anyway, Curve B must be subject to Curve A; that is, A should appeal to B to some extent. Just like price cannot oscillate at will without value, Curve B should not tilt at will without A. Only in this way can we avoid pushing the relativity of distribution according to work to the extreme and thus deviating from the law of distribution according to work. This is just the root cause that we do not deny the absoluteness of distribution according to work as a law while emphasizing the relativity of distribution according to work. However, it is a pity that such deviation from the law of distribution according to work did occur in China. From the 1950s to the 1970s, in particular, the income of the vast majority of employees in China was in a steeple shape, as shown by Curve C; that is, excessive employees (mainly young and middle-aged employees) were in the low-income status. It is very difficult to explain such an extremely distorted status with the relativity of distribution according to work. We can only say that it goes against the objective law of distribution according to work. Therefore, to implement the principle of distribution according to work in actual economic life, we should not allow income distribution to take the bell shape rigidly and should all the more fight off the steeple shape. Instead, the income distribution should be in the skew bell shape.

One problem that should be pointed out incidentally is that in the economic literature in China in the past, the gap between the highest income and lowest income is often used as the only sign to measure the income gap.[3] That is, deviation of laborers' income is measured based only on the gap, which is not comprehensive enough. In the case where the gap between the highest income and lowest income remains unchanged or even is reduced, many unreasonable factors will still be

4   *Some trends of change*

produced due to the change of distribution of laborers with different income levels. The above steepled distribution is just an obvious example. There will be discussions in this regard in Section III of this paper.

II.   Trends of change of income gap between laborers

What kind of trends will the change of the personal income gap between laborers show? This is an issue that the economic circles in China are concerned about. Some comrades pointed out as early as the early 1960s that, according to the actual situations in China, the labor remuneration gap between laborers would undergo a process from small to big and then back to small (the so-called "small-big-small" trend). For example, Comrade Wang Yang points out,

> In the actual conditions of China, the law of distribution according to work will probably undergo a process from insufficiently functioning to fully functioning.
>
> In terms of the trends of change of the gap between labor remuneration, such circumstance would probably occur: Before socialism was built, as most of people's living was greatly improved with the development of productivity, the labor remuneration gap tended to expand on the whole compared to the gap nowadays. In transition to communism after socialism was built, the labor remuneration gap will show a trend of diminishing.[4]

This view, which Comrade Wang Yang put forward beginning more than 20 years ago based on the experience and lessons of China's economic construction in both positive and negative aspects, is quite insightful.

The labor remuneration gap between laborers was small and the income distribution was relatively equal in China in the past (referring to the period before the Third Plenary Session of the 11th Central Committee of the Communist Party of China), which is a fact recognized by the whole world. Let's put aside the views on this situation for the moment, and briefly analyze the reason that caused such a situation first: (1) Due to the low productivity level, the consumable commodities that could be distributed to laborers were small in quantity, and only basic means of livelihood could be guaranteed for working people according to the principle of "food for everyone". (2) In a circumstance where the productivity level was low and the social division of labor and commodity relations were extremely under-developed, different laborers often did similar work (especially in rural areas), their ability in labor was not developed, their differences in labor contributions could not be shown and, naturally, the gap of their labor remuneration could not be widened. (3) Due to the "left" ideology, the principle of distribution according to work was hard hit. In 1958 and 1975, in particular, there were two waves that denied distribution according to work, which separated labor remuneration from labor contributions. (4) The traditional concept of equalitarianism among small producers had a profound social base. Such a concept often confused mass poverty with common prosperity, or even described low pay or even the supply system as the important measure to help eradicate the three major differences, and the important step to help with transition from socialism to communism and from distribution according to work to distribution according to needs. Such an ideologically traditional concept in combination with the political "left" ideology had led to many practices where distribution was forcibly evened up.

Apparently, equalization resulting from the first two factors is an objective necessity caused by the low productivity level and complies with the economic law that relations of production must conform to the level of productive forces. Furthermore, in a circumstance where material conditions were humble, being able to "make overall plans and take all factors into consideration", plus a good job of organization, had guaranteed the minimum living needs of the broad masses of working people, which also reflects the superiority of the socialist system to some extent. Equalization resulting from the second two human factors is actually equalitarianism, which goes against the objective law of distribution according to work. Obviously, only after we make a dialectic analysis of the equal distribution in China in the past can we make relatively comprehensive and scientific comments.

From the perspective of developing the socialist economy, should we maintain the status quo or properly widen the gap then? It is quite obvious that the part of equalitarianism resulting from human factors, which was originally in the state of equalization, goes against improvement of work efficiency and economic development. Such a status quo should definitely be broken. This is an issue of the first level that causes the income gap between laborers to expand. The part resulting from the low level of productive forces, which was originally in the state of equalization, should not be treated statically, either. Within a certain limit, it ensures the basic living needs of people, thus ensuring the normal proceeding of reproduction of labor power, and helps maintain and develop the process of reproduction, which is feasible from the perspectives of both efficiency and equality. However, when a certain limit is exceeded and the level of productive forces is increased to some extent, maintaining the original state of equalization will hinder the development of productive forces. Such a status must be broken to some extent in order to increase efficiency. This is an issue of the second level that causes the income gap between laborers to expand as the socialist economy develops.

Obviously, the policy that allows some laborers to get rich first, which has been implemented since the Third Plenary Session of the 11th Central Committee of the Communist Party of China, accords with China's actual conditions and the development direction of the socialist economy. Correctness of this policy not only has been proved by the five to six years of practice, but it also has been scientifically summarized by the decision of the Third Plenary Session of the 12th Central Committee of the Communist Party of China. The goal of breaking the status quo of mass poverty, allowing some laborers to get rich first and then realizing common prosperity for all the members of society, as summed up in the decision, has clearly sketched the "small-big-small" change trend of the income gap between laborers.

As for whether such tools as the Lorenz curve and Gini coefficient can be used to analyze the income gap and its change trend under the socialist system, there are still different points of view within economic circles.[5] I would like to express my

6   Some trends of change

points of view here and make a comparative analysis. It may be treated differently in the following different circumstances:

1   While the laborers' income gap in China and the income gap in capitalist countries are compared statically using the Lorenz curve and Gini coefficient, we should never make a simple analogy, but such comparison may be used as a reference. For example, under the conditions of capitalist private ownership, labor income and income from exploitation coexist, while under the conditions of socialist public ownership, there is only labor income and no income from exploitation. In terms of the income differences reflected by the Gini coefficient under the two different social systems, they are qualitatively different; furthermore, quantitatively, the capitalist ones are greater than the socialist ones. Another example is that under the current conditions in China, differences of some factors cannot be fully reflected by the Gini coefficient (such as the case of the housing factor, where the rents are too low and allowances are excessive, making it impossible to reflect the actual differences). Therefore, the comparison between the Gini coefficient in China and the Gini coefficient in capitalist countries must consider these incomparable factors. According to Comrade Yang Xiaokai's computation, the Gini coefficient was 0.128 in the six provincially administered municipalities, 0.1545 in the rural areas, and 0.1473 in the prefectural-level towns in Hubei Province in 1981; the result of the weighted algorithm was that the Gini coefficient was 0.1332 in the whole province of Hubei in 1981.[6] According to Comrade Zhao Xuezeng's computation, the Gini coefficient in the 46 cities was 0.178 in the first quarter in 1980, and the Gini coefficient in the 23 counties in Baoding, Hebei Province, was 0.029 in 1978.[7] According to the data of the United Nations, the Gini coefficient in the capitalist countries is between 0.2 and 0.6. Though the Gini coefficient in China cannot be simply compared to that in capitalist countries, the former is far lower than the latter. Is it possible that it is used as a reference index, more or less, to analyze the problem of equalitarianism, which has existed in the income distribution for a long time in China? It is because the guiding ideology for income distribution in China is distribution according to work instead of absolute equalitarianism. It is not our advocacy that the Gini coefficient is the smaller the better, or is even zero. In this case, comparing the Gini coefficient in China to that in other countries is not completely meaningless.

2   When we make a dynamic analysis of the change trend of the income gap between laborers in different stages in China's socialist development, the Lorenz curve and Gini coefficient are definitely applicable because it is a quantitative analysis with quality being the same. Certainly, there is indeed no fixed standard concerning what position is the most suitable for us to set the Gini coefficient in each development stage (it is impossible to set a fixed standard even for the proportion of accumulation and consumption, but we still should study the proper proportional relations of accumulation and

Some trends of change 7

consumption in different development stages). Can we put it this way—that the best joint point for efficiency and equality in a stage of the development of the socialist economy is the suitable point for the Gini coefficient in that stage? When socialism is underdeveloped, greater consideration should be given to equality factors. In the stage where socialism transitions from undeveloped to developed, greater consideration should be given to efficiency factors. In the stage where socialism is developed, it seems that greater consideration again should be given to equality factors. Certainly, the Gini coefficient cannot tell equality in the undeveloped stage from equality in the developed stage as mentioned here. That is, the Gini coefficient cannot tell mass poverty from common prosperity. This is what we should know when using such analytical tools.

3 When we make a dynamic comparative analysis of the change trend of the income gap in China and that in capitalist countries using the Gini coefficient, we should not make a simple analogy, and should take such analysis as a reference only. For example, in the 1950s, Kuznets analyzed the income distribution status in some countries with the help of the Gini coefficient, and put forward the "converse-u hypothesis". According to this hypothesis, developing countries originally have relatively equal income distribution, but they must widen the income gap in order to increase efficiency in the middle and later stages of their development, so as to create inequality in society; and income distribution will tend to be equal again after they become developed countries. However, subsequent facts proved that not all the developing capitalist countries follow this pattern. Some countries have gone from unequal to more unequal (such as Brazil), other countries from unequal to relatively equal (such as Sri Lanka). If Kuznets's analysis and the situations of some developing capitalist countries are used as a reference, it seems we may come up with the following two points of view concerning the change trend of laborers' income gap in China: Firstly, judging by the situations abroad, the countries whose Gini coefficient shows a down trend normally all have a relatively high starting point (about 0.5), that is, changing from "relatively unequal" to "relatively equal". No country has changed from an originally very low Gini coefficient (such as about 0.2) to a still lower Gini coefficient. Therefore, even if the noncomparable factors of different social systems are considered, China's rise from a Gini coefficient lower than 0.2 (that is, widening the gap) accords with the development requirements. Secondly, according to Kuznets's analysis, the Gini coefficient in developing capitalist countries shows a down trend only after it reaches 0.55, while in some countries (and regions), the Gini coefficient drops to about 0.3 from 0.5. Considering the fact that China is a developing socialist country, its highest Gini coefficient should be much lower than that of capitalist countries, though the income gap will be widened to some extent during development. That is to say, though the change of the laborers' income gap in China shows a "small-big-small" trend, the fluctuation will not be too big. On the whole, the characteristics and superiority of the socialist

8 *Some trends of change*

system are reflected not in absolute equalization (Gini coefficient is zero), but in a small Gini coefficient and small changes and fluctuations.

III. Change trend of laborers' income in each age group

Distribution according to work is certainly not distribution according to age. However, each laborer makes different labor contributions in different stages of their working ages. It is just in this limit that we need to make a vertical-section study of the relationship between distribution according to work and age, or of the change trend of laborers' income in each age group.

Within a period of several decades from the time each laborer begins to work until they retire, their labor contributions vary. Normally, the curve of a laborer's labor contributions in his/her lifetime is in the parabolic shape; that is, the contributions are small at the starting point of work, reach the peak in the mature stage, and fall at old age. Certainly, the mature stages are different for laborers who take up different occupations. For example, for coal miners and some sports, literary and art workers, their mature stages are relatively early, and their labor contributions reach the peak earlier than those of laborers in other occupations. However, labor contributions always reach the peak in mature stages if we put aside the exceptional circumstances for some occupations. According to the principle of distribution according to work, generally speaking, the labor remuneration of a laborer in his/her lifetime should also be in a parabolic shape, that is, the labor remuneration is low when he/she begins to work, reaches the peak in the mature stage, and falls afterwards. Whether such a fall of labor remuneration is shown immediately after the mature stage, or is shown when the retirement pension lower than the salary is received after retirement, there are still different points of view. Considering the fact that laborers generally have relatively rich experience in work or labor in the period from the mature stage to retirement, and considering such factors as working years, we may assume that it is practical for remuneration to remain basically stable in the period from the peak of the labor remuneration in the mature stage to retirement. Therefore, in general cases, a satisfactory labor remuneration curve for a laborer in his/her lifetime should be a parabolic curve that matches the labor contribution curve, as shown in Line L in Figure 1.2 (in Figure 1.2, the horizontal axis stands for age, and the vertical axis stands for the labor remuneration level). Assume that the labor remuneration levels of laborers at the work starting point and retirement point are fixed, as shown in Figure 1.2, and then there may be three kinds of basic types of trends of the labor remuneration they get in their lifetime, as shown in Lines L, M and N in Figure 1.2. Apparently, of the three kinds of basic trends, the trend along Line L best accords with the law of distribution according to work. The trend along Line M is actually a way of increasing income based on the number of years, which is inconsiderable; the trend along Line N least accords with the law of distribution according to work, and all the more should be prevented. It is a pity that due to the reasons described, disturbances from the latter two trends had occurred badly in the past economic life. Our Party and Government have made great efforts to overcome the problems left over by the past economic life

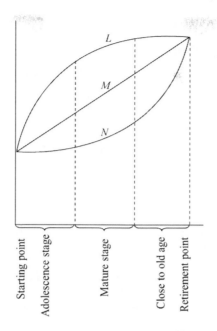

Figure 1.2 The Curve of a Laborer's Labor Contributions in his/her Lifetime

since the Third Plenary Session of the 11th Central Committee of the Communist Party of China. However, Rome was not built in a day. Greater efforts are required and a very long period has to be undergone in order to achieve the trend as shown in Line L through adjustment and reform.

In recent years, public opinion has expressed great sympathy toward middle-aged people, especially middle-aged intellectuals, who get low salaries. Their salaries have been frozen for a long time or have increased very little since they began to work, and such situation is slightly improved after the Third Plenary Session of the 11th Central Committee of the Communist Party of China. The salary of people of this generation, on the whole, changes along the direction as shown in Line N. That is to say, these people are the biggest victims of violation of the law of distribution according to work. They fully deserve the sympathy from public opinion, care from our Party and Government, and remedial measures for them.

Certainly, the disturbances of "leftism" and economic difficulty are the root cause of such distortion of economic relations, but the long-term salary-freezing strategy taken in response to the economic difficulty is also a direct cause of such distortion.

We may design a simple figure to illustrate the impact of salary freezing on employees of different ages. In Figure 1.3, the horizontal axis stands for age, while the vertical axis stands for the salary level. In order to purify the issue, we

10 Some trends of change

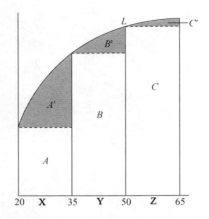

Figure 1.3 The Impact of Salary Freezing on Employees of Different Ages

assume that salary is the only labor remuneration, and the impact of price factors is not taken into consideration. Assume that there are three persons, namely A, B and C. They are under the same conditions, except that they encounter long-term salary freezing at different work ages, and before salary freezing, their respective salary income also accords with the law of distribution according to work—that is, they earn a salary along the direction of Curve L. If A, B and C begin to encounter salary freezing at the age of 20, 35 and 50 respectively, and such salary freezing lasts for 15 years in each case, measured according to the principle of distribution according to work, the impact of salary freezing on them is different. As shown in Figure 1.3, A + A', B + B' and C + C' are the salary amounts that A, B and C should normally get in this period respectively. A, B and C are the salary amounts that A, B and C get respectively during the salary freezing period. A', B' and C' are the sustaining capacity or loading capacity of A, B and C respectively during this period. Apparently, according to the law of distribution according to work, laborers make different labor contributions at different ages, and thus the changes of labor remuneration are different. In Figure 1.3, the slope or skewness of Curve L is different in each stage. The bigger the slope, the bigger the loading capacity, as shown in Figure 1.3: A' > B' > C'. The preceding concerns the absolute loading capacity only. If the different salary levels and total salary of each laborer at each age are also considered, then the differences will be greater. As shown in the figure, the salary amount that Laborers A, B and C get during this period is A, B and C respectively. A < B < C, therefore:

$$\frac{A'}{A+A'} > \frac{B}{B+B'} > \frac{C'}{C+C'}$$

The degree of the above inequation is greater than the degree of A' > B' > C'. That is to say, with salary frozen, the absolute loading capacity for Laborers A, B and

Some trends of change   11

C is different; furthermore, the differences of the relative loading capacity among them are greater.

We summarize this period of history theoretically in order to transform to the normal status more consciously, that is, to cause the labor remuneration of a laborer in his/her lifetime to transform from Curve N to Curve L. Certainly, we should also clearly see that for such issues as salary and price, long-term freezing does no good, and drastic changes are not practical, either. Faced with economic relations that have been distorted for a long time, we can only take the measure of gradual unchoking, and move towards normalization step by step. Some measures have been taken in salary adjustment in recent years. Some of these measures are still unsatisfactory; for example, they tend to increase salary based on the number of years. However, they have broken the ice, gotten rid of the trend of Curve N, and moved along Curve L. The general trend is good. Some measures that increase salary based on the number of years are strategically inadvisable, but they are used as provisional measures to break the ice, which is not hard to understand. As long as we unshakably follow the objective law of distribution according to work, we can gradually normalize and rationalize the change trend of laborers' labor remuneration in their lifetime.

If we can arrange laborers' lifetime labor remuneration according to the above change trend, there will be at least the following two benefits:

1   It will help increase production efficiency and construct socialist material civilization. From the perspective of reproduction of labor power, doing so can ensure that laborers get corresponding material conditions in a timely manner in the period when they can make the biggest labor contributions, which turns distribution into a strong force that pushes forward production development. This will help build up the metabolic function of the entire social and economic organism. Otherwise, labor contributions and corresponding material conditions are separated in terms of time, or only have the nature of "subsequent confirmation", and the entire reproduction process will not be able to proceed smoothly.

2   It will help the young generation to receive prospect education and construct socialist spiritual civilization. Facts have proved that the construction of socialist spiritual civilization and construction of material civilization are inseparable. If it is difficult for young people to become financially independent after 10 to 20 years of hard work, and difficult for them to give birth to and raise children, then it is meaningless to purely accuse them of their material desires. The permanent cure is to change the distorted distribution relations, and to let the new generation understand that they can get corresponding material gains if they make big contributions to the country and society through their hard work during the socialist construction. Only in this way can we plug up all crooked ways and dishonest practices. Only after we overcome the distorted distribution relations at the macro level, can we solve the abnormal "redistribution relations" in families (for example, the old generations bring up the third generations).

12 *Some trends of change*

IV. Change trend of commodity approach (market method) in consumer goods distribution

Distribution of consumer goods may be in the form of physical supply (non-market method) or purchases and sales (market method). For a long time before the economic system reform, the form of physical supply was excessively used while the form of purchases and sales was inhibited, because the system mode of China at that time contained military communism factors.

The supply system factors in consumer goods distribution are mainly reflected in the following two aspects.

A. Rationing based on head count

Rationing, or physical allocation, is conducted for some consumer goods that guarantee people's basic living needs; this is a measure used by many countries in emergency periods, especially in time of war and in the early postwar periods. That is to say, this is a provisional measure in a particular situation. For a variety of reasons, however, this measure was implemented in China for about 30 years before it was changed. The disadvantage of such a practice is that it restricts laborers' freedom as individuals (families) to choose consumer goods and services within the fixed monetary income and thus impairs their economic interests and economic responsibilities. Though consumers also need to pay money when buying rationed goods, money plays a negative role in a circumstance where physical tickets take precedence. That is to say, money is just a computing tool, and the monetary amount does not constitute the basis of choosing. Apparently, under the premise that a laborer's monetary income is fixed, the bigger the range of physical allocation, the smaller the range of free choice. In those days when rationing was the most prevalent in China, some low-income earners among the urban employees could hardly buy other consumer goods except for those rationed ones. In rural areas, there were even some "over-expenditure families" (that is, rationing for a family based on head count exceeded the total income of that family). In this case, freedom to choose consumer goods is certainly out of the question.

B. Free supply based on position

Such free supply differs from rationing as mentioned in the previous section in two aspects: Firstly, it is the excess allocation beyond monetary income, while rationing is the quota allocation within monetary income. Secondly, unlike rationing, which meets the most basic living needs, it meets high consumption needs. However, it is a factor of the supply system like rationing. China switched to the salary system that reflects the requirements of distribution according to work for all the staff of the Party and government organizations in 1956, but kept some residues of the supply system for a small proportion of these people; for example, the free supply of consumable commodities and services, etc., based on executive positions. Such residues of the supply system are not only to the disadvantage of the principle of distribution according to work, but also increasingly unfit for development in actual economic life. The distribution and use of home phones is just a simple example. For a long period of time, home phones in China were distributed free of charge based on administrative posts. However, the needs for home phones cannot be simply measured by administrative posts. In recent years, some users have installed phones at their own expense, which actually is a breakthrough in the original distribution method. As such free supply based on posts is the supply beyond monetary income, it is not economically related to consumers (not associated with their monetary income), nor can it be under monetary supervision, and will definitely waste limited resources and cause other disadvantages.

In addition to the two aspects outlined earlier, greatly subsidizing many consumer goods in a circumstance where price and salary are unreasonable is a kind of supply in a disguised form. The high-amount subsidies not only reduce the portion in the consumption fund that may be directly disposed of by laborers as individuals through distribution according to work, but they also often result in inharmonious new economic interest relations. People who rent more houses can get more benefits through rent subsidies, which is a typical example.

To overcome the disadvantages resulting from the supply system factors just described, the commodity-money relationship must be developed in consumer goods distribution; that is, applications of the market method must be expanded in consumer goods distribution. In this regard, the analysis made by Kornai, a Hungarian economist, has referential meaning.[8] He sorts the methods for distributing consumer goods and services to families in the socialist economy into the market method, the non-market method and the hybrid method. He also uses the experience of Eastern Europe as the background, and divides the development of the socialist economy into three stages: the early period after the victory of the revolution, the relatively peaceful period under the traditional economic management system, and the period after the reform of the economic management system (the experience of Hungary was dominant in this period). He lists the changes of the distribution methods for a number of consumption items in different periods. We can clearly see from what he lists in Table 1.1 that the non-market methods gradually decrease, while the market methods gradually increase. Certainly, situations are not quite the same for different consumption items. It goes like this on the whole: (1) the use of industrial products, Automobile and Entertainment, tourism (referenced in Table 1.1 that follows) have long since been distributed through the market methods; (2) the consumption items concerning education and healthcare are still mainly distributed through the non-market methods; and (3) for the consumption items concerning urban housing, though the non-market methods are kept to a great degree, the market methods are increasing.

The consumer goods distribution methods in China have been changing along this trend in recent years. It is a pity that due to various disturbances, this trend started relatively late in China. However, as long as we summarize our own historical experience and draw on the experience of others, we can completely base the change of distribution methods on a more self-conscious basis. Certainly, quite a number of problems need to be studied further, such as the degree of

14 *Some trends of change*

Table 1.1 Effects of Distribution Methods for Families in Socialist Economy

Method	I	II	III
Period	*Revolution years, civil war or war periods*	*Relatively peaceful period under traditional economic management system*	*Period after reform of economic management system*
Product Category			
Food	Majority: non-market Some: market (legal market and black market)	Market	Market
Clothing	Few: non-market Majority: market	Market	Market
Other industrial products	Market	Market	Market
Urban housing	Non-market	Majority: non-market Few: market (mainly gray market and black market)	Majority: non-market Few: hybrid market
Automobile	—	Mainly: hybrid method Few: market	Mainly: market Few: hybrid market
Entertainment, tourism	—	Mainly: non-market Few: market	Some: market Some: non-market
Education	Non-market	Mainly: non-market Few: market	Mainly: non-market Few: market
Healthcare	Non-market	Mainly: non-market Few: market (legal market or gray market)	Mainly: non-market Few but ever-increasing: market (legal market or gray market)

commercialization, progress and conditions of different consumption items, but this trend is inevitable.

If consumer goods are distributed according to this trend, there will be at least two benefits as follows.

Firstly, it will help boost production and construction through distribution. For example, rationing and price fixing in grain distribution (planned supply) will definitely require rationing and price fixing in grain production and purchase (planned purchase). Economically, the latter often puts grain producers at a disadvantage. Such disadvantage often leads to underproduction of grain, intensifies hardship in grain supply, and forms a vicious circle. In the long run, only after grain distribution and production are gradually commercialized can we turn the vicious circle into a virtuous cycle. Another example is that the supply system factors in housing distribution (such as low rents and high subsidies) definitely lead to the lack of motivation economically in house construction and maintenance, and thus further intensify hardship in the housing supply. Furthermore, such distribution method also encourages people to occupy more houses, occupy good houses or even occupy houses without using them, resulting in a kind of false demand for houses or a demand that exceeds the actual paying ability, and thus leading to sharper contradictions between supply and demand. If the supply system factors in housing distribution are gradually eliminated, and house distribution, construction and maintenance are gradually commercialized, it will definitely help turn the vicious circle into the virtuous cycle.

Secondly, it will help overcome wasting of resources and malpractices. The free supply of some consumption items will definitely result in a waste of limited resources, because it does not concern consumers' economic interests. Waste in the use of home phones is an example. As far as I know, the using of home phones is charged by time even in some developed countries, and people seldom waste time and money in making telephone calls. In China, however, waste can often be seen in the free use of phones, which goes against the principle of socialism and fails to match the backward status of the telephone facility in China. As mentioned earlier, in the long run, the physical supply method in consumer goods distribution fails to solve short supply fundamentally; instead, it will intensify such short supply, and waste and malpractices are often two major coexisting phenomena of the shortage economy. In the shortage economy, shortage in external supply results not only in producers' trend of internal storage, but also in individuals' or families' trend of internal storage as consumers. External shortage and internal storage interact as both cause and effect, and result in a stockpiling-type waste of limited resources. We used to attribute the bad practices or malpractices in housing distribution to some people's ideological problems and did not associate them with the shortage economy's own defects and its distribution method, which should not be enough. If we balance the supply and demand of some consumption items by means of gradual commercialization and stop those people who try to reap unfair gains, it will probably be a fundamental solution.

The study outlined in this paper analyzes the development trend of the consumer goods distribution method at present and for a considerably long time to come. As for the longer-term future, under the premise of overwhelming material abundance, it is possible for some consumption items that reach the full satisfaction level to be distributed in a way other than the market method. Therefore, in the long run, the market method for consumer goods distribution will also show a small → big → small trend.

(Originally published in *Economic Research Journal*, Issue 3, 1985.)

Notes

1 See Jiang Xuemo. (1964). 谈谈按劳分配中的劳动问题 [On Labor in Distribution According to Work]. *Economic Research Journal*, 8; Jin Wen. (1980). 按劳分配在社会主义中的地位 [Role of Distribution According to Work in Scientific Socialism]. *Social Sciences in China*, 4; Qiao Shu. (1981). 坚持按劳分配就要坚持计算劳动量 [Amount of Labor Must Be Calculated for Distribution According to Work]. *China Economic Studies*, 2.
2 See Zhong Jin. (1957). 再来谈谈"按劳分配"问题 [Second Discussion on "Distribution According to Work"]. *XueXi*, 6, and Xu Yi, Wang Zhuo and Dai Yuanchen. (1958). 按劳

16 *Some trends of change*

分配与工资政策 [Distribution According to Work and Salary Policy], *Xin Jian She*, 5; Zeng Qixian et al. (1978). 运用抽象法分析 "按劳分配" 的几点体会 [Some Experience in "Analyzing Distribution According to Work" Using Abstract Method]. In *Collection of Speeches in Three Discussions Regarding Distribution According to Work by Economic Circles in 1977* (pp. 194–195). Beijing: SDX Joint Publishing Company.

3 See the Policy Research Office of State Labor Bureau. (1982). 我国劳动工资问题讲稿 [Lecture Notes on Labor and Salary in China] (pp. 280–281). Beijing: Labor Press.

4 Wang Yang. (1962). 关于按劳分配规律的一点体会 [Some Thoughts on the Law of Distribution according to Work]. *Economic Perspectives*, 22.

5 Li Yining. (1984). 有益的探讨、可贵的起步 [Helpful Discussions and Valuable Starting]. *Economic Research Journal*, 4; Xu Jinsheng. (1984). 关于洛伦茨曲线和基尼系数的应用问题 [On Applications of Lorenz Curve and Gini Coefficient]. *Economic Perspectives*, 12; Li Yining. (1984). 读许金声文章后的一点想法 [Some Thoughts after Reading Xu Jinsheng's Article]. *Economic Perspectives*, 12.

6 Yang Xiaokai. (1982). 社会经济发展的重要指标—基尼系数 [An Important Index of Social and Economic Development: Gini Coefficient]. *Journal of Wuhan University*, 6.

7 Zhao Xuezeng. (1982). 关于我国劳动者工资（工分）分配的洛伦茨曲线和基尼系数的考察 [Observation of Lorenz Curve and Gini Coefficient for Salary (Work Point) Distribution for Laborers in China]. *Journal of Tianjin University of Finance and Economics*, 4.

8 Janos Kornai. (1980). *Economics of Shortage* (p. 440). Amsterdam, New York and Oxford: North-Holland Publishing Company.

2 Two contrasting phenomena in current income distribution

How to view the gap in personal income distribution has become a hot topic nowadays. I would like to express my personal points of view in this regard.

I. What is the problem?

Such remarks can often be heard recently: "Street vendors are getting rich, while workers are getting poor"; "Surgeons are poorer than barbers, and nuclear experts are poorer than tea egg sellers." This indicates that some unreasonable phenomena in income distribution have drawn people's attention. People may list many phenomena to illustrate the unreasonable income gap. For example, taxi drivers have far higher income than bus drivers. Some employees of joint ventures have far higher income than that of the employees of same or similar kinds of state-owned enterprises. Some private enterprises hire many employees, and earn a large amount of non-labor income. The income of some lessees is too high, even if the risk premium is factored in. The income of some employees who do second jobs and some retired people who are re-employed is also on the high side. A small number of people gain sudden huge profits through illegal means, which all the more has aroused dissatisfaction in people. Faced with these phenomena, people are certainly justified to question: what kind of people should be allowed to get rich first?

The unreasonably high income of a small number of people is indeed a pressing economic and social problem we are facing, not just an illusory sense of inequity produced by people's psychology. However, we can never simply conclude on this basis that the problem with personal income distribution in China has transformed from equalitarianism to the excessive income gap. A relatively comprehensive and practicable judgment should be: on the one hand, the chronic illness of equalitarianism in personal income distribution has not yet been cured; on the other hand, the problem of the overhigh income of a small number of people and economic activities has occurred. The latter problem has drawn strong social responses. Actually, these two problems are inseparable. It is just these two completely opposite phenomena that form a strong contrast and cause strong social responses.

The equalitarianism problem is still a non-negligible major aspect in the income distribution in China. The judgment made at the Thirteenth National Party

18   *Contrasting phenomena in income distribution*

Congress that "the prevailing trend in the current distribution is still the egalitarian practice of 'everybody eating from the same big pot' is not outdated yet. The studies conducted by many experts at home and abroad show that the income distribution was relatively equal for both urban residents and rural residents before the reform in China. Measured with the internationally accepted Gini coefficient,[1] its value is much lower than those in many developing countries in the world. As shown by statistics, since the reform, the Gini coefficient in rural areas has slightly risen from 0.2124 in 1978 to 0.2636 in 1985, but the Gini coefficient in cities has slightly fallen from 0.185 in 1977 to 0.168 in 1984. Since the reform, we have emphasized the increase of the income of low-paid employees, and adopted the salary system with a smaller gap after the salary reform for the government departments and public institutions in 1985. For example, the salary income gap between professors, associate professors, lecturers and teaching assistants is much smaller than that in the 1950s, and teachers who have newly earned a professional title are all entitled to the minimum salary for such professional title. Some call this "new equalitarianism", which makes sense to some extent.

People have, in succession, analyzed and tried to summarize the two phenomena. Some comrades hold that the problem of equalitarianism exists in the fields whose main distribution form is distribution according to work, and the problem of an excessive income gap exists in the fields whose main distribution form is not distribution according to work. Some comrades hold that on the whole, equalitarianism is still a main problem in personal income distribution, but the problem of excessive income disparity has occurred on a local scale. The first summary is not accurate enough, because distribution according to work should not be equalitarianism. We can only say that in the fields where distribution according to work is tried, the trend of equalitarianism actually emerges. The second summary is relatively accurate, but it seems to involve only the quantitative aspect, and not the qualitative aspect of the problem. In particular, it does not involve the system. We may make the following summary from another perspective: Within the range where the direct control of the state is available, the old equalitarianism has not been cancelled, and a new equalitarianism has emerged. On the occasions where the State's direct control is unavailable and the indirect control system has not been effectively established and operating, the income of some people and some economic activities is overhigh. Regarding the so-called relations between bus drivers and taxi drivers, workers and street vendors, nuclear experts and egg sellers, first jobs and second jobs, aren't they just the relations between availability and unavailability of direct control?

II.   What is the cause?

Obviously, the problems and phenomena associated with income distribution in China are very complicated. They are different from equalitarianism, a typical phenomenon in the traditional socialist economic system; different from excessive income disparity, a typical phenomenon in the capitalist economy; and greatly different from common prosperity through proper widening of the personal income gap, a goal to be realized by China's economic system reform. In my opinion, the coexistence of new equalitarianism, old equalitarianism, and overhigh income of a small number of people and economic activities is a special phenomenon that emerges in the economic system reform of China. Certainly, we must not regard all these phenomena as inevitable during the economic system reform. We can only say that some are inevitable in the system transformation, some are caused by reform incompatibility and managerial defects, while some are left over by history and need to be further overcome. Here I want to raise several issues, or analyze the cause of these phenomena from several perspectives.

A. Double systems

The economic system reform of China aims to turn the old system, characterized by direct control through administrative measures, into the new system, characterized by indirect control through market parameters. As the transformation from the old system to the new one cannot be achieved overnight, the economic system reform of China has actually taken the road of double systems. Production is double, and is made up of planned production and unplanned production ("plan" here refers specifically to "mandatory planning"). Material supply is also double, and is made up of planned and guaranteed supply and free purchase. Price is also double or multiple. In the planned system, low planned prices are adopted. In the unplanned system, high prices that reflect the law of the market in varying degrees are adopted (floating price, negotiable price and free price). Coexistence of the double systems, especially coexistence of double pricing, has definitely caused a series of contradictions and conflicts in the economic life, made it difficult to coordinate and balance the planned and unplanned economic interest relations, and provided fertile grounds for speculation and profiteering. Furthermore, the unplanned economic activities have not been under effective indirect control, creating a circumstance of drifting and loss of control to some extent. In personal income distribution, the contradictions and conflicts of the double systems are manifested as the income of unplanned economic activities apparently being higher than that of planned economic activities. Obviously, contrasting between these two phenomena is, to a great extent, a manifestation of the contradictions and conflicts of the double systems in personal income distribution during China's economic system reform.

B. Opportunity inequality

In the traditional system, the market mechanism is totally rejected, competition between enterprises and competition between individuals are denied, labor mobility is strictly restricted, and equal competition opportunities are certainly out of the question. Opportunity inequality at that time was covered up by the income distribution of equalitarianism and was not easy to detect. The market mechanism and competitive mechanism have been introduced since the reform and opening-up. However, these mechanisms are quite incomplete, their operations are irregular,

20 *Contrasting phenomena in income distribution*

and the administrative order mechanism of the traditional system is still working. Therefore, the problem of opportunity inequality becomes prominent. People complain about the unreasonable part in income gap widening, often not just about the gap itself, but also about opportunity inequality, which is an important precondition for such an unreasonable gap. Many phenomena about the unreasonable income gap in society are associated with opportunity inequality. For example, the income of a married couple or a pair of sisters whose working ability is almost the same may differ manifold only because one of them works in a state-owned enterprise and the other works in a joint venture. Taxi drivers have a much higher income than bus drivers. Such a gap is caused not by differences in working ability or labor contributions, but by opportunity inequality. As some bus drivers put it, "If we are allowed to do something else, at least 80% of the drivers here will immediately resign and drive taxis." During the reform of ownership diversification, new unequal environments have emerged between economic sectors of different ownership, which is also an eye-catching problem. For example, compared to the private economy, the state-owned economy is often at a disadvantage in terms of such objective conditions as price and taxation. As a result, employees of private enterprises earn a higher income than employees of state-owned enterprises.

C. Disorderly change

Some of the changes in China's income distribution pattern are in line with the reform direction, but some are not. We may call it disorderly change. For example, the policy that allows some laborers to get rich first certainly should also allow some wage earners in the ownership by the whole people to get rich first. In other words, the reform of the salary system should also reflect this policy. However, the reform of the salary system has not reflected this so far. Instead, the income of wage earners shows a trend of being further evened up. The existing salary system is still in the frame of the egalitarian practice of "everybody eating from the same big pot", which does not comply with the new way of reflecting social equity while increasing efficiency. Another example is that there are many physical supply factors in the original income distribution pattern of China. Since the reform, the degree of monetization in the income distribution and consumption expenditure has increased to some extent, and the range of physical supply has significantly reduced in the use of industrial products, automobile and entertainment, tourism, which is in line with the reform direction. However, the long-term freezing measure is still taken for the charging standards for such items as house rent, water and electricity, and public traffic. With residents' monetary income increasing, the share of house rent in the total living expenses of urban employees has dropped from 1.93% in 1978 to 0.90% in 1986, while the share of water and electricity dropped from 1.35% in 1978 to 1.11% in 1986. Certainly, the government has to increase the number of subsidies significantly for this, which has increased the factors for in-kind subsidies in a disguised form. For most people, subsidies and physical supply are always associated with equalitarianism and are unable to reflect the fundamental requirement that distribution should help increase efficiency.

D. Inflation

Inflation, or excessive rise in commodity prices, has emerged since 1989. In this case, a small number of people may profiteer through speculation and put monetary wage earners at a disadvantage. According to the bulletin of the National Bureau of Statistics of China, a survey covering three municipalities and each provincial capital conducted in 1987 shows that the number of households whose real income dropped solely due to price hikes took up 21% of the total households surveyed. Certainly, the subsidies distributed by the state to employees as a remedial measure can, to some extent, make up for employees' losses due to decrease of their real income, but such subsidies have also strengthened the trend of equalitarianism among employees. Inflation definitely further widens the gap between the planned price and unplanned price, widens the gap between the income of the economic activities within the State's direct control and that beyond the State's direct control, and deepens the contrast between the above two phenomena.

III. Where is the way out?

Various factors lead to the aforementioned unreasonable phenomena, and therefore various measures should be taken in order to eliminate such unreasonable phenomena.

Firstly, under ownership by the whole people, especially within the range of the State's direct control, equalitarianism must be resolutely broken, and greater flexibility should be gradually given. Meanwhile, management should be strengthened, so as to achieve the combination of flexibility and control. The sign of the combination of flexibility and control is an economic mechanism that associates income with benefits and associates income increase and gap widening with benefits. If income is increased without the increase of benefits – that is, income is increased based on wealth transfer instead of wealth growth (or even by harming the interests of the state or of others) – isn't that like water without a source? If differences in personal income are widened without the increase of benefits, it goes against the fundamental goal of such widening, and it is like a tree without roots. Nowadays many enterprises are exploring ways to associate gross pay with economic benefits, which is worth advocating. If, within this range, people with good performance and bad performance are treated in the same way, and people are encouraged to ignore their duties and "shift for themselves" from second jobs, this would be like putting the cart before the horse. If a teacher of physics does a good job in teaching but fails to get the corresponding remuneration and has to make a living by selling eggs, then our educational cause will be ruined, and our next generation will be harmed. Some people say, don't western universities just gain profits from their own properties and business activities? Yes, they do this just because they want to ensure economically that professors can be fully devoted to their teaching and research. It is not our advocacy that professors should get into the tower of ivory. However, if our professors have to make a living by spending a lot of time doing things irrelevant to their own work, why should we take

22 Contrasting phenomena in income distribution

the trouble to cultivate so many professors? In my opinion, such philosophy of "shifting for oneself" is not a concept of the commodity economy established on the division of work and socialized mass production, but more like resurgence of the concept of the natural economy established on self-sufficient small production under new conditions.

Secondly, in the fields where the State's direct control system is not available and the indirect control system is extremely incomplete, we should strengthen management as possible and never let things drift. Certainly, perfection of the indirect control system relies on the improvement of the entire economic development level and market growth. However, some managerial defects at present are human-caused and may completely be solved through improvement of work. For example, the wide income gap between state-run, collective and private economic entities caused by lighter-than-usual or heavier-than-usual tax burdens may completely be solved through adjustment of tax burdens. The practice of giving favored treatment to a small number of enterprises regarding taxes, which is based on the will of leading officials, should be stopped by strengthening the rule of law. For those self-employed businesses and private enterprises that have no accounts to be checked, we should improve management from the setup of accounts. For the overhigh legal income, we should strengthen macro adjustment and control through income taxation. For the illegal income gained by illegal means such as counterfeiting and cheating, we should clamp down on it by legal means.

Thirdly, the problem of disorderly change, such as the emerging trend of materialization, which goes against the expanded commodity-money relationship in the income distribution, is mainly caused by the lack of experience and lack of an overall, supporting plan that combines both long-term and short-term measures in the reform. Many subsidy measures taken are just stopgap measures. Only after we strengthen the supporting measures and foreseeability for the reform can we gradually solve the problem of excessive subsidies.

Fourthly, in order to solve the gap in the income distribution, we should avoid focusing on distribution solely. The entire national economy is an organic whole whose links and aspects inter-relate and restrict each other. For example, when the inflation rate is very low, people can hardly feel the impact of prices of commodities on income distribution. However, when the inflation rate is high, or when the price rise rate even exceeds the interest rate and results in a negative interest rate, people will sensitively feel how inflation deepens the contradictions and conflicts between the two unreasonable phenomena in the income distribution. Therefore, fighting inflation and stabilizing commodity prices have become an essential objective condition to rationalize income distribution.

Fifthly, the problem of opportunity inequality, which is an important objective precondition of the unreasonable income distribution, should be solved by taking different measures based on specific conditions. Unequal competitive opportunities caused by human factors (such as unreasonable tax burdens) should be solved as soon as possible through improvement of work. Some problems left over by history (such as restrictions on population movement and flow of personnel) should be gradually solved by creating conditions. Some problems, which are restricted by the economic development and market growth (such as incompleteness of the indirect regulation system and imperfection of the market distribution mechanism, existence of various monopoly and blocking factors), can only be gradually solved during the reform and development.

The analysis in this paper shows that the above problems and phenomena in the currently income distribution in China are quite complicated. It is not easy or possible to solve these problems and eliminate the unreasonable phenomena in just one move, but as long as we figure out the causes and effects and take appropriate measures, we can surely find a way. With the entire economic system reform deepened and the steady growth of the national economy, contrasting between the aforementioned two phenomena in personal income distribution will be gradually reduced, and income distribution will truly take a new path that reflects social equity under the premise that efficiency is increased.

(This paper was written in December 1989, and published in *Cambridge Journal of Economics*, 1990, 14, pp. 345–349.)

Note

1 The Gini coefficient is an index that measures the degree of equality of income distribution. Its value is 1 when the income distribution is absolutely unequal. Between 0 and 1, the higher its value is, the more unequal the income distribution is; the lower its value, the more equal the income distribution.

3 Some special phenomena of income distribution in China's transformation period[1]

I. Introduction

The economic system reform of China has been going on for 12 years. Great changes have taken place in the resident income distribution pattern during this period. This paper focuses on some special phenomena in resident income distribution during the economic system transformation in China. For example, during the reform, as the scope of mandatory planning gradually reduces – or, the part under the State's direct control gradually reduces – the entire economic life is divided into the planned system and the unplanned system ("plan" here refers specifically to "mandatory planning"). Equalitarianism still exists in the former system, while the phenomenon of excessive income gaps emerges in the latter system. These two phenomena are often known as unfair income distribution. Another example is that in a circumstance where the income of urban residents and income of rural residents have greatly increased, the income gap between the two sometimes tends to narrow and sometimes tends to widen. Therefore, how to coordinate the income distribution between urban and rural residents has become an issue of concern. The third example is that during the reform, especially after the focus of the reform was transferred to cities in 1984, the salary part was relatively reduced, while the extra-salary part was relatively expanded in a circumstance where the income of urban employees and urban residents had greatly increased. Such a phenomenon has also aroused people's attention.

In my opinion, such phenomena are not surprising. They indicate only that the practice of the economic life and the reform progress have posed new challenges for us. The purpose of analyzing these phenomena and what they reflect is to rationalize income distribution and advance the reform to a new stage.

Some of the data cited in this paper come from the Income Distribution Project Team of Institute of Economics of the Chinese Academy of Social Sciences (hereinafter referred to as "the Project Team") in its sampling survey on the income distribution of urban and rural residents conducted in 1988,[2] and some of them come from the National Bureau of Statistics of China and other channels. As the sampling survey conducted by the Project Team was only limited to the year 1988, many data from other sources have been used for the dynamic analysis.

II. Coexistence and contrasting of equalitarianism and the excessive income gap

Personal income distribution in China was highly equalized, or equalitarianism was prominent, before the reform, which is generally noted. The investigation report of the World Bank shows that the Gini coefficient was 0.33 nationwide and 0.31 in rural areas in 1979, and was 0.16 in cities in 1980.[3] Some people's calculation shows that the Gini coefficient was 0.237 in rural areas in 1978, and was 0.185 in cities in 1977.[4] The policy that allows some laborers to get rich first has been adopted since the reform, so as to realize the goal of common prosperity by properly widening the personal income gap and by increasing efficiency with the incentive mechanism. This policy is definitely correct. However, the practice of the reform shows that the change of actual situations is much more complex than imagined.

Over the years, the economic reform of China has aimed to turn the old system, characterized by direct control through administrative directive measures, into the new system, characterized by indirect control through market parameters. However, transformation of an old system into a new one cannot be accomplished overnight. Therefore, the new and old systems coexist in the reform. Production is double, and it is divided into planned production and unplanned production. Material distribution is also double and is made up of planned and guaranteed distribution and unplanned free purchase. Price is also double or multiple. In the planned system, low planned prices are adopted. In the unplanned system, high prices that reflect the law of the market in varying degrees are adopted (floating price, negotiable price and free price). Taking a wider look, we can see that double systems, namely planned system and unplanned system, also exist in the field of personal income distribution. Coexistence and conflicts of the two systems also make personal income distribution extremely complicated.[5] Let's study them from the following four perspectives.

A. Unplanned system

In what we call unplanned or beyond-direct-control economic activities, an effective indirect control system has not been established, market rules are imperfect, and tax evasion is prevalent. On the whole, income is relatively high and the income gap is wide in such activities. The result of the sampling survey conducted by the Project Team shows that in 1988, the gap of monetary income per capita per year of the staff members in the private sector (this sector has no mandatory planning and belongs to the unplanned system), including self-employed businesses, private enterprises, joint ventures and foreign-funded enterprises, is quite wide. The result of calculation based on ten equant groups (see Table 3.1) shows that the income of the 20% lowest-income earners accounts for only 3.4% of the gross income, the income of the 20% highest-income earners accounts for 54.1% of the gross income, the latter being 15.9 times the former (as the column for "lowest income of private sector" in Table 3.1 is a negative number, this column is neglected, and Columns 2 and 3 are used instead). The Gini coefficient for this

26 Special phenomena of income distribution

Table 3.1 Monetary Income Level Per Capita Per Year of Staff Members in State Sector and Private Sector Based on Ten Equant Groups in Cities in 1988 (Yuan)

Sequence of ten equant groups (from low to high)	State Sector			Private Sector		
	Lowest	Highest	Average	Lowest	Highest	Average
1 (lowest)	1064.40	791.90	−1180.00	0	93.69	
2	1064.40	1321.20	1204.24	0	331.00	157.80
3	1321.20	1496.80	1414.04	365.00	704.40	546.46
4	1497.60	1644.00	1572.26	708.00	1080.00	913.30
5	1644.00	1790.40	1716.00	1080.00	1404.00	1215.85
6	1790.40	1935.60	1861.69	1412.00	1884.00	1542.26
7	1935.60	2106.00	2016.73	1885.20	2487.60	2167.78
8	2106.00	2336.40	2213.77	2532.00	3360.00	2979.03
9	2336.40	2722.80	2503.96	3385.20	4460.40	3818.65
10 (highest)	2724.00	30092.40	3682.02	4557.60	29231.20	7394.95

Note: The state sector refers to state-owned enterprises, state organs and public institutions. The private sector includes self-employed businesses, private enterprises, joint ventures and foreign-funded enterprises.

sector is up to 0.4929. Some typical cases released in newspapers and periodicals have also indicated the same situation. According to the survey conducted in Beijing, the income of employers is 10 times higher than that of employees. There are about one thousand private enterprises and 15,000 employees in Shanghai. The private enterprise owners all have an annual income of more than 10,000 yuan. Some employers that hire many employees may earn an annual net income of up to 50,000 or even 100,000 yuan. The Chinese managers of some foreign-funded enterprises also earn an exceptionally high income.

B. Planned system

The income distribution gap in the planned system or within the range of the State's direct control is larger than that in the unplanned system. The result of the sampling survey conducted by the Project Team shows that the monetary income[6] gap between the staff members in the state sector (including state-owned enterprises, state organs and public institutions) is much smaller than that in the private sector. Among the staff members in the state sector, the income of the 20% lowest-income earners accounts for 10.52% of the gross income; the income of the 20% highest-income earners accounts for 32.60% of the gross income, the latter being 3.1 times the former (see Table 3.1). The Gini coefficient for this sector is 0.2321.

We may produce Table 3.2 according to this calculation. Table 3.2 clearly shows the small income gap in the planned system and the big income gap in the unplanned system.

Income equalization in the planned system may also be seen from the situation after the salary reform in 1985. The composite salary system was adopted in 1985;

Special phenomena of income distribution 27

Table 3.2 Income Gap in the Planned System and Income Gap in the Unplanned System in 1988

	Share of the 20% lowest-income earners (%)	Share of the 20% highest-income earners (%)	Gini coefficient
Planned system	10.52	32.60	0.2321
Unplanned system	3.40	54.08	0.4929

Table 3.3 Salary Income Ratio of Senior and Junior Personnel before and after Salary Reform

	Before salary reform (1985)	After salary reform (1988)
Universities: teaching assistants and professors	1:4.1	1:21
Research institutes: research apprentices and research fellows	1:3.0	1:2.0
Hospitals: doctors and senior doctors	1:3.0	1:2.2
Middle schools: third-grade teachers and senior teachers	1:3.0	1:1.8
State organs: clerks and directors	1:3.1	1:1.6

Source of data: A sampling survey covering 45 cities conducted by the National Bureau of Statistics of China. Quoted from Li Xuezeng et al.'s *Establishment of the Efficiency-Oriented Salary System*, Economic Research Journal, Issue 2, 1989.

that is, a salary was divided into four parts, namely base pay, job pay, seniority pay (allowance) and bonus pay. Later, the first two parts were collectively called the standard pay. According to the data of the National Bureau of Statistics of China, the salary reform in 1985 further narrowed the salary income gap among urban employees. The salary income ratio for junior and senior staff members dropped from 1:3 to 1:2 on the whole (see Table 3.3). Some people call this "new equalitarianism", which makes sense to some extent.

C. Between the two systems

The Project Team's sampling survey shows that the average income gap between the staff members of the two systems is not very big. The average monetary income was 1876 yuan for the staff members in the state sector and 2200 yuan for the staff members in the private sector in 1988, the latter being higher than the former by 14.7%. But why has the public strongly responded to the overhigh income in the unplanned system in recent years? In my opinion, the reasons are as follows:

1   *Regional distribution.* Most people with the overhigh income in the unplanned system are located in the economically developed regions, especially coastal

28   *Special phenomena of income distribution*

open regions; therefore, the income differences between the two systems vary with regions. Table 3.4 shows that in some cities in the economically developed regions, the income of self-employed persons differs greatly from that of employees under ownership by the whole people. Naturally, Table 3.4 lists only the salary income of the employees under ownership by the whole people; it does not include the extra-salary income. If adjustment is made according to the proportion of extra-salary income estimated in the second half of this paper, the gap between the two will be smaller but still considerable.

2   *Structure.* As the income distribution in the unplanned system is quite unequal, a tiny minority of people get abnormally high income, which causes not only the high-income earners in the planned system, but also the low- and middle-income earners to make comparison. It must be pointed out here that in the unplanned system, not all people are rich. Take self-employed entrepreneurs as an example. In the central and western regions of China, most self-employed entrepreneurs earn a very low income. Even if in big cities like Shanghai, the self-employed entrepreneur whose income is significantly overhigh (annual income of up to 10,000 yuan) account for only 20% of the total number.

3   *Statistics.* Statistics in this paper include statistics of the National Bureau of Statistics of China and the sampling surveys conducted by the Project Team, and they should not be considered as very complete. Resource losses caused by the conflicts between the dual economy and their impact on income distribution are not included in these statistics, which is just one of the focal points for people to complain about unfair income distribution. Therefore, we must conduct the analysis at the fourth level.

D.   Gap between the two systems

The concentrated expression of the dual economy is the dual pricing system. The drop height of dual pricing (difference between list price and market price) creates

Table 3.4 Salary Income Comparison between Self-Employed Entrepreneurs and Employees under Ownership by the Whole People in 1988

City	(1) Income of earners in private economy (yuan)	(2) Salary of employees under ownership by the whole people (yuan)	(3) Comparison: (1)/(2)
Beijing	7458	1725	4.32
Shanghai	6000	2060	2.91
Shenyang	7608	1648	4.62
Qingdao	8479	1681	5.04
Baotou	5000	1495	3.34
Jingdezhen	4440	1511	5.18

Special phenomena of income distribution 29

Table 3.5 Comparison of Annual Per Capital Income of Urban and Rural Households

Year	(1) Annual per capital income of rural households (yuan)	(2) Annual per capital income of urban households (yuan)	(3) Comparison 1 (per capita income of rural residents is 1)	(4) Comparison 2 (per capita income of urban residents is 100)
1957	73	254	3.48	29
1964	102	243	2.38	42
1978	134	316	2.36	42
1979	160	377	2.36	42
1980	191	439	2.30	44
1981	223	500	2.24	45
1982	270	535	1.98	50
1983	310	573	1.85	54
1984	355	660	1.86	54
1985	398	749	1.88	53
1986	424	910	2.15	47
1987	463	1012	2.19	46
1988	545	1192	2.19	46
1989	602	1388	2.31	43
1990	630	1523	2.42	41

Source of data: *China Statistical Yearbook* (1981, 1983, 1989, 1990 and 1991); *Statistical Abstract of National Economy* 1984. Specifically, the value of 1979 is the mean value of 1978 and 1980 (see Zhu Ling's *Characteristics of Personal Income Distribution in China's Economic Reform*, Reform, Issue 5, 1991).

a huge difference. According to some scholars' research and estimate, such a difference (which may be called "rent" in a broad sense) is as high as about 356.9 billion yuan in China in 1988. Specifically, the total list-and-brand price difference of state-controlled commodities is about 150 billion yuan, the total list-and-brand interest margin of loans from state banks is about 113.881 billion yuan, and the list-and-brand exchange rate difference of the foreign exchange used in imports is about 93.043 billion yuan. The summation of the three items accounts for about 30% of the national income in that year.[7] It is just through the seam of the double systems that these rents outflow. These estimation methods may be further discussed, and the specific rent amount may also be overestimated. However, existence of the huge sum of rents is definitely an important soil for rent-seeking activities, corruption and unfair income distribution.

The analysis in this section shows that the aforementioned phenomena in the income distribution in China are different from equalitarianism, a typical phenomenon in the traditional socialist economic system; different from excessive income disparity, a typical phenomenon in the traditional capitalist economy; and greatly different from "common prosperity through by widening the income gap and increasing the economic efficiency", a goal to be realized by China's economic system reform and strategy of economic development. The coexistence of new

30 *Special phenomena of income distribution*

equalitarianism, old equalitarianism, and overhigh income of a small number of people and economic activities, is a special phenomenon that emerges in China's economic system reform.

III. First narrowing, then widening of income gap between urban and rural residents

Before the reform, the income gap between urban and rural residents was big. As shown in Table 3.5 and Figure 3.1, in 1957, which was the golden age for the traditional system before the reform, the income of urban residents was 3.48 times that of rural residents; in other words, the latter was 29% of the former. By 1978, just before the reform, the income of urban residents was still 2.36 times that of rural residents, or, the latter was 42% of the former. Creation of such a gap is apparently inseparable from the dual economic structure in developing countries; that is, the entire national economy is obviously divided into two systems – the modern industry sector and traditional agriculture sector. The former is capital intensive and is mostly in cities. The latter is labor intensive and is distributed in rural areas. Furthermore, this gap is also closely related to the system and policy factors. For example, before the reform, China had been adopting the low-price policy for agricultural products, and took it as one of the means to accumulate capital required for industrialization. Meanwhile, China adopted the household registration system that strictly restricted rural residents from migrating to cities, which further segmented the urban and rural economic systems. According to the research of the World Bank, "the urban-and-rural-income ratio in China is far greater than that in other low-income countries (about 1.5 on average), and slightly greater than that in middle-income countries (about 2.2 on average)".[8] See Table 3.6 for a comparison of specific countries. The income gap between urban and rural residents in China before the reform was greater than that in other developing low-income countries, which should be more directly related to the system and to policy factors.

Table 3.6 International Comparison of Income Inequality between Rural Areas and Cities

Country	Ratio of urban average income to rural income (per capita)
China (1979)	2.5
India (1973–1974)	1.4
Bangladesh	1.5
Philippines	2.1
Thailand (1975–1976)	2.2
Brazil (1976)	2.3
Colombia (1970)	2.3

Source of data: Investigation report by the World Bank: "China: Development of the Socialist Economy" (1981), Chinese version, p. 49.

Special phenomena of income distribution 31

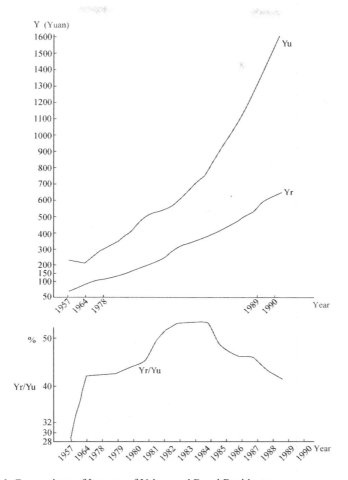

Figure 3.1 Comparison of Income of Urban and Rural Residents

The change of the income gap between urban and rural residents has undergone two distinctly different stages: the gap between the two showed a trend of narrowing before 1984, then showed a trend of widening again after 1984. As shown in Table 3.5 and Figure 3.1, the ratio of the income of urban residents to that of rural residents dropped from 2.36 in 1978 to 1.85 in 1983; or, the proportion of the income of rural residents in the income of urban residents rose from 42% to 54% in the same period; From 1984 to 1990, the ratio rose from 1.86 to 2.42, and the proportion dropped from 54% to 41%. That is to say, the income gap between urban and rural residents in 1990 had greatly exceeded the minimum gaps in 1983 and 1984 since the reform, and slightly exceeded the gap in 1978 just before the reform.

32 *Special phenomena of income distribution*

The main reasons for the substantial increase of the income of rural residents and the substantial narrowing of the income gap between urban and rural residents in the first stage include: (1) the state substantially increased the planned purchase price of agricultural products, and reduced the proportion of planned purchase of agricultural products, so that peasants can get more profit from the higher planned price and higher market price; and (2) the system of contracted responsibility linking remuneration to output for peasants was adopted, which greatly increased peasants' production enthusiasm, substantially increased the output of agricultural products, and offered the material premise for the increase of peasants' income.

The reasons for widening of the income gap between urban and rural residents in the second stage include: (1) the previous two factors boosting the substantial increase of peasants' income were strongly compensatory (substantial increase of purchase price of agricultural products) and abrupt (system change boosts the release of potential capacity), which cannot last long; (2) the focus of the economic system reform shifted to cities from 1984, allowing the income of urban residents to increase substantially; and (3) the rise in price of the agricultural means of production increased the production cost of agricultural products, which accordingly inhibited the increase of peasants' net income.

This analysis of the change of the income gap between urban and rural residents over the past 12 years is based on the data of The National Bureau of Statistics of China. The income of urban and rural residents is further analyzed based on the data of the sampling survey conducted by the Project Team in 1988.

Firstly, the income level of urban and rural residents in 1988 is observed. According to the sampling survey conducted by the Project Team, the annual per capital income of urban households was 1837.01 yuan in 1988, and the annual per capital income of rural households was 778.44 yuan, compared to the numbers released by The National Bureau of Statistics of China, which were 1192 yuan and 545 yuan respectively. The reason of such difference is that the Project Team survey data tried to count in all kinds of subsidies, especially housing subsidies and price subsidies for consumables, while the data of the statistical bureau normally took no account of the subsidy factor. The subsidies for urban residents increased significantly after 1984; therefore, the income gap between urban and rural residents was greater after subsidies were counted in. The ratio of the income of urban residents to that of rural residents in 1988 is 2.36 instead of 2.19 released by the statistical bureau; and the proportion of the income of rural residents in the income of urban residents is 42% instead of 46% released by the statistical bureau.

Secondly, let's compare the three Gini coefficients. According to the sampling survey conducted by the Project Team, we may calculate and come up with three Gini coefficients, for cities, for rural areas and for the whole country. Due to the small differences in the calculation of housing subsidies, calculation of the Gini coefficients also varies. When the housing subsidies are overestimated, the Gini coefficients are 0.232 for cities, 0.333 for rural areas and 0.385 for the whole country. When the housing subsidies are underestimated, the Gini

Special phenomena of income distribution 33

Table 3.7 Respective Proportion of Urban and Rural Households in Ten Equant Groups of National Households

Sequence of ten equant groups (from low to high)	Urban households		Rural households	
	Number of households	Percentage (%)	Number of households	Percentage (%)
1 (lowest)	8	0.42	1912	99.58
2	26	1.35	1894	98.65
3	83	4.32	1837	95.68
4	236	12.29	1684	87.71
5	717	37.34	1203	62.86
6	1280	66.67	640	33.33
7	1525	79.43	395	20.57
8	1658	86.35	262	13.65
9	1725	89.84	195	10.16
10 (highest)	1751	88.12	236	11.88

Note: Total number of households: 19,267, including 9009 urban households and 10,258 rural households.

coefficients are 0.213 for cities, 0.338 for rural areas and 0.351 for the whole country. The Gini coefficient for the whole country is not only significantly higher than the Gini coefficient for cities, but also higher than the Gini coefficient for rural areas. The income gap between urban and rural residents is rather big in China at present.

Thirdly, the income gap between urban and rural residents may also be observed from the respective proportion of urban and rural households in the ten equant groups of national households. As shown in Table 3.7, the 19,267 households in the sampling survey nationwide are made up of 9009 urban households and 10,258 rural households. Specifically, in the 20% lowest-income households, 34 urban households account for 0.18%, and 3806 rural households account for 19.75%. In the 20% highest-income households, 3476 urban households account for 18.04%, and 431 rural households account for 2.24%. In other words, the highest-income households are mostly in cities, while the lowest-income households are mostly in rural areas.

Such imbalanced distribution is more clearly shown in Figure 3.2, which is plotted according to Table 3.7. In Figure 3.2, the horizontal axis stands for the income level, while the vertical axis stands for the household percentage. High-income households are mostly in cities and low-income households are mostly in rural areas; therefore, X appears to be high in the figure. We may presume that if the income gap between urban and rural residents is very small, then X in Figure 3.2 will be short and flat.

The first-narrowed-then-widened status of the income gap between urban and rural residents over the past 12 years, as well as the current income gap between urban and rural residents, were analyzed earlier in this paper. According to the

34 *Special phenomena of income distribution*

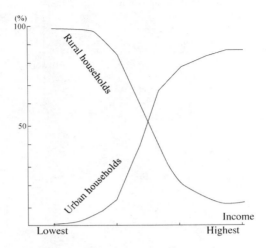

Figure 3.2 Distribution of Urban and Rural Households by Income Level

actual conditions, the following points of view are put forward from the perspective of summarizing experience of the reform and development:

Firstly, the intensity of effects of the factors that influence the income of urban and rural residents is different in different periods; therefore, it is inevitable for the change of the gap between the two to fluctuate within a short period of time. However, within a long period of time, such as 12 years as mentioned previously, is it inevitable for the gap between the two to narrow first and then widen? I don't think it is. We should sum up experience and lessons and help to narrow the gap between the two while setting the strategy of economic development, especially the strategic objective for long-term development. Certainly, we should not always expect the miracle of substantial narrowing of the gap between the two that occurred from 1978 to 1984, nor hope that substantial widening of the gap between the two that occurred from 1984 to 1990 occurs again in future development. We hope that under the premise of the general trend of gradual narrowing, the change of the gap between the two will be smaller, and development will be more stable.

Secondly, fluctuations of the aforementioned changes are apparently associated with the steps of China's economic reform, namely starting in rural areas first and then shifting to cities. As the reform cannot be accomplished overnight, it is inevitable that the reform measures come out in sequential order. The development sequence from rural areas to cities for the reform of China is successful on the whole. However, the fluctuation of the change of the aforementioned income gap between urban and rural residents shows that the supporting reform measures are still not enough. Before the reform, the traditional system divided cities and rural areas into two systems that are relatively closed to each other. After the reform, some measures have been taken to make the two systems open to each other, but the degree and steps of such opening are still subject to various constraints. In periods of economic difficulty and economic adjustment, in particular, segmentation

Special phenomena of income distribution 35

measures had to be strengthened, such as strictly restricting peasants from entering cities. The quickly widened income gap between urban and rural residents as mentioned earlier apparently is closely related to the improvement, rectification and contraction measures taken in recent years. We hope that with the improvement and rectification period coming to an end and with the promotion of new reform and development measures, the trend of a widening income gap between urban and rural residents will be inhibited and reversed.

Thirdly, the income gap between urban and rural residents and its change actually reflect the economic relations between cities and rural areas and between industry and agriculture from the side. In order to gradually narrow the income gap between urban and rural residents, the most fundamental way is to increase farm labor efficiency and gradually realize agricultural modernization. Only in this way can we provide a satisfactory base for the further development of cities and industry. Therefore, to coordinate income distribution relations between urban and rural residents, we should, in the final analysis, coordinate the relations between agriculture and industry and between rural areas and cities. To coordinate these relations, and to make them in a virtuous cycle that helps each other move forward, will help realize the goal of four modernizations.

IV. Relative narrowing of salary part and expansion of extra-salary part in income structure of urban employees

The income of urban employees has increased significantly since the reform, especially since the reform focus shifted to cities. In the process of growth, a remarkable phenomenon is that in the income structure of urban employees, the extra-salary income has grown faster than the salary income. As a result, the proportion of the extra-salary income has grown larger and larger, and the proportion of the salary income has fallen relatively in the gross income of urban employees.

According to existing statistical methods in China, a salary is normally divided into three parts, namely standard pay, allowance and bonus, which are collectively known as the salary income. An extra-salary income is made up of four parts: (1) other income from the employer, including monetary income and income in kind, such as bath and haircutting fee, traffic allowance, single child allowance, travel allowance, etc.; (2) other labor income, such as part-time income, author's remuneration and lecture fee; (3) transfer income, including alimony income, give-away income, etc.' and (4) other income in kind, which refers to the income converted from all kinds of material objects obtained from units other than the employer.

It is impossible to calculate the extra-salary income very accurately. Based on surveys on the household income of urban residents conducted by The National Bureau of Statistics of China and according to banks' receipts and disbursements, the salary income and extra-salary income of urban employees are listed in Tables 3.8 and 3.9 respectively.

Though the results of these two kinds of calculation vary, they indicate one thing: the proportion of extra-salary income is increasing. According to the first calculation, the proportion of extra-salary income in salary income has increased

36 *Special phenomena of income distribution*

Table 3.8 Salary Income and Extra-Salary Income of Urban Employees (1)

	(1)	(2)	(3)	(4) Comparison 1	(5) Comparison 2
	Salary income (yuan/person)	Extra-salary income (yuan/person)	Gross income (1) + (2)	(2)/(1)(%)	(2)/(3)(%)
1985	1056.92	269.56	1326.48	25.50	20.32
1990	2057.12	713.97	2771.09	34.70	25.76

Source of data: A sampling survey conducted by the National Bureau of Statistics of China.

Table 3.9 Salary Income and Extra-Salary Income of Urban Employees (2)

	(1)	(2)	(3)	(4) Comparison 1	(5) Comparison 2
	Salary income (yuan/person)	Extra-salary income (yuan/person)	Gross income (1) + (2)	(2)/(1)(%)	(2)/(3)(%)
1978	523.6	93.8	617.4	17.91	15.19
1985	1386.58	399.96	1786.54	28.85	22.39
1990	3067.88	1394.93	4462.81	45.47	31.26

Source of data: Calculated according to banks' cash receipts.

from 25.5% in 1985 to 34.7% in 1990; the proportion of extra-salary income in gross income has increased from 20.32% in 1985 to 25.76% in 1990. According to the second calculation, the proportion of extra-salary income in salary income has increased from 17.91% in 1978 to 28.85% in 1985 and to 45.47% in 1990; the proportion of extra-salary income in gross income has increased from 15.19% in 1978 to 22.39% in 1985 and to 31.26% in 1990.

The proportion of extra-salary income is a bit larger than the prior two calculation results, mainly because such calculation does not include rent subsidies and price subsidies. If such subsidies are included, the proportion of extra-salary income will be even higher. Xue Muqiao holds, "The total subsidies for commodity prices and rent subsidies granted by the state are roughly equal to the salary amount for employees. Therefore, China actually adopts the half-salary and half-supply system."[9]

Extra-salary income has two very distinctive characteristics: low transparency, and high degree of materialization. Salary income, on the contrary, is featured by transparency and monetization. Therefore, if we compare the monetary income and income in kind of urban residents, it will supplement and verify the earlier analysis of the relations between salary income and extra-salary income of urban employees. Now the relationship between the income in kind and monetary income of the urban residents in Zhejiang Province in 1988 is taken as an example for study.

As shown in Table 3.10, the per capita income in kind is equivalent to 585.82 yuan; the monetary income (living expenditure income) is 1453.31 yuan for the

Special phenomena of income distribution   37

Table 3.10 Income in Kind of Urban Residents in Zhejiang Province in 1988

Item	Total (100 million yuan)	Per capita amount (yuan)	Equivalent to per capita living expenditure income* (%)
(1) Price subsidies	11.31	180.29	12.41
(2) Internal benefits in kind of employer	8.79	140.12	9.64
(3) Rent subsidies	16.65	65.41	18.26
Total	36.76	585.82	40.31

Source of data: Zhejiang Economic Information Center: *Prediction and Analysis*, Issue 38, April 13, 1990.

* The per capita living expenditure income of the urban households in Zhejiang Province in 1985 is 1453.31 yuan (see "Zhejiang Statistical Yearbook").

urban residents in Zhejiang Province in 1988. The income in kind is 40.31% of the monetary income, and 28.73% of the gross income.

These facts show that judging by the relationship between salary income and extra-salary income of urban employees, or by the relationship between monetary income and income in kind of urban residents, the proportion of extra-salary income and income in kind has reached a very high level in China at present.

Why is the proportion of extra-salary income and income in kind higher than that in the traditional system? We can look for the cause only from the transition from the old system to the new one. During this transition, diversification of both income channels and distribution subjects are inevitable. However, corresponding regulatory mechanisms are often not available for the extra-salary distribution and distribution in kind. As distribution subjects, enterprises and employers often lack the self-regulating mechanism.

With the distributable resources fixed, the share distributed in salary channels and monetary forms will reduce accordingly if more resources are distributed in extra-salary channels and in-kind forms. On the contrary, when the state exercises strict control over the distribution in salary channels and monetary forms, some distributable resources are often lost in extra-salary channels and in-kind forms. For example, when the state controls overissue of bonuses by means of the "bonus tax", some enterprises distribute food to employees in the name of "purchase by employees' dining hall", and distribute articles to employees in the name of "labor protection for employees", or even evade the State's control and supervision by distributing "retail vouchers".[10] Certainly, some problems are caused by insufficient support of reform measures. For example, the monetary income of urban residents has increased since the reform, but the housing rent is still frozen. As a result, the state continues to increase invisible subsidies for urban residents, and accordingly, urban residents get more invisible income or income in kind. The proportion of the housing rent expenditure of urban residents per capita per year in gross living expenses has kept decreasing over the past years (already to less than 1%), which clearly indicates this (see Table 3.11).

Only a fraction of the extra-salary income (such as author's remuneration) is associated with labor contributions, and most of the extra-salary income is

Table 3.11 Proportion of Housing Rent Expenditure Per Capita Per Year in Gross Living Expenses Per Capita Per Year for Urban Residents

Item	1957	1964	1981	1982	1983	1984	1986	1987	1988	1989	1990
Living expenses of urban residents per capita per year (yuan)	220.00	220.68	456.84	505.92	559.44	673.20	798.96	884.40	1103.98	1210.95	1278.89
Housing rent expenditure of urban residents per capita per year (yuan)	5.16	5.76	6.36	7.98	7.80	6.48	7.20	7.74	7.873	8.82	9.36
Comparison (2)/(1) (%)	2.32	2.61	1.39	1.50	1.52	1.39	0.96	0.90	0.88	0.71	0.73

Source of data: *China Statistical Yearbook* (1987, 1988, 1989 and 1991).

distributed by head count, status or position, which can hardly stimulate the increase of labor efficiency. Furthermore, such a distribution pattern has low transparency, which not only goes against the State's statistics and supervision, but also enhances people's sense of unfairness. Therefore, how to increase the proportion of salary income, monetary income and visible income and to decrease the proportion of extra-salary income, income in kind and invisible income is indeed a task before us.

V. Epilogue

The three phenomena analyzed in this paper are essentially the special phenomena that occur during system transformation. Therefore, only by unshakably pushing forward the reform, overcoming various disordered states during system transformation and enabling the entire economic system to enter the orbit of the new system, can we solve problems fundamentally. Certainly, reform and development are closely related to each other. The issue concerning narrowing the income gap between urban and rural residents, in particular, depends not only on reform, but also on modernization of the entire rural economics; that is, both the dual economy problem and also the dual economic structure problem must be solved. In order to solve the problem of unfair income distribution, the problems concerning population movement and talent flow must also be solved, which are not only the reform issues, but also the development issues.

In the choice of reform and development strategies in the future, the awareness of comprehensive supporting reform measures and long-term considerations must be available so as to help solve the above problems. The so-called comprehensive supporting reform measures mean that various measures should coordinate with each other. Not only should the reform in rural areas coordinate with the reform in cities, but the reform in each field, such as salary reform, price reform, housing reform, tax reform and social security reform, must all coordinate with each other. The so-called long-term considerations mean that short-term behaviors should be avoided. For example, damping down inflation by increasing subsidies can only lead to distorted income distribution relations, so such a method should be avoided or minimized.

Control and management over the unplanned income and extra-salary income must be strengthened. This concerns two aspects: on the one hand, the government must work hard to establish and perfect the market rules, especially the tax system, in order to perfect the indirect control system. On the other hand, enterprises and institutions, etc., which are the subjects of income distribution, must be made to set up the self-regulating mechanism.

In deepening reform, it is an arduous task to increase transparency of income distribution. In a circumstance where market rules are unsound, it is certainly difficult to plug up various channels of invisible losses, but turning invisible subsidies (housing subsidies and subsidies for commodity prices, etc.) into visible rise (salary rise), namely reducing subsidies and increasing salary, is a practical measure.

As long as we pull through the transition period of the economic system reform after various efforts, we believe that the goal set in the early stage of the reform,

40 Special phenomena of income distribution

namely "realize common prosperity by properly widening the gap and thus increasing efficiency", will definitely be realized.

(This paper was written in December 1991; it was originally published in Issue 1 of *Economic Research Journal* in 1992.)

Notes

1 Comrade Li Shi gave strong support to the calculation of some data in this paper, which is appreciated.
2 The data in this paper are all quoted from the results of the sample surveys by the Project Team, except for those whose sources are indicated.
3 Quoted from Liu Guoguang. (1984). *中国经济发展战略问题研究* [A Study of China's Economic Development Strategies] (pp. 388–389). Shanghai: Shanghai People's Publishing House.
4 Li Chengrui. (1986). 关于中国近几年的经济政策对居民收入的消费状况影响的统计 [Statistical Report on the Impact of China's Economic Policies in Recent Years on Resident Income and Consumption]. *Statistical Research*, 1.
5 See Zhao Renwei. (1990, September). Contrast between Two Phenomena in China's Income Distribution. *Cambridge Journal of Economics*. Though the planned and unplanned systems here generally refer to the whole national economy, they normally do not include rural economic activities due to the special features and relative segmentation of the rural economic activities that are to be analyzed hereinafter.
6 The monetary income of the employees in the state sector in the sample survey by the Project Team can basically reflect the employee income status in the planned system.
7 Hu Heli. (1989). 1998 年我国租金价值的估算 [Estimation of Rental Value in China in 1988]. *Comparative Economic & Social Systems*, 5.
8 中国：社会主义经济的发展 – 世界银行经济考察团队中国经济的考察报告 [China: Development of the Socialist Economy: Investigation Report by Economic Investigation Group of the World Bank] (p. 49). (1981). Chinese version.
9 Xue Muqiao. (1989). 谈谈劳动工资制度的改革 [On the Reform of the Labor and Salary System]. In *中国社会主义劳动工资问题* [Issues on Socialist Labor and Salary in China] (pp. 11–12). Beijing: Labor and Personnel Publishing House.
10 For details regarding some employers' issuance of "retail vouchers" to employees, and issuance of retail vouchers, which is banned by explicit order by the General Office of the State Council, see the report in *People's Daily* on June 2, 1991.

4 Residents' income distribution in China

In cities, rural areas and regions

Some gratifying achievements have been in the research project concerning income distribution in China, which was jointly carried out by the Income Distribution Project Team of Institute of Economics of the Chinese Academy of Social Sciences, and the scholars from the University of California and Columbia University in the United States and the University of Oxford in Britain. The cooperation members of both sides held a symposium in Xi'an, China, on December 28–30, 1991, and submitted 19 theses, including some excellent ones. Based on a large number of survey data and using the analysis method of modern economics, these theses make the empirical analysis and study of some problems in income distribution in China that the domestic and foreign scholars and policy makers are concerned about, and offer some policy implications and views that deserve attention. This paper comments on these research findings.

Fundamentally speaking, the economic issues of China may be summed up into two major themes: reform and development. This is the case not only at present, but also for quite a long time to come, and the issue is the one that economic circles and economic policy makers are most concerned about. The status of resident income distribution, as one of the economic reform and economic development achievements, not only constitutes an important system standard that assesses the result of reform and development, but also will speed up or delay the progress of economic reform and economic development.

I. General description

Great changes have taken place in the pattern of resident income distribution in China since the economic reform began 12 years ago. Under the impact of evolution of a number of ownership structures, and with the two major economic systems in urban and rural areas separated from each other, it is very difficult to make a general judgment of the income distribution pattern of Chinese residents and to analyze it with a uniform theoretical framework while the labor market is still in the early development stage during the economic mechanism transition and while local economic segmentation is quite influential today. Both the historical change process of resident income distribution in China, as indicated by time series data, and the relative importance of some explanatory variables in resident income decisions and income distribution, as indicated by cross-section data, carry the traces of the original economic system and the factors of the growing new economic system.

42   *Residents' income distribution in China*

The survey data on the income of urban and rural residents in 1988, which the Income Distribution Project Team acquired, has provided an experiential grounding for judging the basic income distribution pattern in China. According to the result of data analysis and other data concerned, the basic pattern of resident income distribution in China may be summed up by the following aspects:

In the past decade, inequality of resident income distribution in China showed a trend of continuous expansion. Our sample data show that the Gini coefficient of the resident income nationwide in 1988 is 0.382. This number is apparently higher than the Gini coefficient 0.33, which was estimated by the World Bank for resident income in China in 1980.[1] Though estimation of the Gini coefficients for the two years is based on different sources of data and different income definitions,[2] a large part of the differences between the two should be interpreted as having been caused by such factors as the widened income gap between urban and rural areas, increased income inequality in cities and in rural areas and a widened inter-regional income gap.

The time series data released by the National Bureau of Statistics of China prove that in the past ten-plus years, the income gap between urban and rural residents in China has undergone a U-shaped process; that is, the income gap between urban and rural residents narrowed first from 1978 to 1984, and then gradually expanded from 1984 to 1990.[3] It is worth pointing out that the income gap between urban and rural residents in 1990 exceeded that in 1978 just before the reform. Furthermore, the widened income gap between urban and rural areas is also a major factor that causes the increase of resident income inequality nationwide. Our analysis of the 1988 sample data shows that the level of per capita income in cities may explain 82.5% of the resident income differences nationwide, but the level of per capita income in rural areas can only explain that for 11.4%[4] in the income composition of rural residents, the pseudo-Gini coefficients of other income items, except for individual salary income, are all smaller than the national Gini coefficient. That is to say, these income items all narrow the resident income gap nationwide. In contrast, all the composition items of the income of urban residents have very high pseudo-Gini coefficients (0.69–0.84), and the relative rise of income level in cities can only lead to widened resident income inequality nationwide.

The income distribution inequality in urban residents in China also shows a trend of continuous expansion. According to the estimate of the World Bank, the Gini coefficient of the income of urban residents in China is 0.16 in 1980.[5] Estimated based on our samples, the Gini coefficient of the income of urban residents in China is 0.233 in 1988, up by about 46% compared to 1980. If the widened income gap of urban residents is characterized by the abnormally high income of some people, then the other characteristic of the urban income distribution is new equalitarianism.

The income gap of rural residents in China has also undergone a process of first narrowing and then widening. The World Bank's estimation of the Gini coefficient for the rural areas in China for the 1978–1986 period shows that from 1978 to 1982, the income gap of rural residents was gradually narrowed, with the Gini coefficient falling from 0.32 to 0.22; the income gap of rural residents was widened year by year from 1983, with the Gini coefficient rising to 0.31 in 1986. Estimated based on our samples, the Gini coefficient of the income of rural residents is 0.338 in 1988. An important reason for the intensified income inequality in rural areas of

China is the imbalance of inter-regional economic development. Such imbalance grows out of the evolution of the industrial structure within the regions, especially the differences in the development scale and speed of rural industries.

The inter-region (inter-provincial) income gap in China also shows a trend of continuous expansion. According to the data of the National Bureau of Statistics of China, the inter-provincial income gap in rural areas shows a trend of almost perpendicular rise from 1980 to 1990, whether measured with the inter-provincial Gini coefficient calculated based on the per capita net income in the rural areas in each province, or measured with the ratio of the rural per capita income of the highest province to the rural per capita income of the lowest province. The widened inter-regional income gap is also an important factor that leads to the widened national income gap. Our analysis of the 1988 samples shows that 81.87% of the overall differences of the income of rural residents nationwide can be interpreted as inter-provincial income differences, while the remaining 18.13% can be interpreted as intra-provincial income differences.

From the vertical perspective, the resident income gap in China shows a trend of continuous expansion, whether in cities or rural areas, whether between cities and rural areas or between regions. From the horizontal perspective, however, the degree of resident income inequality in China (Mainland China) is apparently lower than other Asian countries, except that it is higher than Taiwan (province) and slightly higher than a small number of countries or regions such as South Korea. It is noteworthy that in other Asian countries, the degree of income distribution inequality in cities is generally greater than that in rural areas, while the opposite is true in China. In contrast, China's degree of income distribution equality in cities is the highest, and degree of income distribution equality in rural areas is at the moderate level among the Asian countries.

II. Income distribution in cities and towns: roles of planning and market

The study of the income distribution of urban residents in China may be conducted in a context where the two major systems, namely planning and market, and two different regulatory mechanisms coexist and interact with each other. Planning and market not only will directly lead to the significant differences in income distribution for the employees working in these two major systems, but they also will change the relative importance of the other factors and variables that determine employees and residents' household income and income distribution.

A. Composition and distribution of income of urban residents

According to the different sources of income, the disposable income of urban residents in China may be divided into eight parts, namely: monetary income from salary, monetary income of retired people, income of non-employed (non-retired) people, subsidies and monetary income, depreciation allowance of owner-occupied housing, income of self-employed persons and private enterprise owners, asset income, and other income (such as transfer income). Table 4.1 lists the degree of distribution equality of various kinds of income and their proportion of gross

44 *Residents' income distribution in China*

Table 4.1 Income Gap of Urban Residents and Its Sources

Income and its composition	1. Proportion of each income Ui (%)	2. Gini coefficient or pseudo-Gini coefficient (Gorgi)	3. Uigi absolute contribution	4. Uigi/G(%) relative contribution
1. Monetary income of in-service employees	44.42	0.178	0.079	33.9
2. Monetary income of retired people	6.83	0.335	0.023	9.8
3. Income of non-employed persons	0.47	0.433	0.002	0.9
4. Subsidies and income in kind, including:				
a. Various ticket subsidies	5.26	0.13	0.007	2.9
b. Housing subsidies	18.14	0.311	0.056	24.2
c. Other subsidies and income in kind	15.68	0.208	0.033	14.0
5. Depreciation allowance of owner-occupied housing	3.9	0.338	0.013	5.7
6. Income of self-employed or private entrepreneurs	0.74	0.413	0.003	1.3
7. Asset income	0.49	0.437	0.002	0.9
8. Other income	4.06	0.377	0.015	6.6
Gross income	100.00	0.233	0.233	100.00

income, which shows the relationship between the distribution equality degree of gross income and that of various kinds of income.

In the numeric comparison, three aspects are worthy of attention.

1   The monetary salary income of in-service employees accounts for only 44.42% of the gross income of urban residents. Though it is the biggest share of resident gross income, it does not have a big proportion.
2   Resident subsidy income, which is mainly composed of housing subsidy, food subsidy and employees' subsidy-type monetary income, ranks second among various income sources in terms of its proportion of gross income, up to 39.08%. If the medical subsidy is added, the subsidized income of urban residents will be roughly the same as the monetary salary income of employees.
3   The Gini coefficient of the per capita gross income of urban residents is 0.233, which indicates that the degree of income equality is overhigh. The degree of distribution inequality of the monetary salary income of in-service employees (pseudo-Gini coefficient of 0.178), various ticket subsidies (pseudo-Gini coefficient of 0.130) and other subsidies and income in kind

(pseudo-Gini coefficient of 0.208) is lower than that of gross income, while the degree of distribution inequality of other subitem income is higher than that of gross income.

In addition, it is obvious that the distribution of employee salary income and subsidies, subject to much planning and administrative control, shows a high degree of equality; while the distribution of income of self-employed persons and private enterprise owners and asset income, subject to greater market influence, shows a low degree of equality.

B. Comparison of internal income gaps in sectors of different ownership

Through comparing the income level and income gap of internal employees in sectors of different ownership, we may further understand the different effects of planning and market on the income distribution pattern. The comparison between employees of state-owned enterprises subject to excessive planning and administrative intervention, on one hand, and employees of individual enterprises, joint ventures and foreign-funded enterprises subject to excessive market regulation (collectively known as the "private sector") on the other, shows that there are not big differences between the two in terms of average monetary income level. According to our sample data, 1988 monetary income is 1876 yuan for the former and 2200 yuan for the latter. If the good remuneration for state-owned sector employees, such as housing conditions, medical treatment and labor protection, is considered, then the real income of the two is almost the same. However, the state-owned sector and private sector have apparently different income distribution patterns. The monetary income gap of the employees in the state-owned sector is not obvious, with the Gini coefficient being 0.232. The income gap in the private sector is more obvious, with the Gini coefficient as high as 0.493.

Our further study of employees' income composition shows that the state-owned sector's distribution mechanism is different from that of the private sector. The regression analysis, covering ten groups of dummy variables such as sex, age group, national status, educational level, pattern of ownership, job type, employment nature and province of employer, shows that the monetary cash income of the joint-venture employees is 19% higher than that of the employees of state-owned enterprises, and the former's base pay is 31% higher than that of the latter; but its income other than base pay is 8% lower than the latter. This indicates that the former tends to pay employees in the form of salary, while the latter tends to pay employees in the form of welfare.

The state-owned sector is subject to much planning control as well as receives much preferential treatment from the planning system. In comparison, the collective ownership sector is subject to control but does not enjoy preferential treatment. Compared to the state-owned sector, the average monetary income of collective-ownership employees is 17% lower, but the degree of equality of monetary income distribution is almost the same between the two. The monetary income differences

46 *Residents' income distribution in China*

between the employees of the state-owned sector and those of the collective ownership sector grow mainly out of the differences in labor resource allocation, labor quality and enterprise size between the two sectors. Compared to the state-owned sector, the collective ownership sector has a higher percentage of female employees, smaller enterprises and lower degree of education of employees.

C. Rate of return to education and "income misplacement between intellectual and manual workers" hypothesis

The hypothesis of "income misplacement between intellectual and manual workers", which has been debated for a long time within economic circles in China, has been challenged in this research project. Theoretically, to answer the question of whether income is misplaced between intellectual and manual workers is to estimate an individual's rate of return to education. If the estimated result shows that an individual's rate of return to education is a positive value, then the issue of income misplacement between intellectual and manual workers in a general sense does not exist; otherwise, the issue exists.

Internationally, an individual's rate of return to education is mostly estimated using the J. Mincer formula,[6] which is:

$$LY = b_0 + b_1 S + b_2 E + b_3 E^2 + u \tag{1}$$

Where LY is the logarithm of personal income, S is the number of educational years, E is the number of working years (normally in years), and u is the error term. The economic meaning of the formula is that when the direct expenses of education are not considered, the coefficient b_1 stands for the earning rate of human capital, or earning rate of foregone income (also known as "individual's rate of return to education") that the income earner has obtained during education; b_2 and b_3 are the earning rates of human capital that individuals at work have obtained (including on-the-job training). Through regression analysis of the monetary income of 17,981 employees in cities and towns and their number of educational years and work experience, using the above formula and our 1988 samples, we get the estimated value of each variation coefficient. The result shows that each estimated value is highly significant. The estimated value of b_1, which stands for an individual's rate of return to education, is 3.8%. It shows that on average, provided that the working years are the same, every additional year of education may increase an employee's personal income by 3.8%. This result is a negative answer to the hypothesis of "income misplacement between intellectual and manual workers".

The positive value of an individual's rate of return to education means that there is no absolute income misplacement between intellectual and manual workers in the present stage, but that does not mean such rate of return is reasonable. The individual's rate of return to education in China is not only lower than that in other developing countries,[7] but it is also lower than the interest rates of bank deposits in China. This indicates that the income mechanism's compensation for education or human capital is insufficient. It is not difficult to imagine that with direct expenses of education (tuition and related costs, etc., paid by individuals) on the rise in the future, education is losing its economic appeal.

The individual educational return in China is on the low side mainly because of the salary policy and salary increase mechanism in China. Firstly, China's salary policy does not set the differential starting salaries for new employees whose educational level is below technical secondary school (or senior high school). Therefore, for employees whose educational level is senior high school, junior high school or even primary school, working years rather than educational-level differences determine their salary differences, unless employees with a higher degree of education have more chances of promotion. Secondly, the several rounds of "rigid-uniformity-style" general salary adjustment and the inter-region or inter-department salary rises after the "Great Cultural Revolution" basically took no account of employees' educational differences, which further narrowed the salary gap between employees with different educational levels.

Another way to study the relationship between educational level and income level is to regard education as a dummy variable and put it into a regression model together with other characteristic variables of employees for estimation. The estimation result shows the income differences of employees with different levels (grades) of education when other characteristic variables remain unchanged (or the same). The result shows that employees' educational levels are highly positively correlated to their income levels. With primary school education of less than three years as the benchmark, the employees earn a monetary income of 0.6% higher if they have more than three years of primary school education, 3.79% higher if they graduate from primary school, 9.14% higher if they graduate from junior high school, 9.78% if they graduate from senior high school, 11.21% higher if they graduate from technical secondary school, 12.77% higher if they graduate from junior college and 18.10% higher if they graduate from university. Obviously, such results also go against the hypothesis of "income misplacement between intellectual and manual workers".

The planning and market income determination mechanisms assess the contributions made by education to income differently. The comparison between Guangdong Province, whose marketization degree is high, and Henan Province, whose marketization degree is low, shows that in determining employee income, Guangdong Province attaches greater importance to the variable of education. In Guangdong Province, employees whose degree of education is above university earn an income which is 35.89% higher than illiterate and semiliterate employees; while in Henan Province, this number is only 13.59%. Such comparison also shows, more or less, that the market mechanism is more sensitive than the planning mechanism in assessing human capital.

D. Reassess the function of subsidies

We should not underestimate the impact of subsidies received by urban residents on the income distribution of urban residents and the income gap between urban and rural residents, whether from the perspective of the absolute amount or from

48 *Residents' income distribution in China*

that of the relative amount. The study of the latter issue mainly concerns the absolute level of subsidies, which will be described in Section IV of this paper. The former issue concerns not only the proportion of subsidies in resident income, but also the distribution of subsidies among residents (distribution). Here we will discuss the role played by subsidies in the income distribution of urban residents from these two aspects.

Due to differences in the methods of estimating housing subsidies and medical subsidies, there is not a very accurate value concerning the total subsidies that urban residents get in various ways. According to the calculation that overestimates housing subsidies and excludes medical subsidies, the per capita subsidies each urban resident household in China received in 1988 totaled 719.84 yuan, equivalent to 39.08% of its disposable income. According to the calculation that includes medical subsidies and underestimates housing subsidies, the amount of subsidies each urban resident household received was equivalent to 41.12% of its gross income. Among various subsidies, the housing subsidy comes out on top. On average, it is equivalent to 18.14% of the per capita disposable income of each resident household, and 13.5% of the gross monetary income of each resident household.

What effects do subsidies have on the income distribution of urban residents? Do they widen or narrow the income gap? In the ten equant groups of urban residents divided based on per capita income, the degree of inequality of subsidy distribution is slightly higher compared to the gross income of residents. This indicates that high-income resident households get a bigger proportion of subsidies, while low-income residents get a smaller proportion of subsidies. A further breakdown of various subsidy items shows that various subsidies have different effects on the gross income gap (see Table 4.2). Among various subsidies, the housing subsidy deserves a special description. The housing subsidy has the obvious effect of widening the income gap of urban residents. The pseudo-Gini coefficient of the

Table 4.2 Income Distribution Effects of Subsidies

	Proportion of highest-income group and lowest-income group in ten equant groups
Gross income	4.023
Various subsidies	
1. Non-staple food price subsidy	2.812
2. Traffic allowance	6.696
3. Other monetary subsidies	3.164
4. Ticket and income in kind	6.605
5. Housing subsidy	3.671
6. Medical subsidy	2.569
7. Grain and oil subsidy	1.863
8. Non-staple food subsidy	3.121
9. Other consumption subsidies	4.647

Residents' income distribution in China 49

housing subsidy, which is calculated according to the sequence of the per capita disposable income of residents, is as high as 0.311 – far higher than 0.233, which is the Gini coefficient of the disposable income of urban residents. Because the housing subsidy takes up a considerable proportion of residents' disposable income, its distribution may explain 24.2% of the degree of inequality of this income.

Inequality of subsidy distribution and its effect of widening the income gap have posed two questions. Firstly, what is the function of subsidies? In most of the market economy countries, subsidies are mainly a kind of compensatory income for low-income people, so as to allow them to possess and sustain necessary survival conditions and to narrow the obvious income gap caused by the market mechanism. Such a function was taken into consideration when China started to set the subsidy policy, and it had played a positive role. Why has the function of subsidies in narrowing the income gap developed in the opposite direction as time goes by? It is impossible to answer this question before we study in depth the subsidy mechanism in China. Secondly, why can't planning and administrative means distribute subsidies on a relatively equal basis or in favor of low-income earners? Some subsidies, such as the grain and oil subsidy for residents, still have a high degree of distribution equality since they were implemented more than 30 years ago, which, to some extent, is associated with the long-term unchanged grain and oil ration. For some subsidies in which increments are created constantly, such as the housing subsidy, the distribution mechanism keeps changing as time goes by, and ultimately a subsidy distribution mechanism that helps widen the income gap will be created, though such a mechanism, in name, is still controlled by administrative means (or planning means).

E. *High-income class and rent-seeking[8] activities*

As mentioned earlier, the income gap of urban residents in China is not prominent, but that does not mean that high-income earners do not exist in society, though the relative proportion of these people is not high. According to our 1988 samples, of the ten equant groups, the per capita disposable income is about 3868.2 yuan for the highest-income household, which accounts for 21% of the gross income of the samples, and 921 yuan for the lowest-income group, which accounts for 5% of the gross income of the samples after various subsidies and income in kind are considered. The ratio of the highest-income group to the lowest-income group is 4.2:1. People's empirical estimation shows that high-income earners are mostly self-employed persons and private enterprise owners, which has been proved by many typical surveys. In our samples, private, the average monetary income is 7394.95 yuan in the highest-income group of employees in the private and self-employed sectors. This number is double that in the highest-income group of employees in the state sector. It cannot be denied that the high-income earners among the self-employed persons and private enterprise owners will underreport their operating income due to worry about policy changes and for the purposes of tax evasion. From the study perspective, if we know their general psychology of underreporting and the empirical proportion of what they report to their actual income, then we may estimate their average actual income on a relatively practical basis.

50 *Residents' income distribution in China*

Some high-income earners can be felt by people in real life but cannot be reflected by sampling surveys and statistical data. These people are mainly rent-seekers during the system transition. The rent-seeking income of these people varies with each individual and is therefore greatly invisible. Therefore, it is very difficult to estimate their income levels. However, the study of the relationship between rent-seeking activities and income distribution is of great significance.

Logically, the relationship between rent-seeking activities and income distribution may be studied at three levels. The first level is the estimation of the total rental of the whole society, which involves determination of the definition of rent-seeking activities, and calculation methods for the rental. The second level is the estimation of rental losses of the society; that is, study of the percentage of the total social rental that is ultimately possessed by individuals. The third level is the distribution of rental losses; that is, ultimately the rental is possessed by the high-income class or low-income class, or is distributed uniformly, because different distribution of rental losses will have different effects on the resident income distribution of the whole society. The study at the second and third levels requires accurate survey data as the basis, but it is difficult to get such data in the present stage. Therefore, our discussion is limited to the first level.

Regarding the estimation of rental, the central point of the argument is whether the total rental should be estimated based on the difference between the planned price and market price, or based on the difference between the planned price and equilibrium price. According to the first kind of calculation, the total rental is about 356.9 billion yuan in 1988, which is equivalent to 30% of the national income in that year.[9] The second kind of calculation does not give a specific estimated value, because the equilibrium value is just a theoretical price. In the case where a perfect competitive market is not available, it is difficult to know the accurate equilibrium price. The rationality of the first calculation scheme is its assumption that in reality, market share and market transaction volume do not vary with the increase of rent-seeking activities; therefore, the market price remains unchanged even if it is distorted. In addition, it regards the rental amount as a potential amount instead of a realized amount. The second calculation scheme assumes that the market share will expand with transformation of the potential rental into the realized rental and thus lead to the drop in the market price. When the market share is expanded to a certain scale, the market equilibrium price will emerge. Therefore, the realized rental comes only from the difference between the planned price and equilibrium price. It is not difficult to know that the rental amount estimated according to the second calculation scheme is far lower than that estimated according to the first calculation scheme.

F. Role played by age in income determination

The regression analysis using our sample data in 1988 shows that among urban employees in China, the relationship between monetary income and age structure is manifested as a converse-U. That is, monetary income rises with age, especially the years of working, reaches the highest point at a certain age and then begins to decline. This relationship exists in almost all economies. Mainly two theories explain this converse-U relationship between income or salary and age. One holds that work experience helps create human capital, and the salary rise and change are completely determined by the life-cycle change of human capital. The other holds that enterprises are willing to pay the seniority salary solely because they want to reduce chances of "job-hopping" by their old employees. Both explanations assume that the labor market exists and that enterprises have the right to decide the salary at their discretion. Such an assumption apparently fails to comply with the actual situation in China. Therefore, the converse-U relationship can be explained only by China's unique salary system.

In China, the importance of seniority in the salary increase mechanism for employees is common knowledge. In a very wide age bracket for employees, the power of seniority exceeds that of the number of educational years in explaining monetary income differences. Such high correlation between seniority (or age) and income levels is, to a large extent, the result of the long-term combination of a social culture mindset and the administrative salary management system. In a society where experience is advocated and the old are respected, increasing salary based on seniority can be regarded as the most effective measure for the centralized and unified salary management system. The biggest advantages of this method are its minimum decision-making and operation costs and minimum social conflicts. Meanwhile, with no labor market, an employee's other individual characteristic variables, such as occupation, job department and degree of education, almost all become fixed values, and only age is a natural variable. Only by associating the age (or seniority) variable with the salary variable can we ensure continuity of the salary policy and allow all employees to anticipate the salary increase. Furthermore, if we assess it from the perspective of the whole life cycle, such a distribution result seems relatively equal.

Some analytical results provide some proof for our explanation. If all the monetary income of employees is divided into base pay and other monetary income, the relationship between the two kinds of income and employees' age structure is a converse-U, but the highest points of the two kinds of income are at different ages. The highest point of base pay is in the 55–60 age group, which indicates that employees' base pay is maximized before retirement. The highest point of other monetary income is in the 41–45 age group; it then drops by 13% between age 45 and retirement. The first kind of income is mainly determined by planning control, while the second kind of income is mainly determined by enterprises and affected by the market.

III.   Rural income distribution during development

If the income distribution pattern of urban residents results from the coexistence and interaction between the planning mechanism and market mechanism, then the income distribution pattern of rural residents is the concrete reflection in economic development. Compared to that in cities and towns, the degree of inequality of income distribution is high in rural areas. The Gini coefficient of the income of rural residents, which is calculated based on our data of 1988, is 0.338, about 50% higher than that in cities and towns. Furthermore, the experimental data in recent years show that the degree of inequality of income distribution of rural residents

52 *Residents' income distribution in China*

in China tends to expand continuously. Therefore, we must study in depth those factors that widen the income gap in rural areas. What coexists with the inequality of rural income distribution is rural poverty. Analyzing the cause and mechanism of rural poverty and coming up with effective policies and measures to eradicate poverty on this basis are significant, whether for rural economic development or for narrowing the income gap. In the long term, studying the relationship between income distribution and property distribution of rural residents helps to understand the change trend of income distribution. Therefore, we will turn to the latter two aspects after assessing some research findings on the influential factors of rural income determination and income distribution.

A. *Analysis of various income sources that affect income gap*

The disposable income of peasants may be divided into different subitems of income according to different study purposes. In our study, the disposable income of peasants is divided into the household production and operation income (including cash income and self-produced and self-marketed products), individual salary income, depreciation allowance of house property, non-salary income from collectives and enterprises, asset income, net subsidy and other income (such as transfer income), depending on the sources. For the degree of equality of gross income and various incomes, see Table 4.3.

Table 4.3 shows that the household production and operation income constitutes the major part of the gross income of a rural resident household, accounting

Table 4.3 Distribution of Gross Income and Subitem Income of Rural Residents

Gross income and its composition	*1. Proportion of each income Ui (%)*	*2. Gini coefficient or pseudo-Gini coefficient (G or gi)*	*3. Absolute contribution Uigi*	*4. Relative contribution Uigi/G (%)*
1. Household production and operation income	74.21	0.282	0.209	61.8
including: a. Cash income	−33.08	−0.436	−0.144	−42.6
b. Self-produced and self-marketed products	−41.13	−0.159	−0.065	−19.2
2. Individual salary income	8.73	0.710	0.062	18.3
3. Depreciation allowance of house property	9.67	0.281	0.027	8.0
4. Non-salary income from collectives and enterprises	2.4	0.487	0.012	3.6
5. Asset income	0.170	0.484	0.001	0.3
6. Net subsidy	−1.9	0.052	−0.001	−0.3
7. Other income (transfer income, etc.)	6.71	0.418	0.028	8.3
Gross income	100	0.338	0.338	100

Residents' income distribution in China 53

for 74.21%. Its distribution is relatively equal, and the pseudo-Gini coefficient is 0.282, about 20% lower than the Gini coefficient of the gross income (0.338). However, in the household production and operation income, the two parts also have different degrees of distribution inequality. Cash income shows a high degree of inequality, and its pseudo-Gini coefficient is −0.436, about 29% higher than that of gross income. Self-produced and self-marketed products have a very low degree of distribution inequality, and the pseudo-Gini coefficient is only −0.159. Household production and operation income, as a whole, has a low degree of inequality; therefore, its explanatory power for the degree of inequality of the gross income is 61.8%, lower than its proportion of gross income. Individual salary income accounts for 8.73% of gross income, but it has a very high degree of distribution inequality, with the pseudo-Gini coefficient being 0.710. Therefore, its explanatory power for the degree of inequality of the gross income is 18.3%, far higher than its proportion of gross income. Last, the distribution of the depreciation allowance of house property is noteworthy. Depreciation allowance of house property is estimated mainly based on the present value of the house. Its low degree of inequality (pseudo-Gini coefficient of 0.281) reflects the equality of rural residents in possession of house property.

If peasants' production and operation income is further divided into the agricultural production and operation income and non-agricultural income, and their pseudo-Gini coefficients are estimated respectively, then we may see that the degree of inequality of the latter (pseudo-Gini coefficient of 0.398) is apparently higher than that of the former (pseudo-Gini coefficient of 0.242). Based on the high inequality of individual salary income, we may make the following judgment: peasants' non-agricultural economic activities are a major cause of the inequality of rural income distribution. However, such process of income inequality reflects, on the one hand, the evolution of the rural industrial structure in China, and on the other hand, the imbalance of regional economic development.

B. *Multi-variable regression analysis of income determination*

Here we mainly review the estimation results of the two groups of regression models that explain the determination of income of rural residents in China. In the first group of regression models, the explained variables of the three models are peasants' gross income, household production and operation income, and individual salary income respectively. The explanatory variables of the three models are almost the same. Specifically, the dummy variables include the job type, province and Party member status. The continuous variables include the ratio of male labor, degree of education, value of productive fixed assets, land area, value of other assets, amount of chemical fertilizer applied, sideline rate and commodity rate.[10] The result of model estimation shows that the following aspects are of significance. Firstly, the average degree of education of the laborers of a peasant household has a prominent impact on gross income. Among the eight levels of education, from illiterate and semiliterate to above a university degree, every level increase for a peasant household's members may increase the gross income

54 *Residents' income distribution in China*

of the household by 34.97 yuan. Likewise, the correlation between the degree of education of the laborers of the peasant household and the household production and operation income is highly prominent. However, in the analysis of the salary income function, the estimated value of the coefficient of labor's degree of education is very low and statistically non-significant. Secondly, the ratio of male labor in a peasant household does not prominently impact gross income. Every increase of the ratio of male labor by 1/3 can help increase the peasant household's gross income by only 50 yuan. However, the impact of a household's population size on the gross income is prominent. Assume that other factors remain unchanged. On average, every additional member of a peasant household may help increase its gross income by 239 yuan, which is equivalent to 31% of the peasant household's per capita income, and accordingly will reduce the per capita income of the household by 11%. Assume that other variables will vary with the expansion of a household's population size, and then every additional member of a peasant household may help increase its gross income by 576 yuan and will reduce the per capita income by 4% only. Considering the economy in consumption resulting from a household's population size, expanding this population size will have no adverse impact on the household's actual income. This also indicates that peasants' strong inclination to expand household size is not economically self-limited. Thirdly, the impact of productive fixed assets on the peasant household's gross income, especially on household production and operation income, is prominent. The annual rate of return of productive fixed assets is 6% to gross income and 9% to household production and operation income. In contrast, the contribution of the land area to the peasant household's gross income and household production and operation income is negligible. Though the estimated coefficient value of the variable is statistically significant, its value is extremely low. Every additional mu (= 0.0667 hectares) of land can increase household production and operation income by 1.18 yuan only. This result may be caused by the following factors:

1   The per capita quantity of land is inversely proportional to the regional economic development level. This inverse relationship exists not only between provinces but also in each province. Therefore, in the regression model where "province" is used as a dummy variable, it is difficult to completely eliminate the impact of such inverse relationship.
2   The differences in land quality are not reflected in the regression model, because such differences will affect the linear relation between land productivity and land area.
3   The land area perhaps does not constitute the factor that causes the gap of household production and operation income in reality. This is associated with the allocation method of land, which is a scarce factor. The current land allocation in rural areas may be based on the quantity of supporting agricultural assets possessed by the peasant household in order to ensure the highly efficient use of land. In this case, the contributions of land to income are hidden in other productive assets. Therefore, the direct effects of land on income are not obvious.

4   The low rate of return of land is an actual situation. With the continuous decline in relative prices of agricultural products and the continuous rise in prices of agricultural inputs, the marginal productivity of land has declined to a very low level. These explanations need to be further estimated before they are verified.

Fourthly, the sideline rate, which manifests a peasant household's diversification of production, statistically does not have a prominent impact on household's gross income, and its estimated coefficient value is very low (1.40). The commodity rate, which reflects the degree of market development, has a highly prominent impact on peasants' gross income, with an estimated coefficient value of up to 1642.8. This indicates that every 10% increase in the commodity rate will accordingly help increase the peasant household's gross income by 164.28 yuan.

In the second group of regression models, the explained variable is peasants' per capita income. The explanatory variables include the ratio of labor in household population, per capita educational level in the household, ratio of salary income earners in labor, percentage of non-agricultural income in gross income, average age of family members, productive fixed assets, percentage of irrigable land, commodity rate, geographical location (specifically, Sichuan, Guizhou, Yunnan, Shaanxi, Gansu, Qinghai and Ningxia are regarded as western regions, and other provinces as non-western regions) and Party member status. Judging by the estimated coefficient value of the explanatory variable, the labor ratio has a highly prominent impact on the peasant household's per capita income. In a family of five people, every additional laborer may help increase the peasant household's gross income by 357 yuan. The increased ratio of salary income earners in laborers will also increase the peasant household's gross income more significantly. For example, in a peasant household of three laborers, every additional salary income earner may help increase the peasant household's per capita income by 226 yuan. This, to some extent, reflects the significant differences between peasants working in township enterprises and peasants engaged in agricultural operations. The ratio of irrigable land is also an important variable that affects the income of a peasant household. Every 10% increase of the irrigable land ratio may help increase the peasant household's per capita income by about 22 yuan. In addition, the estimation result of some other explanatory variables is roughly the same as that of the first group of models.

C.   Analysis of property distribution of peasant household

On the one hand, residents' property value is the result of the long-term accumulation of their income, whose distribution equality reflects the equality of resident income distribution within a long period in the past to some extent. On the other hand, residents' property value will have a certain impact on resident income in the current period and on income distribution equality. The property distribution of rural residents in China may be studied at two levels: firstly, the pure study of the equality of resident property distribution itself; secondly, the analysis of the relationship between property distribution and income distribution.

56 Residents' income distribution in China

Table 4.4 Property Distribution of Rural Resident Households (1988)

Per capita property	Percentage (%)	Gini coefficient	Pseudo-Gini coefficient
Gross property	100	0.311	0.311
Land (value)	58.8	0.310	0.268
House property (value)	31.2	0.488	0.380
Productive fixed assets	7.7	0.559	0.250
Financial assets	3.1	0.859	0.500
Non-housing liabilities	−0.8	0.934	−0.014

The property of a peasant household in China is mainly composed of land, house property, productive fixed assets, financial assets, etc. Table 4.3 shows the distribution inequality of gross property and subitem property.

Table 4.4 shows that the distribution of total assets of peasant households is highly equal, with a Gini coefficient of 0.311. Among the property items, the distribution of land value is the most equal, with the Gini coefficient of 0.310; the distribution of financial assets is the most unequal, with the Gini coefficient of up to 0.859, which indicates that such assets are mostly in the hands of a small number of peasant households. The pseudo-Gini coefficient of each property item, which is calculated according to the gross property sequencing, shows the relationship between its distribution and that of total assets. The pseudo-Gini coefficients of land and productive fixed assets are both lower than the Gini coefficient of total assets, which indicates that their distribution helps narrow the distribution inequality of the gross property of peasant households. The pseudo-Gini coefficients of house property and financial assets indicate that their distribution pattern shows the sequence of peasant households' accumulation of property: they first invest in productive fixed assets that go with land, then in real estate and finally in financial assets. On the whole, the degree of inequality of rural property distribution in China is far lower than that in other developing countries, and also lower than the degree of inequality of rural income distribution in China. For the second situation, it is difficult to find a precedent in other countries in the world.

There are two kinds of explanations for the relatively equal property distribution of peasant households in China. Firstly, the land distribution equality is determined by the institutional factor. As the land value accounts for a large proportion of the gross property of peasant households, the high equality of land distribution will naturally reduce the distribution inequality of the gross property. Secondly, as land is distributed equally, the distribution of agricultural fixed assets that go with land is unlikely to show a high degree of inequality under the impact of such factors as limited land scale in household operations, and continuous decline of relative prices of agricultural products. This, to a large extent, is determined by production technology relations.

D. Rural poverty

The study of income distribution cannot avoid the poverty problem. The size of poverty-stricken population and poverty degree in a country or region not only reflects the economic development level of the country or region, but also is associated with their income distribution inequality. The increase of economic development levels will help reduce poverty, while the widened income gap will aggravate poverty.

In the past decade, China has made great achievements in reducing rural poverty, and it gained much valuable experience, particularly in developing poverty-stricken areas and helping them shake off poverty.[11] However, it is still a very arduous task to eradicate poverty from the rural, poverty-stricken population. In the early 1980s when the rural economic reform in China was in its prime, the size and degree of the rural poverty-stricken population both declined substantially. The rural poverty problem was aggravated in 1984 and 1985. Furthermore, for a long time, China has focused only on the poverty-stricken areas and neglected the scattered poverty-stricken population in non-poverty-stricken areas. Based on our samples, it is estimated that about two-thirds of the rural poverty-stricken population lived in non-poverty-stricken areas in 1988.

In the study of poverty, a very important task is to determine the poverty line. The two methods that are normally used in this regard are the nutritional standard method and the income standard method. According to the first method, it is estimated that about 17.8% of the rural resident households in China lived below the poverty line in 1988. According to the income standard method, and considering such factors as price change, regional disparity, consumption economy of household size, the rural poverty line in China was about 330 yuan in 1988. Accordingly, it can be determined that the percentage of poverty households is 12.1%, while the percentage of the poverty-stricken population is 13%.

According to the study of the income level and income distribution of the rural poverty-stricken population, the general characteristics of rural poverty in China may be described as follows. Firstly, the distribution of per capita income of the poverty households is relatively centralized, with most being within the range of 200–300 yuan (poverty line). The Gini coefficient of the income of the poverty-stricken population is 0.164, which is equivalent to half of the general Gini coefficient (0.338) of the rural areas. Secondly, the poverty degree, which is measured with the per capita poverty gap (92 yuan),[12] is not very serious. The poverty gap in 1988 is equivalent to 38% of the average income of the poverty-stricken population. Thirdly, due to the first two characteristics, the tax burden required in poverty eradication is light. To help the poverty-stricken population reach the poverty line and higher, we need only to levy a tax of about 1.6% from the non-poverty-stricken population in rural areas, or a tax of about 1.8% from the urban population, and transfer it to the poverty-stricken population. Fourthly, for the majority of the poverty-stricken population that is scattered in non-poverty-stricken areas, other poverty alleviation policies, except for such measures as relief and subsidies, are more difficult to implement.

58 Residents' income distribution in China

Compared to non-poverty households, poverty households have their different economic and social characteristics. According to the analytical result of our 1988 sample data, three characteristics of rural poverty households are noteworthy. First is big household population size. The population size is 5.29 people for poverty households, and 4.95 people for non-poverty households. Second is the low percentage of possession of irrigable land – 35.5% for poverty households, compared to 63.6% for non-poverty households. Third is low possession of assets. For example, the value of financial assets of poverty households is equivalent to 44.3% of that of non-poverty households, and the value of house property of the former is equivalent to 45.5% of that of the latter.

Simulated calculation of some regression models may help produce some policy means for poverty alleviation. Firstly, the most effective measure is to develop township enterprises in poverty-stricken areas and to allow poverty households greater opportunity to enter industrial activities in rural areas. Every 33% rise in the percentage of industrial laborers among poverty households may help reduce the poverty rate from 13% to 0.7%. Secondly, another way to reduce rural poverty is to improve water conservancy facilities of farmland and to increase the percentage of irrigable land. Every 10% increase in the percentage of irrigable land among poverty households may help reduce the poverty rate by 2.3%. Thirdly, developing diversified economies and increasing the commodity rate also help reduce poverty. Every 10% rise in the commodity rate may reduce the poverty rate by 4–6%. Fourthly, increase the educational opportunities for the poverty-stricken population. Every additional year in per capita education for poverty households may reduce the rural poverty rate by 0.6%.

IV. Inter-regional and intra-regional income gap

In a broad sense, the study of inter-regional resident income distribution in China should include three major aspects: the study of the income gap between cities and rural areas, the study of the income gap between regions or between provinces, and the inter-regional or inter-provincial comparative study of the income gap within a region or province. The huge inter-regional differences in terms of income and income distribution are one of the consequences of inter-regional unbalanced economic development and are also associated with the economic development strategy tilting towards cities that China has been implementing for a long time, which reflects some common features of the dual economic structure in developing countries.

A.   Great contrast of urban and rural income

The distribution inequality of the income of urban and rural residents is a prominent problem in the income distribution field in China.

The time series data show that though these data have greatly underestimated the actual income of urban residents, the income gap between urban and rural residents is obvious and shows a trend of "first narrowing then widening" in the past 12 years

Residents' income distribution in China   59

Table 4.5 Percentage of Urban and Rural Resident Households in Ten Equant Groups of National Resident Households

Unit: %

		Ten equant groups by per capita income * (from low to high)									
		1	2	3	4	5	6	7	8	9	10
Percentage of urban and rural resident households in each group	Cities and towns	0.42	1.35	4.32	12.29	37.34	66.67	79.43	86.35	89.84	88.12
	Rural areas	99.58	98.65	95.68	87.71	62.66	33.33	20.57	13.65	10.16	11.88

Note: Total number of households: 19,267, including 9009 urban households and 10,258 rural households.

of reform. Based on our data, the comparison of residents' disposable income shows that the income ratio of urban and rural residents in China in 1988 is 2.41:1, higher than the 2.17:1 ratio released by the National Bureau of Statistics of China. If urban and rural resident households are divided into ten equant groups by income level, we may see the respective distribution of urban and rural resident households in different income groups. As shown in Table 4.5, urban resident households are mostly in the high-income group, while rural resident households account for an extremely high proportion among low-income earners.

Judging by the income composition, the income gap between urban and rural residents comes mainly from the high subsidies and high welfare of urban residents, instead of the nominal labor remuneration income of urban employees. In 1988, the per capita amount of various calculable subsidy and welfare income that urban residents get (such as retirement pension) is up to 854.5 yuan, accounting for 46.39% of their gross income and equivalent to 112% of the rural per capita income. If welfare income that is hard to calculate is added, the actual subsidy amount that urban residents receive will be higher. It is noteworthy that subsidies, especially housing subsidies for urban residents, not only widen the income gap in the income distribution of urban residents, but also widen the resident income gap between cities and rural areas more prominently. In the analysis of the relationship between the Gini coefficient of the national resident gross income and the pseudo-Gini coefficient of the subitem income, the subsidies for urban residents account for 16.8% of the national resident gross income, but they can explain 32.4% of the national resident income inequality.

The interaction of the urban and rural income inequality with the inequality of educational opportunities between urban and rural residents (human capital) may aggravate the two kinds of inequality themselves. According to our survey data, the educational level differences between urban and rural residents are prominent. With all other conditions being equal, urban residents receive 4.5 years more

60 *Residents' income distribution in China*

education than rural residents on average. As the national educational fund tilts towards cities and towns, education in rural areas is in a state of relative under-supply and low quality. The first situation leads to difficulty in attending school, while the second one leads to a low rate of return to education in rural areas, which, in turn, affects peasants' needs for education. In such an economy where labor income is the main income source of resident households in China, the human capital amount will become a major factor that affects the resident income gap with the formation of the labor market. Therefore, the prominent differences between urban and rural residents in terms of educational levels and educational opportunities in China at present will further become an important factor that widens the income gap between urban and rural residents in the future.

One direct effect of the great contrast between urban and rural resident income is the transfer of laborers from rural areas to cities. China restricts the outflow of rural laborers through the household registration system and strict administrative means in the present stage, but in the current circumstance where the income gap exists between cities and rural areas, it is possible to predict the trend of flow of rural laborers by means of modeling. With Todaro's labor flow model[13] and our survey data of 1988, it is possible to calculate the intention or probability of the rural laborers in each region flowing to the cities in that region as well as to cities in other regions. The calculation result shows that the probability of the rural laborers' intention to flow to cities is at least 70% in each province. Once the administrative restrictions on the flow of rural laborers are lifted, the labor markets for free flow are formed in cities, and the jobs in cities are open to rural laborers, then the strong trend of flow of rural laborers, as predicted earlier, may become reality. Certainly, with the outflow of rural laborers, their trend of flow will weaken gradually, because this outflow will, on the one hand, squeeze down the prices of urban laborers and increase the marginal productivity of rural laborers; while, on the other hand, increase difficulty of job hunting in cities. This is not considered in the application of the model. In addition, the model also neglects the restrictive effects of some non-economic factors, such as dialect and cultural habit, on labor flow.

B. *Analysis of inter-provincial income gap*

As urban areas and rural areas are two seriously divided operating systems, the study of the inter-provincial resident income gap should also be divided into urban and rural parts.

The inter-provincial income gap of rural residents is more prominent in China. Calculation based on the data of the National Bureau of Statistics of China shows that the inter-provincial Gini coefficient of the per capita net income of rural residents in China was 0.188[14] in 1988. In addition, the inter-provincial income gap of rural residents has showed a trend of continuous expansion in the past 10 years. The inter-provincial Gini coefficient rose from 0.137 in 1980 to 0.197 in 1990, and the inter-provincial income gap has widened by 44%. As mentioned earlier, the inequality of inter-provincial income of rural residents has become a major cause of the income differences among rural residents. The analysis conducted using other sources of data has also proved this. In the analysis of the income differences of 2400 counties nationwide in 1987, the estimated Their Index shows that inter-provincial differences may explain 71% of the inter-county income differences, while intra-provincial differences can explain only 29%.

On the whole, formation of the inter-provincial income gap of rural residents may be attributed to the inter-provincial unbalanced economic development. The detailed analysis shows some factors of different levels that affect such a gap.

According to peasant households' income sources, individual salary income and non-agricultural income play prominent roles in widening both the entire rural income inequality and the intra-provincial inequality. Based on this, we may further infer that salary income and non-agricultural income are also the major factors that lead to the widened inter-provincial income gap. Such an inference still needs further verification. There are two concrete methods for argument. Firstly, the correlation analysis of the proportion of the per capita income and salary income in each province in the gross income may be conducted, so as to judge whether the inference is true according to the value of the correlation coefficient. Secondly, the inter-provincial pseudo-Gini coefficient of the provincial per capita salary income may be calculated according to the sequence of the provincial per capita income, so as to judge whether the inference is true according to its explanatory power for the inter-provincial per capita income differences.

Is the widened inter-provincial resident income gap a staged phenomenon, or a constant consequence in the economic development? It is difficult to make an accurate judgment based on the existing data. According to the data over the past ten-plus years, a high correlation exists between the growth of the rural per capita income and the size of the inter-provincial income gap. However, this correlation does not mean that there is inevitable causation between the two. The comparison between the growth rate of the rural per capita income and the inter-provincial income gap in 1980–1990 shows a very low degree of correlation between the two. This indicates that the quick economic growth is not a factor that accelerates widening of the income gap. If we assume that the inference is true that the widened inter-provincial income gap mainly comes from the unbalanced development of rural industries in each province, then as undeveloped provinces keep expanding the percentage of their rural industries, the inter-provincial income gap will show a trend of constantly narrowing after a certain time point. In addition, as the flow of rural laborers between provinces falls under fewer and fewer restrictions of administrative factors and policy factors, the relatively high labor prices in rich regions will attract more and more laborers from backward regions. Meanwhile, the resource advantages and relative short supply of capital and technical personnel in backward regions will attract the capital, technologies and talents in rich regions to flow in. Such process of to-and-fro flow also helps narrow the inter-provincial income gap.

The inter-provincial income gap is smaller in cities than in rural areas. According to our 1988 survey data, among the ten sample provinces surveyed, the per capita income in cities is 3016 yuan in the highest province (Guangdong Province) and 1379 yuan in the lowest province (Shanxi Province). The former is 2.19 times

62   *Residents' income distribution in China*

that of the latter. This number is 3.72 times in rural areas. The inter-provincial per capita income differences in cities reflect the differences in the developmental level, industrial structure and labor quality between provinces and also reflect, to a large extent, some differences in the ownership structures and market roles of each province. The big proportion of the self-employed, private, foreign and joint venture sectors is in line with the high per capita income level of a region. For example, the per capita income in Guangdong Province is 67.5% higher than that in Jiangsu Province, while the per capita income of self-employed persons and private enterprise owners of the former is 87.5% higher.

In addition, the inter-provincial per capita income differences in cities are also associated with the monetary income differences of employees. In the multi-variable regression analysis of the monetary income of urban employees, the differences of inter-provincial per capita monetary income of employees are also prominent. The per capita monetary income of employees in the highest province is 52.6% higher than that in the lowest province. In contrast, the inter-provincial differences of base pay in monetary income are far smaller than those of other parts of monetary income. For example, for the former, the highest-income province is 18% higher than the lowest-income province, and this number is 109% for the latter. As base pay tends to be subject to greater administrative control and other monetary income tends to be affected by the market, the proportion of the two in gross monetary income reflects, to some extent, the market utilization degree of a region. Though the correlation between the market growth degree of a region and the per capita income of the region is unlikely to be proved by such an example, the impact of the former on the latter is undeniable.

C.   Intra-provincial income distribution and inter-provincial comparison

Intra-provincial income distribution and the inter-provincial comparison are significant in at least two aspects. Firstly, they may judge whether some determinants of intra-provincial income distribution are general or special. This helps to understand the income distribution pattern across the country and in the whole rural or urban areas. Secondly, they may aid in studying the relationship between the intra-provincial income inequality and its income level, the result of which helps determine the long-term change trend of the income inequality nationwide. Considering the availability of our samples, we focus here on the comparison of the intra-provincial income gap in rural areas of China.

Judging by the analytical result of the available data of 28 provinces and cities, the income gaps in rural areas vary with provinces. In some provinces (such as Jiangsu Province), the Gini coefficient is as high as 0.383. In other provinces (such as Jiangxi province), the Gini coefficient is as low as 0.230. Fundamentally speaking, the size of the income gap in a province is determined by the degree of unbalanced economic development in the province. Specifically, the development speed, size and distribution of township enterprises and non-agricultural industries are the major factors that explain the degree of intra-provincial income

Residents' income distribution in China 63

differences. For the five provinces with the highest Gini coefficients, the average explanatory power of the salary income and non-agricultural income for the gross income inequality is 41%, while the explanatory power of the agricultural operation income is 45.4%. For the five provinces with the lowest Gini coefficients, the corresponding numbers are 30.2% and 53.2% respectively. It is obvious that the size of the intra-provincial income gap is associated with the share and distribution equality of the two kinds of income.

Is each intra-provincial income gap associated with its income level? If the answer is yes, is this relationship linear or nonlinear? To answer these two questions, we may use by-province cross-section data to verify whether Kuznets's "converse-U hypothesis" exists in rural areas of China. Though this hypothesis has had a history of more than 30 years, it is still being verified and falsified now. Some scholars have verified the authenticity of this hypothesis using the empirical data of some countries, while some scholars have got the negative answer using the empirical data of different countries.[15] If this hypothesis is verified, its policy implication is quite definite. Some scholars have analyzed the relationship between the intra-provincial Gini coefficient and intra-provincial rural per capita income and other variables using the by-county data of rural areas in China in 1987. The result cannot demonstrate any regularity between the intra-provincial income gap and its per capita income level. Likewise, according to the analytical result of our 1988 sample data, the inequality of rural income distribution of each province in China is irrelevant to its per capita income. Even if different provinces are sorted by geographical location and degree of diversification of production structure, there is still no correlation between the two variables. It shows that it is difficult to prove the converse-U relationship between regional economic development and resident income distribution in rural areas of China using the by-province cross-section data.

However, this proof does not fundamentally deny the existence of the converse-U relationship in rural areas of China, because the analysis using by-province cross-section data has certain limitations. Firstly, Chinese provinces cover a wide range, with large internal differences. Therefore, the change of intra-provincial income gaps is affected not only by the industrial structure and development process, but also by intra-provincial area differences to a greater extent. In view of such an inference, if the regression analysis of the per capita income level and its income gap in a county is conducted using the sample data, the impact of intra-provincial area differences on the income gap may be narrowed. Secondly, the limitation of the analysis using the cross-section data is that it assumes that all areas have the same dynamic development track and each area is just at a different point on the track. Apparently, such an assumption is questionable. The analysis using time series data may avoid this limitation, and its result will be more convincing. It is a pity that the data released by China's existing sample surveys on rural residents can hardly offer help to such analysis.[16] However, even if the time series data of the past ten-plus years are available, it may be still difficult to prove the existence of the converse-U relationship, because the economic growth in the Chinese rural areas featuring economic structure transformation emerged only

64   *Residents' income distribution in China*

10 years ago, and it is possible that we are still in the ascent stage on the converse-U track. It is impossible to predict when the "turning point" will emerge based on the existing time series data.

After the earlier introduction and remarks, we have come up with the following views on the study of resident income distribution in China:

Firstly, the study of many economic issues, especially the issue of income distribution, must be based on a large number of facts and on the empirical analysis, so that the reliable factual basis is available for the normative analysis and the scientific basis is available for policy advice. The research result of this project does not offer a directly operable scheme to economic policy making, but its policy implication is very obvious. Therefore, we hope that such a research result can play an active role for future economic policy making, directly or indirectly, and on a short-term or long-term basis.

Secondly, the issue of income distribution is an important perspective of the whole national economy issue, but is only a perspective. It reflects the operation status of the whole national economy from a perspective, and meanwhile restrains the progress of economic reform and economic development. Therefore, we must see the role of income distribution clearly. In other words, to improve income distribution status, we should not focus solely on distribution. Only when we think big and focus on the big picture can we think small and come up with practical policy advice on income distribution. Without the concept of a big picture, it is often difficult for a certain reform measure for income distribution (such as salary reform in government departments and public institutions) to become effective.

Thirdly, income distribution also concerns the micro aspects. It seems that people have thus far focused their attention on the income distribution of urban residents, especially on the issue of unfair income distribution. However, the studies presented here have shown that the income distribution of rural residents and inter-regional income distribution, especially the income distribution gap between urban and rural residents, are important issues in income distribution. Rationalization of the income distribution relations between urban and rural residents, in the long run, will affect improvement of the income of urban residents, or even affect consolidation of agriculture, which is the foundation of the national economy, and the whole industrialization progress.

Fourthly, the study of the economic issues of China, especially issues on income distribution, should not only introduce advanced analysis methods from foreign countries, but also be rooted in the national conditions of China. The research findings presented here show that some advanced modern analysis methods can indeed help deepen understanding of the national conditions of China. Certainly, the study in this regard is just an attempt, whether in the application of modern analysis methods and the study of the national conditions of China, or in the combination of the two. This study cannot in the nature of things be free from error. However, such an attempt is definitely helpful. It is helpful not only in the economic construction practices, but also in increasing the level of economics. We hope that the achievements of this study can serve as a modest spur to others in the study of issues on income distribution in China.

(This paper was co-written with Li Shi based on joint discussions. Li Shi wrote, and Zhao Renwei revised. It was originally published in the periodical *Reform*, Issue 2, 1992.)

Notes

1 The World Bank. (1983). *China: Development of the Socialist Economy* (Vol. 1, pp. 83–95). Washington, DC.
2 Firstly, the World Bank's estimation of the Gini coefficient of resident income in China is based on the grouped data of the National Bureau of Statistics of China, while our calculation is based on raw data. Secondly, the income definition used by the National Bureau of Statistics of China in the household income survey is somewhat different from the income definition we used. The income of urban residents used by the National Bureau of Statistics of China is mainly the monetary income. The income we used includes the income in kind and various subsidies that include housing subsidies estimated based on market prices. The definition of the income of rural residents that we used differs from that used by the National Bureau of Statistics of China, mainly because our income definition includes the depreciation allowance of owner-occupied housing of rural residents. In addition, our estimation of those agricultural products for self-consumption is based on market prices.
3 See National Bureau of Statistics. (1981–1991). 中国统计年鉴 [China Statistical Yearbook], China Statistics Press.
4 For a certain sample group, the gross income and Gini coefficient may be expressed with the pseudo-Gini coefficient of their subitem income (or concentration ratio). The specific formula is $G = \Sigma uigi$, where G is the Gini coefficient of the gross income; ui is the proportion of Item 1 in the gross income; gi is the pseudo-Gini coefficient of Item 1, which is the Gini coefficient of Item 1 sequenced and calculated based on the gross income; uigi is the absolute contribution of the income of Item 1 to the inequality degree of the gross income; therefore, uigi/G is its relative contribution. For details in this regard, also see Nanak Kakwani. (1980). *Income Inequality and Poverty* (pp. 175–181). New York: Oxford University Press.
5 The World Bank. (1983). *China: Development of the Socialist Economy* (Vol. 1, pp. 83–95), Washington, DC.
6 Jacob Mincer. (1974). *Schooling, Experience and Earnings*. New York: Columbia University Press.
7 According to the World Bank's estimation of income of employees in the public sectors in 11 countries and their educational levels, an individual's rate of return to education is about 10% on average. See George Psacharopoulos. (1985). Returns to Education: A Further International Update and Implications. *Journal of Human Resources*, 585.
8 Rent-seeking refers to activities that seek the rental. The so-called "rental" here normally refers to the price difference of the market price minus the planned price, or in some people's opinions, the price difference of the equilibrium price minus the planned price, in the double-track price system.

66 *Residents' income distribution in China*

9 Hu Heli. (1989). 1988 年我国租金价值估算 [Estimation of Rental Value in China in 1988]. *Comparative Economic & Social Systems*, 5.

10 The sideline rate = ratio of gross sales of household industrial and sideline products to gross sales of agricultural products; the commodity rate = ratio of total product sales of households to their income of production and management.

11 See the World Bank. *Poverty: World Development Report 1990* (p. 72). Oxford: Oxford University Press.

12 The poverty gap (T) is normally used to measure the poverty degree. Its calculation formula is: $T = q(Z - \breve{Y}p)$, where q = poverty-stricken population, Z = poverty line and $\breve{Y}p$ = average income of poverty-stricken population. The per capita poverty gap may be derived on this basis: $G = T / q = (Z - \breve{Y}p)$.

13 In the Todaro model, the probability of labor flowing from rural areas to cities is the function of the difference between the expected income in cities and the current period income in rural areas, while the expected income in cities is the function between the current period income of urban employees and the acquisition of job opportunities in cities.

14 The inter-provincial Gini coefficient regards each province as a calculation unit and calculates the provincial per capita income as the unit income level.

15 For the results of the major empirical studies concerning the "converse-U hypothesis", see Ramaswamy Meenatchi Sundrum. (1990). *Income Distribution in Less Developed Countries* (pp. 77–88). London and New York: Routledge.

16 For example, the sample survey data on the rural resident households in China released by the *China Statistical Yearbook* employ not the equal division method, but the income range method in grouping the resident households. Therefore, it is difficult to infer any index on the income gap of rural residents from this.

5   Widening of Chinese residents' income gap and cause

I.   Introduction

China's economic system reform has been going on for about 20 years. Great changes have taken place in the income distribution pattern among residents during this process.

This paper attempts to study the changes in the income distribution pattern, especially widening of the income gap. As the income distribution covers a wide range, this paper focuses on some important aspects of the income distribution changes. It will briefly review and analyze the characteristics of the resident income distribution in China before the reform in order to better study the income distribution changes since the reform, and to have a basic understanding and judgment of the starting point and background of such changes.

China's economic reform goes hand in hand with the economic development and growth. In other words, China's transformation from planned economy to market economy has interwoven with its transformation from the dual economy to a modern economy. The changes of the pattern of resident income distribution in China have taken place during these two transformations. Therefore, this paper also attempts to analyze the cause of the income gap changes from the economic development, economic reform, and policy factors concerned.

Last, we try to come up with some suggestions with policy implications on how to improve the income distribution in the future.

Some of the data cited in this paper come from the Income Distribution Project Team of Institute of Economics of Chinese Academy of Social Sciences (hereinafter referred to as "the Project Team") in its sampling surveys on the income distribution of urban and rural residents conducted in 1988 and 1995. Other data come from the National Bureau of Statistics of China and other channels. Data that do not indicate their sources all come from the above two sample surveys.

II.   Characteristics of income distribution before the reform

"Before the reform" here refers to the 20-plus years from establishment of the planned economy system in 1956 to proposing the reform in 1978. On the whole, China before the reform was a society with a high degree of equality (or a very low

68   *Widening of Chinese residents' income gap*

degree of inequality), but also with some unequal factors. Why do we say that China before the reform was a society with a very high degree of equality? A lot of research literature shows that just before the reform or in the early stage of the reform, China's Gini coefficient of the income distribution was lower than that in most of the developing countries in the world. Its urban Gini coefficient was below 0.2; its rural Gini coefficient was slightly higher but was mostly estimated to be between 0.21 and 0.24 (see Table 5.1). In many developing countries, the urban Gini coefficient was 0.37–0.43, and the rural Gini coefficient was 0.34–0.40 (see Table 5.2).

At least three factors explain why China had a high degree of income equality before the reform. Firstly, the system factor. The socialist system is characterized by public ownership of the means of production. Therefore, after the gradual socialization of means of production from 1949 to 1956, residents had hardly any property income except for a small amount of saving deposits and interest income. Secondly, the policy factor. The decision makers held that socialism pursues the goal of social equity and that people should accumulate more and consume less in the early stage

Table 5.1 Various Kinds of Estimation of Degree of Income Inequality before the Reform (Gini Coefficient)

Cities	Rural areas	Nationwide	Estimator
0.16	0.31	0.33	(The World Bank, 1983)
(1980)	(1979)	(1979)	
0.185	0.237		(Li Chengrui, 1986)
(1980)	(1978)		
0.16	0.212		(Ren Caifang, Cheng Xuebin, 1996)
(1978)	(1978)		
0.165	0.222		(Irma Adelmen, David Sunding, 1987)
(1978)	(1978)		

Note: See the references at the end of this paper for the estimator's sources of data.

Table 5.2 Degree of Income Distribution Inequality in Some Asian Countries

Country and year	Gini coefficient		
	Rural areas	Cities	Nationwide
India (1975–1976)	0.34		0.42
Bangladesh (1985–1986)	0.36	0.37	0.37
Indonesia (1976)	0.40		
Thailand (1975–1976)	0.39		0.47
Philippines (1985)	0.37	0.43	0.43
South Korea (1971)	0.325		0.36

Sources of data: Kahn et al.: Income of Chinese Resident Households and Its Distribution, published in *Study of Resident Income Distribution in China* written by Zhao Renwei and Keith Griffin, China Social Sciences Press, 1994 Edition, p. 86.

Widening of Chinese residents' income gap 69

of construction of New China; the labor income should also be low and equalized. Thirdly, the bonds of the equalitarianism concept "inequality rather than want is the cause of trouble" in the Chinese cultural tradition. Such concept advocates fairness without considering efficiency, does not intend to make the "cake" bigger for distribution, and often mixes up common prosperity with widespread poverty.

If we make a further study, we may find that even in a circumstance with a very high degree of equality, some unequal factors still exist or stay in concealment. For example:

1   The income gap between urban and rural residents was big. According to the calculation of the World Bank, the per capita income ratio of urban residents to rural residents was 2.5 (1979), higher than that in other low-income Asian countries (about 1.5 on average), and slightly higher than that in middle-income countries (about 2.2 on average) (see Table 5.3).

The income gap between urban and rural residents was big in China before the reform. The general reason is that China had the dual economic structure like other developing countries; that is, the modern industry sector coexisted with the traditional agriculture sector. The special reason for the big gap is that China's decision makers implemented special policies at that time, especially the low-price purchase policy for agricultural products, and used them as one of the means to accumulate the capital required for industrialization. Meanwhile, they implemented the household registration system that strictly restricted rural residents from immigrating into cities, which further enhanced segmentation between the urban and rural economic systems (Zhao Renwei, 1992). It is obvious that with the income distribution highly equalized, especially when the degree of equality in urban areas was higher than that in rural areas in those days, the unequal factors still existed for rural residents due to the big income differences between cities and rural areas.

Table 5.3 International Comparison of Income Inequality between Rural Residents and Urban Residents

Country	Ratio (per capita income in cities/per capita income in rural areas)	Year
China	2.5	1979
India	1.4	1973–1974
Bangladesh	1.5	1966–1967
Philippines	2.1	
Thailand	2.2	1975–1976
Brazil	2.3	1976
Colombia	2.3	1970

Source of data: investigation report by the World Bank: *China: Development of the Socialist Economy* (1981), Chinese version, p. 49.

70 *Widening of Chinese residents' income gap*

2   In terms of the distribution pattern of consumables, the pattern of distribution in kind, namely the supply system, was emphasized, while the market distribution pattern (buying with money) was restrained. In a circumstance where distribution in kind was emphasized, the monetary income gap was smaller than the actual income gap among residents. The distribution in kind is actually an invisible welfare subsidy system. The original purpose of such a subsidy system was to compensate the low-income class so as to narrow the income gap. However, it was not the case, according to the result of such implementation. Firstly, the rural residents who account for about 80% of the population were not entitled to the subsidies that urban residents were. Secondly, even for the urban residents, their subsidies were distributed according to the principle of equalitarianism only for those consumer goods that were rationed per capita (such as grain, cotton and oil). For those consumer goods that were supplied by position (such as houses, automobiles and phones), the subsidy distribution was highly unequal. Such a subsidy system or benefit system should be an unequal factor that is covered up by equalitarianism.

3   Long-term freezing of salaries resulted in an unfavorable income distribution pattern for the young generation. Salaries were basically frozen from 1956 to 1976, before the reform. Certainly, the prices of basic consumer goods during this period were also basically frozen. Superficially, everyone was equal before such "freezing" of salaries and prices of commodities, because everyone lost the opportunity of the rise in salaries. But actually, the long-term salary freezing had different income distribution effects on people of different generations. It resulted in intergenerational inequality and created an unfavorable income distribution pattern for the young generation (Zhao Renwei, 1985, 1991). The consequence resulting from such a situation even became a prominent social problem in the early 1980s. It should be said that in non-war times, substantial freezing of salaries that lasted for such a long time was quite special. This was also an unequal factor covered up by equalitarianism.

Then again, on the whole, China was still a society with prevalent equalitarianism at that time, despite the aforementioned unequal factors that existed in its income distribution before the reform. As Professor Li Siqin put it, China had a highly equalitarian economy in its income distribution before the reform (Carl Riskin, 1987). Inequality existed in such equality, while equality existed in inequality, which indicates the complex economic situations of Chinese society. Such complexity is analyzed in order to have an in-depth understanding of the starting point and background of the reform.

III.   Some important aspects of changes of resident income gap in China since the reform

The prevailing trend in income distribution in China before the reform was to emphasize fairness but ignore efficiency, and there were some seemingly fair inequity factors. As a result, the necessary incentive mechanism was not available

Widening of Chinese residents' income gap 71

in the economic life, which led to the low efficiency in production. Therefore, China's decision makers put forward the policy of "allow some people to get rich first" right from the beginning of the reform, with the purpose of overcoming equalitarianism in the income distribution, strengthening the incentive mechanism, increasing efficiency, and ultimately realizing common prosperity based on a bigger "pie". The experience of reform and development over the past 20 years shows that the general trend has followed the goal set in the early stage of the reform. However, very complex situations emerged during the system transformation, and the income distribution changes are much more complex than imagined. Here, we attempt to study some important aspects of the income distribution changes since the reform.

A. General trend of changes: obvious widening of income gap

We first study the changes of the rural and urban Gini coefficients in China since the reform using the time series data released by the National Bureau of Statistics of China, then make further verification according to the data of the two sample surveys conducted by the Project Team in 1988 and 1995.

Table 5.4 and Figure 5.1, the latter plotted according to Table 5.4, show that since the reform, the income gap as reflected by the Gini coefficient has shown an

Table 5.4 Gini Coefficients of Income of Rural and Urban Residents from 1978 to 1995

Year	Rural areas	Cities and towns
1978	0.212	0.16
1979	0.237	—
1980	—	0.16
1981	0.239	0.15
1982	0.232	0.15
1983	0.246	0.15
1984	0.258	0.16
1985	0.264	0.19
1986	0.288	0.19
1987	0.292	0.20
1988	0.301	0.23
1989	0.300	0.23
1990	0.310	0.23
1991	0.307	0.24
1992	0.314	0.25
1993	0.320	0.27
1994	0.330	0.30
1995	0.340	0.28

Source of data: Li Shi et al.: *Changes of Income Distribution in China's Economic Reform*, a thesis prepared for the symposium in August 1997.

72 *Widening of Chinese residents' income gap*

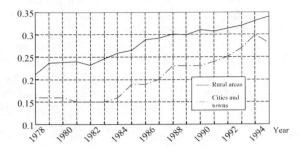

Figure 5.1 Gini Coefficients of Income of Rural and Urban Residents from 1978 to 1995

Table 5.5 Gini Coefficients in 1988 and 1995

Year	Rural areas	Cities and towns	Nationwide
1988	0.338	0.233	0.382
1995	0.429	0.286	0.445

upward trend on the whole, whether in rural areas or in urban areas, despite the gap narrowing in certain years. Specifically, the Gini coefficient of the income of rural residents rose from 0.212 in 1978 to 0.340 in 1995, while the Gini coefficient of the income of urban residents rose from 0.16 in 1978 to 0.28 in 1995.

Table 5.5 shows the Gini coefficients calculated according to the two sample surveys conducted by the Project Team. Their values differ from what was released by the statistical bureau to some extent, but the general trend of the increased Gini coefficient and widened income gap is the same, whether in rural areas or in urban areas. Specifically, the rural Gini coefficient rose from 0.338 in 1988 to 0.429 in 1995. In the same period, the urban Gini coefficient rose from 0.233 to 0.286, while the national Gini coefficient rose from 0.382 to 0.445.

B. Income gap between urban and rural residents: old problem

We still use the time series data released by the National Bureau of Statistics of China and the data of the two sample surveys conducted by the Project Team to study the income gap between urban and rural residents.

With regard to the income gap between urban and rural residents, Table 5.6 and Figure 5.2 show a narrowing trend in the early 1980s and a widening trend from the mid-1980s to the mid-1990s. The ratio of the urban and rural actual income per capita was 2.15 in 1983, returned to the 1978 level just before the reform in 1987, and reached the peak of 2.93 in 1994.

According to the two sample surveys conducted by the Project Team, if we divide all the residents in the samples into ten equant groups by income level, the rural residents are mostly distributed in the low-income group, while the urban

Table 5.6 Income of Urban and Rural Residents and Gap from 1978 to 1995

Year	Nominal per capita income (yuan)		Actual per capita income (yuan)		Urban and rural per capita income ratio	
	Rural areas	Cities and towns	Rural areas	Cities and towns	Actual	Nominal
1978	134	316	134	316	2.36	2.36
1979	–	–	–	–	–	–
1980	191	439	146	401	2.75	2.30
1981	233	458	161	408	2.53	2.05
1982	270	500	191	433	2.27	1.83
1983	310	526	210	451	2.15	1.70
1984	355	608	231	507	2.19	1.71
1985	398	685	238	510	2.14	1.72
1986	424	828	240	577	2.40	1.95
1987	463	916	246	586	2.38	1.98
1988	545	1119	247	594	2.41	2.05
1989	602	1261	228	575	2.52	2.10
1990	686	1387	249	625	2.51	2.02
1991	709	1544	252	662	2.63	2.18
1992	784	1826	266	721	2.71	2.33
1993	922	2337	275	794	2.89	2.54
1994	1221	3179	295	864	2.93	2.60
1995	1578	3893	325	906	2.79	2.47

Source of data: *China Statistical Yearbook*, 1986 and 1996; Li Shi et al.: *Changes of Income Distribution in China's Economic Reform*, a thesis prepared for the symposium in August 1997.

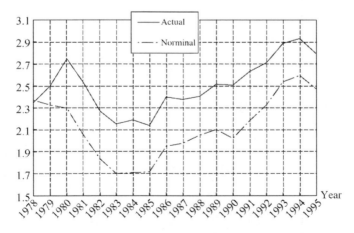

Figure 5.2 Ratio of Income of Urban and Rural Residents from 1978 to 1995

74 *Widening of Chinese residents' income gap*

residents are mostly distributed in the high-income group, whether in 1988 or in 1995. Table 5.7 and Figure 5.3 (the vertical axis stands for the percentage of residents, and the horizontal axis stands for the income level, in Figure 5.3) show that such distribution does not change significantly between 1988 and 1995. Interestingly, there is hardly any change in the low-income and lower-middle-income

Table 5.7 Percentage of Urban and Rural Residents in Ten Equant Groups by Income

Unit: %

Sequence of ten equant groups	1988		1995	
	Rural residents	Urban residents	Rural residents	Urban residents
1 (lowest)	99.24	0.76	99.36	0.64
2	97.94	2.06	97.41	1.59
3	95.37	4.63	94.95	5.05
4	89.30	10.70	90.36	9.64
5	77.53	22.47	76.95	23.05
6	56.71	43.29	55.53	44.47
7	36.37	63.63	34.16	65.84
8	24.87	75.13	23.10	76.90
9	20.47	79.53	18.92	81.08
10 (highest)	19.55	80.45	23.78	76.22

Note: Number of residents: 83,179 persons in 1988; 56,435 persons in 1995.

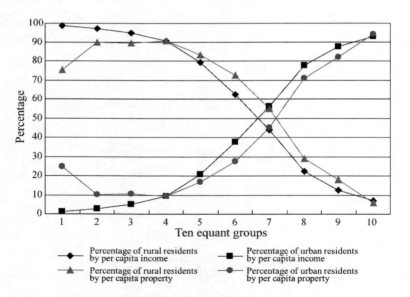

Figure 5.3 Distribution of Urban and Rural Residents by Income Level

Widening of Chinese residents' income gap 75

groups; some tiny changes take place in the upper-middle-income groups (widening the gap) and in the highest-income group (narrowing the gap). This is perhaps because the rapid development of township enterprises in rural areas allows a small number of enterprise owners to enter the highest-income group quickly. However, even if the employees of township enterprises can enter the middle- and high-income groups, their income growth is still slower than that of the urban middle- and high-income groups due to restrictions of their personal ability and systematic factors.

C. Inter-regional resident income gap: many controversial issues

The issue on the inter-regional income gap, including whether the gap (especially the relative gap) has been widened and how to view the widened income gap, has always been controversial in the academic community (Liu Shucheng et al., 1994; Hu Angang, 1994; Yu Genqian, 1996). Here, we study the changes of the inter-regional income gaps in rural areas and in cities respectively, based only on the two sample surveys conducted by the Project Team.

Tables 5.8 and 5.9 show that from 1988 to 1995, there is an obvious growth in the per capita income in all the three major regions in rural areas, but Eastern China grows the fastest, Central China comes next, and Western China grows the slowest. The changes of the Gini coefficients of the three major regions

Table 5.8 Per Capita Income in Three Major Regions in Rural Areas and Its Changes (in 1988 and 1995, Based on the Prices in 1988)

	1988		*1995*		*Absolute difference of intra-regional income (yuan) (3)–(1)*	*Relative difference of intra-regional income (3)/(1)*	*Relative difference of inter-regional income (based on 100 in Western China)*	
	Per capita income (yuan)	*Gini coefficient*	*Per capita income (yuan)*	*Gini coefficient*			*1988*	*1995*
Eastern China	891	0.34	3150	0.45	2260	3.54	161.7	243.9
Central China	606	0.3	1599	0.33	993	2.64	110.0	123.8
Western China	551	0.29	1292	0.38	742	2.35	100	100

Note: The three major regions are divided as follows (they included 28 provinces and cities in 1988, and 19 provinces and cities in 1995; names in italics stand for the 19 provinces and cities in the 1995 survey):

Eastern China: *Beijing*, Shanghai, Tianjin, *Liaoning, Hebei, Shandong, Jiangsu, Zhejiang*, Fujian, *Guangdong*, Guangxi, Hainan

Central China: *Shanxi*, Inner Mongolia, *Jilin*, Heilongjiang, *Anhui, Jiangxi, Henan, Hubei, Hunan*
Western China: *Sichuan, Guizhou, Yunnan*, Shaanxi, *Gansu, Qinghai*, Ningxia

76 Widening of Chinese residents' income gap

Table 5.9 Rural Per Capita Income in Jiangsu and Gansu and Its Changes (in 1988 and 1995, Based on the Prices in 1988)

	1988		*1995*		*Absolute difference of intra-provincial income (yuan) (3)–(1)*	*Relative difference of intra-provincial income (3)/(1)*	*Relative difference of inter-provincial income (based on 100 in Gansu)*	
	Per capita income (yuan)	*Gini coefficient*	*Per capita income (yuan)*	*Gini coefficient*			*1988* 年 *1988*	*1995* 年 *1995*
Jiangsu	843	0.38	3444	0.349	2610	4.13	186.6	334.7
Gansu	447	0.28	1029	0.338	582	2.30	100	100

show that the income gap in such regions has widened to some extent. The relative difference of inter-regional income shows that the income gap between the three major regions has also widened. Such changes of the inter-regional income gap are more prominent in the economically developed Jiangsu Province and the economically backward Gansu Province. However, the changes of the Gini coefficients of the two provinces in the past seven years show that widening of the intra-provincial income gap is more prominent in Gansu Province than in Jiangsu Province.

As the sample surveys in cities have a small coverage, we conduct the study by dividing the samples into the coastal area group and inland area group only.

Tables 5.10 and 5.11 show that from 1988 to 1995, there is also an obvious growth in the per capita income in coastal and inland cities. The changes in the Gini coefficients show that the income gap has widened within both coastal areas and inland areas. The relative difference of the inter-regional income shows that the income gap between coastal areas and inland areas and the income gap between Jiangsu, a coastal province, and Yunnan, an inland province, have both widened.

If we further compare the rural and urban inter-regional income gaps, then the data show that the degree of widening of the rural inter-regional income gap is significantly higher than that of the urban inter-regional income gap.

D.   *Property income gap: a new problem*

As mentioned earlier, Chinese residents had hardly any property income except for a small amount of interest income of personal savings before the reform. Residents' property income, especially urban residents' property income, has been growing rapidly and distributed unequally since the reform, a new problem that concerns people. As urban residents' property income is closely related to the housing subsidy and rental valuation of owner-occupied housing, it is necessary for us to study them together.

Widening of Chinese residents' income gap   77

Table 5.10 Per Capita Income in Coastal Areas and Mainland China Cities and Its Changes (in 1988 and 1995, Based on the Prices in 1988)

	1988		1995		Absolute difference of intra-regional income (yuan) (3) − (1)	Relative difference of intra-regional income (3)/(1)	Relative difference of inter-regional income (based on 100 in inland areas)	
	Per capita income (yuan)	Gini coefficient	(Per capita income (yuan)	Gini coefficient			1988	1995
Coastal areas	1584	0.213	2502	0.277	918	1.58	134.6	149.0
Inland areas	1177	0.22	1679	0.247	502	1.43	100	100

Note: The coastal areas and inland areas are divided as follows (they included 10 provinces and cities in 1988, and 11 provinces and cities, with Sichuan Province added, in 1995):

Coastal areas: Beijing, Guangdong, Jiangsu, Liaoning

Inland areas: Shanxi, Henan, Anhui, Sichuan, Hubei, Yunnan, Gansu

Table 5.11 Urban Per Capita Income in Jiangsu and Yunnan and Its Changes (in 1988 and 1995, Based on the Prices in 1988)

	1988		1995		Absolute difference of intra-provincial income (yuan) (3)–(1)	Relative difference of intra-provincial income (3)/(1)	Relative difference of inter-provincial income (based on 100 in Gansu)	
	Per capita income (yuan)	Gini coefficient	Per capita income (yuan)	Gini coefficient			1988	1995
Jiangsu	1412	0.174	2251	0.23	839	1.59	111.4	123.7
Gansu	1268	0.198	1820	0.21	552	1.44	100	100

Table 5.12 shows that the proportion of property income of urban residents in personal gross income raised from 0.49% in 1988 to 1.3% in 1995. The housing subsidy and rental valuation of owner-occupied housing have changed most prominently. Specifically, the housing subsidy dropped by 4.21%, from 18.14% in 1988 to 13.93% in 1995; the rental valuation of owner-occupied housing rose by 6.38%, from 3.9% in 1988 to 10.28% in 1995. Apparently, such rise and drop is closely associated with the housing commercialization reform carried out since the end of the 1980s, namely the increase in owner-occupied housing and decrease of the housing subsidy. Public-owned housing is sold to residents at an extremely low price, the housing subsidy is also cancelled at the time of such sales, and residents who buy houses also pay a certain price. However, there is a huge difference between the market price of housing and the actual selling price.[1] This indicates

78 *Widening of Chinese residents' income gap*

Table 5.12 Property Income, Subsidy and Rental Valuation of Owner-Occupied Housing of Urban Residents

	1988		1995	
	Ui	Ci	Ui	Ci
Property income	0.49	0.437	1.3	0.489
Subsidy and income in kind				
Housing subsidy	18.14	0.331	13.93	0.322
Income in kind	2.21	0.233	0.99	0.284
Ticket subsidy	5.26	0.13	–	–
Rental valuation of owner-occupied housing	3.90	0.338	10.28	0.371

Source of data: Li Shi et al.: *Changes of Income Distribution in China's Economic Reform*, a thesis prepared for the symposium in August 1997.

Ui is the proportion of such income in personal gross income (percentage).

Ci is the concentration ratio of such income, namely the degree of distribution inequality of such income.

that housing commercialization means turning public property into personal property all at once.[2] Therefore, if rental valuation of owner-occupied housing is also counted as a kind of property income, then the property income of urban residents had already reached 11.58% in 1995, up by 7.19% compared to 4.39% in 1988. In addition, not only does the property income in a narrow sense have a very high concentration ratio (0.489 in 1995), but so does the rental valuation of owner-occupied housing (0.371 in 1995). Interestingly, the rental valuation of owner-occupied housing has a higher concentration ratio than the housing subsidy (0.322 in 1995). Table 5.12 also shows that the concentration ratio of the above three types of income is all higher than the Gini coefficient of the income distribution of urban residents (0.286 in 1995). We will discuss the effects of housing commercialization on income distribution in the next section.

In addition to the rental valuation of owner-occupied housing, personal property income is mainly in the forms of interest, dividend and rental, etc., in China at present. According to the data of the National Bureau of Statistics of China, the interest income of personal savings alone was only 600 million yuan in 1978, accounting for only 0.3% of the personal income; by 1995, however, the interest income already reached 300 billion yuan, accounting for 7.9% of the personal income (project team for "Income Distribution Issues" of National Bureau of Statistics of China et al., 1996).

Inequality of the property income results from inequality of the property distribution. Table 5.13 and Table 5.14 show that since the beginning of the 1990s, the financial assets of Chinese urban residents have grown extremely rapidly. The financial assets per household have increased from 7,869 yuan at the end of 1990 to 30,982 yuan at the end of June 1996, and the actual financial assets per household have increased from 7,869 yuan at the end of 1990 to 14,715 yuan at the end of June 1996, up by 87%. Furthermore, their distribution is quite unequal. In five equant groups, the financial assets per household of the highest 20% households are 12 times those of the lowest 20% households.

Widening of Chinese residents' income gap 79

Table 5.13 Financial Assets of Urban Residents and Their Changes

	End of 1990			End of June 1996			
	Total (100 million yuan)	Per household (yuan)	Composition (%)	Total (100 million yuan)	Per household (yuan)		Composition (%)
					Nominal	Actual	
Financial assets of residents	5404	7869	100.0	27110	30982	14715	100.0
Including:							
Bank deposit	4084	5941	75.5	22718	25961	12331	83.8
Marketable securities	1052	1532	19.5	2467	2821	1338	9.1
Cash on hand	272	396	5.0	1085	1233	586	4.0
Others	–	–		840	970	461	3.1

Source of data: National Bureau of Statistics of China: *Statistical Report*, Issue 21, November 8, 1996.

Note: The actual financial assets per household in 1996 are calculated with the consumer price index of urban residents in 1990 as the base period.

Table 5.14 Distribution of Financial Assets of Urban Residents (in Five Equant Groups, June 30, 1996)

Sequence of five equant groups of urban households (from high to low)	Financial assets per household (yuan)	Proportion in total financial assets of residents (%)
1 (highest)	74359	48
2	35629	23
3	24786	16
4	13942	9
5 (lowest)	6192	4

Source of data: National Bureau of Statistics of China: *Statistical Report*, Issue 21, November 8, 1996.

E. High-income class and rent-seeking activities: a difficult problem

The issue on the high-income class has been arousing a strong social response since the reform, but how to ascertain the size of the high-income class and their actual income level has always been a difficult, troubling problem. Our limited data in hand are made up of two types: various case surveys in society, and the two sample surveys we have been using here. The defect of the first type is that the national representativeness is unknown. The defect of the second type is that many high-income people cannot be covered by the sample surveys at all.

According to a study conducted in Wenzhou City, Zhejiang Province, in the ordinary private enterprises, the entrepreneur's annual income is 21 times that

80 *Widening of Chinese residents' income gap*

Table 5.15 Distribution of Salary Income Per Capita in Cities and Ratio Change (Yuan) in 1988 and 1995

	1988	*1995*	
		Nominal	*Actual*
1. Highest 3% income group	5567.4	19447.70	8533.3
2. Lowest 10% income group	724.4	1644.69	721.6
3. Lowest 20% income group	1131.4	3081.41	1352.1
Ratio 1 (3% / 10%)	7.69	11.82	
Ratio 2 (3% / 20%)	4.92	6.31	

Note: The actual income in 1995 is calculated with the consumer price index of urban residents in 1988 as the base period.

of ordinary employees; in the private enterprises whose assets are worth at least one million yuan, the entrepreneur's annual income is 79 times that of ordinary employees (Zheng Dajiong, 1994). In addition, according to the survey conducted by the Institute of Sociology of the Chinese Academy of Social Sciences, the number of households with an annual income of up to one million yuan has reached one million in China (Gao Xiaoyan, 1995). People who get rich first consist of ten-plus types of people, such as private enterprise owners and Chinese managers of joint ventures, as well as singers and film stars who command high appearance fees.

The two sample surveys conducted by the Project Team do not sufficiently cover representative high-income people, but Table 5.15 shows that the ratio of the high-income group to the low-income group has risen prominently: The ratio of the highest 3% income group to the lowest 10% income group has risen from 7.69 in 1988 to 11.82 in 1995; the ratio of the highest 3% income group to the lowest 20% income group has risen from 4.92 in 1988 to 6.31 in 1995.

As for rent-seeking activities, only two articles have estimated the total rental in 1988 and 1992 so far (Hu Heli, 1989; Wan Anpei, 1995). It is impossible to conduct an accurate study of rental distribution and losses at present. However, it is generally believed that the rental distribution is extremely unbalanced.

We analyzed earlier the expanded income gap or increasing income inequality among Chinese residents since the reform. It is worth pointing out; however, that poverty was significantly mitigated in China during the same period. The poverty-stricken population in China has dropped from 250 million in 1978 to 65 million in 1995 (Zhu Fengqi et al., 1996). This coexistence of increasing inequality and decreasing poverty mainly results from the high economic growth since the reform. In other words, expansion of the resident income gap since the reform occurs after the "pie" is growing bigger and bigger. Concerning the relationship between economic growth, inequality and poverty, the report of the World Bank makes an analysis from the perspective of international comparison (Development Report of the World Bank, 1996).

IV. Cause of widened income gap and value judgment

It is a complicated task to analyze the cause of the widened income distribution gap since the reform. For a long time, people have been using economic growth or development to explain expansion of the income gap. The converse-U hypothesis proposed by Simon Smith Kuznets, in particular, has been used to explain the income gap expansion in developing countries during their economic takeoff (Simon Kuznets, 1955). Even Taiwan's experience, where relatively equal results are achieved in income distribution after rapid economic growth, and which is an exception of such hypothesis, focuses on the study of the relationship between economic growth and income distribution; that is, the study of whether economic growth will result in income gap expansion. However, according to China's actual situations, we believe that the impact of the following three factors on income distribution should be observed: (1) economic growth or development; (2) economic reform or system change; and (3) economic policies and their changes (see Table 5.16). Certainly, these three factors both widen and narrow the income distribution gap. The widening effect has been dominant in the past ten-plus years; therefore, the income distribution gap has been widened on the whole. In addition, the three factors are inter-related. We now analyze the impact of these factors on the income distribution gap one by one.

A. Economic growth or development

The facts since the reform show that in terms of economic growth or development, the rapid development of the non-state-owned economy in cities (compared to the state-owned economy) and the rapid development of non-agricultural industries in rural areas (compared to agricultural industries) are two strong factors that caused the income gap expansion. The results in Tables 5.17 and 5.18 are calculated according to the two sample surveys conducted by the Project Team. The tables show that in cities, the Gini coefficient in the non-state-owned sectors is obviously higher than that in the state-owned sectors, and that in rural areas, the Gini coefficient in the non-agricultural industries is obviously higher than that in agriculture. Therefore, with the rapid development of the non-state-owned economy and non-agricultural industries, widening of the income gap is a quite natural phenomenon. It should be pointed out that not all the economic growth factors cause widening of the income gap. For example, the rapid development of agricultural production from 1979 to 1983 significantly narrows the income gap between cities and rural areas. In terms of its impact on the inside of the rural areas, it is hard to make a comprehensive judgment. According to some calculations (Li Shi et al., 1997), the income gap inside rural areas is slightly widened. However, it is hard to say that this is caused by the development of agricultural production, because it may be caused by the unbalanced development of the non-agricultural industries.

Table 5.16 Impact of Growth, Reform and Policy on Income Distribution

Factors	Impact on income distribution gap	
	Within cities or within rural areas	Between cities and rural areas
1. Economic growth or economic development		
Rapid development of non-state-owned economy	+	+
Rapid development of non-agricultural industries in rural areas	+	−
Development of agricultural production (especially from 1979 to 1983)		−
2. Economic reform or system changes		
A. Orderly changes		
Price reform in rural areas	−	−
Household contract responsibility system in rural areas	−	−
Labor flow in rural areas		−
Reform of housing system in cities	+	+
B. Disorderly changes		
Rent-seeking activities	+	+
Control by insiders	+	+
Monopoly	+	+
Corruption	+	+
3. Economic policies and their changes		+
Low-price purchase of agricultural products		
Agricultural tax		+
Nontax burden on peasants		+
Personal income tax	−	−
Subsidy decrease in cities		
A. By head count	+	−
B. By position	−	−
Welfare of urban residents transformed into personal property	+	+

Note: "+" stands for gap expansion, namely increased inequality; "−" stands for gap narrowing, namely decreased inequality. Some factors, whose impacts are complex and difficult to tell, are indicated with blanks.

Table 5.17 Gini Coefficients of Salary Income of Staff Members in State-Owned Sectors and Non-State-Owned Sectors in Cities

	1988	1995
State-owned sectors	0.222	0.283
Non-state-owned sectors	0.286	0.347

Table 5.18 Gini Coefficients of Agricultural Income and Non-Agricultural Income in Rural Areas

	1988	1995
Agriculture	0.242	0.239
Non-agricultural industries	0.390	0.512

B. *Economic reform or system change*

As China adopts gradual reform, double systems coexist in the system transformation. Plus the impact of some non-economic factors, some disorderly problems occur in the economic reform or system change. Therefore, it is feasible to divide the system change factors into orderly changes and disorderly changes.

The price reform and the household contract responsibility system implemented in the early 1980s, especially the practice of fixing farm output quotas on the household basis, have brought benefits to most peasants. Therefore, these reform measures narrow the gap within rural areas and, all the more significantly, narrow the urban and rural income gap.

As for the flow of rural laborers, it obviously narrows the urban and rural income gap, but its impact on income distribution within rural areas is relatively complicated, because the regions from which rural laborers flow out are distributed in an extremely unbalanced manner. Therefore, it widens the income gap for rural areas as a whole but narrows the income gap within a certain residential community. That is why we do not make indications in Table 5.16.

The housing system reform in cities that has been implemented since the late 1980s is a very important reform measure. Some scholars hold that its significance is equivalent to that of the household contract responsibility system implemented in rural areas in the past. Though this reform is still in process, its preliminary impact on income distribution has been quite prominent. As mentioned earlier, the concentration ratio of rental valuation of owner-occupied housing is not only higher than the urban Gini coefficient, but also higher than the concentration ratio of housing subsidies. Therefore, the reform of the housing system has widened the income distribution gap. This reform does not take into careful consideration the inequality factors that are produced in the original public housing distribution. For example, it does not carefully consider the differences between people who own public houses and people who don't, people who own good houses and people who own inferior houses, and people who own big houses and people who own small houses, according to the principle of market economy. As a result, it widens not only the income distribution gap of urban residents, but also the income distribution gap between urban and rural residents. Furthermore, the most unequal part of the original public housing distribution has not been reformed thus far. If policies on the housing commercialization reform, especially the price policy, remain unchanged, then one can expect the income distribution gap to widen further as

84   *Widening of Chinese residents' income gap*

the housing reform is further promoted. It should be pointed out that fundamentally speaking, the housing system reform is a process of visualizing the invisible income inequality in the original system. However, when the inequality of the rental valuation of owner-occupied housing exceeds the inequality of housing subsidies, we should note that this is the additional inequality in the process of visualization and is a noteworthy problem in the reform process.

As for the impact of disorderly factors in the system change on income distribution, that issue is the most difficult to ascertain through investigation, as well as one that has aroused strong social repercussions.

Among the disorderly factors, rent-seeking activities are especially eye-catching. As mentioned previously, there has been no accurate study concerning rental distribution, but it is generally believed that rental distribution is extremely unbalanced. Therefore, it should be unquestionable that rent-seeking activities widen the income gap and are an important factor that creates the high-income class.

Insider control (Aoki Masahiko, Qian Yingyi, 1995) is also an important disorderly factor in the system change. During the system transition, centralized control over public assets is gradually loosened, and all departments, local authorities and enterprises have the right to control public assets. The interests resulting from different amounts of public assets possessed are often transformed, through insider control, into the interests of the department, region, unit or even individual concerned. The distribution of such interests is considerably non-transparent and unequal. The massive loss of state-owned assets is all associated with insider control.

All kinds of monopolistic behaviors during the system transition, including departmental monopoly and trade monopoly, are also the factors that result in the increased income distribution inequality. Some economists call profiteering through monopolistic behaviors rent-making activities, which are more serious than rent-seeking activities. Unequal distribution resulting from corruption, especially unequal distribution resulting from power-for-money deals, is particularly hated and a factor that is hard to ascertain through investigation.

This analysis shows that not all the factors of the system change widen the income distribution gap. On the contrary, some factors in the orderly changes outlined here narrow the gap. Therefore, it is not proper to attribute widening of the income gap to the economic reform itself. Certainly, we should see that all the factors of disorderly changes widen the income gap. Such disorderly changes, in a sense, can be regarded as the price or cost of the reform. However, to what extent we should pay the price, or, which price is inevitable and which one is avoidable, still remains an issue to be discussed.

C.   *Economic policies and their changes*

In addition to the economic growth and system changes outlined previously, the impact of economic policies and changes in income distribution is also non-negligible. Here, we want to analyze the relationship between economic policies and the urban and rural income gap. As mentioned earlier, the trend of widening

Widening of Chinese residents' income gap 85

the urban and rural income gap lasted for about ten years, from the middle 1980s to the middle 1990s, since the reform. The turning point emerged after 1995, but it lasted for a short time and did not form a trend. Given that, what is the major factor that caused the ten years' trend of widening? Seemingly, it is hard to say that it is mainly caused by the economic growth factor. International experience shows that as developing countries transform from the dual economy to the modern economy, the urban and rural gap shows a trend of gradual narrowing. China's own experience shows that the progression of rural industrialization is mainly manifested as the rapid development of non-agricultural industries in rural areas, which narrows the urban and rural income gap. As for the system change factors, the orderly changes often narrow the gap, while the disorderly changes are not easily reflected in the sample surveys conducted by the National Bureau of Statistics of China and the Project Team. Therefore, it is hard to say that widening of the income gap between urban and rural residents, as reflected by the above data, is mainly caused by the economic reform or system change factors. We believe that the ten-year widening of the urban and rural income gap is closely related to the "policy inertia" in the original system to a great extent. The long-standing urban-rural segmentation is a kind of policy product in the original system. The low-price purchase policy for agricultural products, tax policy for peasants, nontax burden policy for peasants, welfare subsidy policy for urban residents and policy on restricting peasants from entering cities are all important parts of the original policy. These policies have loosened and changed to some extent since the reform but still have a distance to go from fundamental changes. The policy on substantially increasing the procurement prices for farm products since the early 1980s and in 1995 has effectively narrowed the urban and rural income gap, which, from another perspective, indicates the important role of policy factors in that gap. It should be noted that if welfare of urban residents based on subsidies is transformed into personal property (such as the housing reform), then this policy will further widen the income gap between urban and rural residents.

There are all kinds of value judgments and social responses concerning the widening of the income gap. One opinion holds that though the income gap in China has widened since the reform, it has not exceeded the reasonable range, and so we cannot say that prominent "polarization of the rich and the poor" has emerged. Widening of the income gap is one of the costs of economic growth, and is acceptable if it can be controlled to the extent that social stability and normal operation are ensured (Li Peilin, 1995). The report of the World Bank also holds that, "Widening the salary, income and wealth gaps to a certain degree is an integrated part of transition, because allowing the market to decide salaries will create motivators that increase efficiency, and such motivators are vital to a successful reform" (Development Report of the World Bank, 1996). Another opinion holds that internationally, it is generally accepted that the Gini coefficient of 0.3–0.4 indicates the moderate gap between the rich and the poor. In China, the Gini coefficient has exceeded 0.4. Within a short period of ten-plus years, China has transformed into a country with a moderate degree of inequality in the world from

86 *Widening of Chinese residents' income gap*

a country with prevalent equalitarianism, and its degree of inequality has exceeded even that of the United States, which is therefore worrying (Li Qiang, 1995).

We put forward the following two points of view in this regard:

Firstly, we should not hold a simplistic view when measuring the degree of inequality with the Gini coefficient. For example, it is difficult to use the range of 0.3—0.4 as a standard to measure whether the degree of equalization in a country is reasonable or not. In fact, such factors as population size, territorial area, and socio-economic homogeneity will all affect the level of the Gini coefficient. China is a country with a big population size and territorial area and very low socio-economic homogeneity, and its Gini coefficient is naturally higher than those in the countries and regions that have different situations.

Secondly, we must differentiate whether widening of the income gap is temporary and non-constant, or long-term and relatively constant. For example, according to the two sample surveys conducted by the Project Team, the Gini coefficient of the monetary income of the staff in the private sector in cities was 0.49 in 1988 and dropped to 0.40 in 1995. It seems that such change is associated with the increasing number of staff in the private sector, gradual increase of competitive mechanisms, and gradual improvement of the market rules. Therefore, we may say that the big income gap in the private sector in 1988 is a short-term, non-constant transient phenomenon. Therefore, what China will become in terms of income distribution depends on the next step of the reform. If an economy, which has both the fundamental function of the market mechanism and the effective macroeconomic control of the government, is established by deepening the reform, the income gap may tend to be rationalized. If the disordered status in the transitional period cannot be effectively overcome, the widening trend and status of the income gap goes on, a turning point cannot be found and such status is solidified and stereotyped, then it will turn China into a truly polarized society. It is obvious that we cannot form a judgment hastily based on some phenomena in the transitional period, nor can we ignore the serious consequences that may result from the widening trend of the income gap.

D.   *Some suggestions in epilogue*

We have analyzed the widening status of the income distribution gap and its causes and effects in this paper. Given this analysis, how should we improve the income distribution status?

1   Firstly, we must focus on deepening reform. Only by deepening reform can we fundamentally solve the problem of income inequality caused by the disordered status in the transitional period. On the one hand, we must not deny the reform orientation or even require returning to the old system

Widening of Chinese residents' income gap   87

because of widening of the income gap. On the other hand, we must not slow down the reform step because China chooses gradual reform, thus increasing the reform cost or even solidifying some transient phenomena of the transitional period.

2 Secondly, we must focus on development. Only when the economy develops and the "cake" is made bigger can we lay a solid material base for equitable distribution and poverty alleviation. Judging by China's situation, we should attach particular importance to the development of the rural economy and speed up transformation from the dual economy to the modern economy. Only by speeding up this process can we create the necessary conditions for narrowing the urban and rural income differences and regional income differences. We should attach importance to the development of the rural economy from a strategic perspective – we should not only provide food security and maintain social stability, but we should also narrow the urban and rural income differences and realize nationwide modernization.

3 We should also improve a series of policies and measures, such as: (a) The policy on personal income tax. This is an important policy and measure that narrows the income gap between the high-income class and ordinary people. In order to give play to this policy, firstly, we should increase the income transparency, and secondly, we should ensure that people accept it with pleasure. (b) The social security policy. This is the most important policy and measure that solves disparity between the rich and the poor as a result of such factors as unemployment, diseases and senility. (c) The labor flow policy. This provides a premise for narrowing the income gap – equal opportunity. (d) The educational policy. We should increase input in the human capital, especially input in basic education. Only in this way can we increase the population quality and provide another premise for narrowing the income gap – narrowing the gap in the educational background.

4 The government should give play to its function effectively in income redistribution. In a mature market economy, taxation and welfare (especially subsidies) are the important means for the government to redistribute income. In principle, regulation by means of taxation and welfare, namely redistribution of income, should be able to narrow the income gap. In the planned economy era, however, the net tax policy was implemented in rural areas, and the net welfare and net subsidy policy was implemented in cities. As a result of such "retro regulation" policy, as people call it, the income gap was widened. This situation has shown some improvement in the transitional period, but further efforts are still needed in order to enable these two means to get on the macroeconomic control track in the market economy. It must be particularly noted here that we must use these two means in combination and avoid attending to one thing and losing another. For example, if a progressive income tax is imposed on a certain high-income group in order to narrow the income gap, but high welfare and high subsidies are also given to this group at the same time, then the income tax will be turned into the negative income tax and lose its meaning.

88 *Widening of Chinese residents' income gap*

In conclusion, improving income distribution status is indeed an extremely arduous task. However, the outlook of such an improvement should be good, as long as we strive to push forward reform and development and regard it as part of a great undertaking.

Notes

1 The differences between the actual selling prices and market prices of public-owned housing vary with regions. Generally speaking, the differences of small and medium-sized cities are smaller than those of big cities. In the prime locations of megacities, the differences are very big. The market prices are one to two times higher than the actual selling prices in general cases, and ten times higher in extreme cases (Wang Lina, 1997).
2 In fact, Chinese urban residents are not allowed to transfer houses immediately after they buy them; that is, it takes time to transfer property rights.

References

Aoki Masahiko, Qian Yingyi. (Eds.). (1995). 转轨经济中的公司治理结构 [Corporate Governance Structure in Transition Economy]. Beijing: China Economic Publishing House.

Aziz Raman Kahn et al. (1994). 中国居民户的收入及其分配 [Income of Chinese Resident Households and Its Distribution]. In Zhao Renwei, Keith Griffin (Eds.), *Study of Resident Income Distribution in China*. Beijing: China Social Sciences Press.

Carl Riskin. (1987). *China's Political Economy*. Oxford: Oxford University Press.

Development Report of the World Bank. (1996). 从计划到市场 [From Plan to Market]. Beijing: China Financial & Economic Publishing House.

Gao Xiaoyan. (March 18, 1995). 变动着的中国阶层 [Changing Social Hierarchy in China]. *China Business Times*.

Hu Angang. (1994). 中国地区差距报告 [Report on Regional Gaps in China]. printed by Research Center for Eco-Environmental Sciences, Chinese Academy of Sciences.

Hu Heli. (1989). 1988 年我国租金价值的估算 [Estimation of Rental Value in China in 1988]. *Comparative Economic & Social Systems*, 5.

Income Distribution Project Team by National Bureau of Statistics of China et al. (1996). 目前收入分配中存在的主要问题和对策 [Main Existing Problems in Current Income Distribution and Strategies, Scientific Institute of National Bureau of Statistics of China]. *Research Reference*, 94.

Irma Adelmen, David Sunding. (1987). Economic Policy and Income Distribution in China. *Journal of Comparative Economics*, September.

Li Chengrui. (1986). 关于中国近几年的经济政策对居民收入和消费状况影响的统计报告 [Statistical Report on the Impact of China's Economic Policies in Recent Years on Resident Income and Consumption]. *Statistical Research*, 1.

Li Peilin. (1995). 经济转型、分配差距与社会公平 [Economic Transformation, Distribution Gap and Social Equity]. *Modernization Research* (Taipei), October.

Li Qiang. (1995). 中国大陆的收入差距问题 [Income Gap Problems on Mainland China]. A thesis for the International Symposium on Income Distribution.

Li Shi, Zhao Renwei, Zhang Ping. (1997). 中国经济改革中的收入分配变动 [Changes of Income Distribution in China's Economic Reform]. A thesis prepared for the Symposium in August.

Liu Shucheng et al. (Eds.). (1994). 中国地区经济发展研究 [Study of Regional Economic Development in China]. Beijing: China Statistics Press.

Ren Caifang, Cheng Xuebin. (1996). 从城镇居民收入看分配差距 [Distribution Gap from the Perspective of Income of Urban Residents]. *Review of Economic Research*, Issue 157.

Simon Kuznets. (1955). Economic Growth and Income in Equality. *The American Economic Review*, March.

Wan Anpei. (1995). 租金规模的动态考察 [Dynamic Observation of Rental Scale]. *Economic Research Journal*, 2.

Wang Lina. 中国的住房价格和收入分配 [Housing Price and Income Distribution in China]. A thesis prepared for the Symposium in August 1997.

The World Bank. (1983). 中国: 社会主义经济的发展 [China: Development of the Socialist Economy]. Washington, DC.

Yu Genqian. (April 19, 1996). 地区收入差距问题 [Regional Income Gap Problems]. *Economist Intelligence*.

Zhao Renwei. (1985). Some Trends of Change of Personal Income Distribution of Laborers. *Economic Research Journal*, 3.

Zhao Renwei. (1991). The Trend of Changes in the Distribution of Workers' Income. *International Journal of Social Economics*, England, Special Issue, 18, Numbers 8/9/10.

Zhao Renwei. (1992). 中国转型期中收入分配的一些特殊现象 [Some Special Phenomena in Income Distribution in China's Transitional Period]. *Economic Research Journal*, 1.

Zheng Dajiong. (1994). 从私营企业主、百万富翁与职工的收入情况看社会收入差别的变化 [Changes of Social Income Differences from the Perspective of Income of Private Enterprise Owners, Millionaires and Employees]. A thesis prepared for the Symposium on Equity Issues and Strategies in the Period of Social Transition.

Zhu Fengqi et al. (1996). 中国反贫困研究 [Study of Anti-Poverty in China]. Beijing: China Planning Press.

(This paper was written jointly with Li Shi: written by Zhao Renwei and calculated by Li Shi. It was originally published in *Economic Research Journal*, Issue 9, 1997.)

6 Context of the income gap among Chinese residents

At the turns of the century and the millennium, it is quite significant to review and give some prospective thoughts on the issue of resident income distribution in China, especially on the income gap problems. In this short thesis, we firstly make a retrospective analysis of the characteristics of the income distribution pattern before the reform and opening-up. These characteristics reflect the legacy left by the Chinese-style planned economy and may be regarded as the starting point of the reform in this field. Secondly, we analyze, within the radius of our capacity, the changes in income distribution pattern during the past 20 years since the reform and opening-up, as well as the prominent problems associated with such changes. Last, we give some prospective thoughts on the cause and effect of widening of the income according to the policy implication.

I. Legacy left by the planned economy

What are the characteristics of China in terms of income distribution before the reform and opening-up (it refers to the 20-plus years from the establishment of the planned economy system in 1956 to the initiation of the reform in 1978)? Using the simplest language, we may summarize it this way: China before the reform was a society with a very high degree of equality, or a very low degree of inequality, where some unequal factors coexisted in a hidden way.

Why do we say that China before the reform was a society with a very high degree of equality? A lot of research literature shows that just before the reform or in the early stage of the reform, China's Gini coefficient of the income distribution was lower than that in most developing countries in the world. Its urban Gini coefficient was below 0.2; its rural Gini coefficient was slightly higher, but was mostly estimated to be between 0.21–0.24. In many developing countries, the urban Gini coefficient was 0.37–0.43, and the rural Gini coefficient was 0.34–0.40.

There are at least three factors that explain why China had a high degree of income equality before the reform: Firstly, the system factor. The socialist system is characterized by public ownership of the means of production. Therefore, after the gradual socialization of means of production from 1949 to 1956, residents had hardly any property income except for a small amount of saving deposits and interest income. Secondly, the policy factor. The decision makers hold that socialism

The income gap among Chinese residents 91

pursues the goal of social equity and that people should accumulate more and consume less in the early stage of construction of New China; the labor income should also be low and equalized. Thirdly, the bonds of the equalitarianism concept "inequality rather than want is the cause of trouble" in the Chinese cultural tradition. Such concept advocates fairness without considering efficiency, does not intend to make the "cake" bigger for distribution, and often mixes up common prosperity with widespread poverty.

However, if we make a further study, we may find that even in a circumstance with a very high degree of equality, some unequal factors still existed or were hidden. For example:

1   The income gap between urban and rural residents is big. According to the calculation of the World Bank, the per capita income ratio of urban residents to rural residents was 2.5 (1979), higher than that in other low-income Asian countries (about 1.5 on average), and slightly higher than that in middle-income countries (about 2.2 on average).

The income gap between urban and rural residents in China was big before the reform. The general reason is that China had the dual economic structure like other developing countries; that is, the modern industry sector coexisted with the traditional agriculture sector. The special reason for the big gap is that China's decision makers implemented special policies at that time, especially the low-price purchase policy for agricultural products, and used them as one of the means to accumulate the capital required for industrialization. Meanwhile, they implemented the household registration system that strictly restricted rural residents from immigrating into cities, which further enhanced segmentation between the urban and rural economic systems. It is obvious that with the income distribution highly equalized, especially when the degree of equality in urban areas was higher than that in rural areas in those days, the unequal factors still existed for rural residents due to the big income differences between cities and rural areas.

2   In terms of the distribution pattern of consumables, the pattern of distribution in kind, namely the supply system, was emphasized, while the market distribution pattern (buying with money) was restrained. In a circumstance where distribution in kind was emphasized, the monetary income gap was smaller than the actual income gap among residents. The distribution in kind is actually an invisible welfare subsidy system. The original purpose of this subsidy system was to compensate the low-income class so as to narrow the income gap. However, it was not the case according to the results of such an implementation. Firstly, the peasant residents who accounted for about 80% of the population were not entitled to the subsidies that urban residents were. Secondly, even for the urban residents, their subsidies were distributed according to the principle of equalitarianism only for those consumer goods that were rationed per capita (such as grain, cotton and oil). For those consumer goods that were supplied by position (such as houses, automobiles and phones), the subsidy distribution was highly unequal. Such

92 *The income gap among Chinese residents*

a subsidy system or benefit system should be an unequal factor that is covered up by equalitarianism.

3 Long-term freezing of salaries resulted in an unfavorable income distribution pattern for the young generation. Salaries were basically frozen from 1956 to 1976, before the reform. Certainly, the prices of basic consumer goods during this period were also basically frozen. Superficially, everyone was equal before such "freezing" of salaries and prices of commodities, because everyone lost the opportunity of the rise in salaries. But actually, long-term salary freezing had different income distribution effects on people of different generations. It resulted in intergenerational inequality and created an unfavorable income distribution pattern for the young generation. The consequence resulting from such situation even became a prominent social problem in the early 1980s. In non-war times, substantial freezing of salaries that lasted for such a long time was quite special. It did not happen even in the Soviet Union and Eastern Europe countries in those years. It should be said that this was associated with the special background resulting from the period of the late 1950s to the 1970s, and can be regarded as a special phenomenon produced by the special Chinese-style planned economy. Such a phenomenon is also an unequal factor covered up by equalitarianism.

Then again, overall, China was still a society with prevalent equalitarianism at that time, despite the aforementioned unequal factors that existed in its income distribution before the reform. Inequality existed in such equality, while equality existed in inequality, which indicates the complex economic situation of Chinese society. Such complexity is analyzed in order to have an in-depth understanding of the starting point and background of the reform.

II. Changes since the reform

Targeting such a complicated background and starting point, China's decision makers put forward the policy that "allows some people to get rich first" right from the beginning of the reform, with the purpose of overcoming equalitarianism in income distribution, strengthening the incentive mechanism, increasing efficiency, promoting economic development, and ultimately realizing common prosperity based on a bigger "pie".

The goal of this policy is the principle known as "efficiency first and consideration to fairness". In my opinion, such a principle is definitely a feasible alternative for a certain development stage with equalitarianism as the starting point. In addition, this is similar in some way to the first stage of the "converse-U hypothesis" of Simon Kuznets that has been discussed a lot internationally. However, experience over the past 20 years shows that the change in the income distribution pattern is much more complicated than expected. The income gap is indeed widened, but actually it exceeds the range of overcoming equalitarianism. In addition, some widening of the gap has nothing to do with efficiency promotion.

The income gap among Chinese residents 93

The changes in income distribution of Chinese residents may be summarized in the following five aspects:

1 The general trend of changes included an obvious widening of the income gap. According to the survey conducted by the Project Team of the Institute of Economics, Chinese Academy of Social Sciences, the national Gini coefficient already reached 0.445 in 1995. According to the survey conducted by the Institute of Economics at Nankai University, the national Gini coefficient from 1994 to 1997 all exceeded 0.5 if illegal and abnormal income was included.

2 The income gap between urban and rural residents first narrowed, then widened. This gap was narrowed to some extent in the early stage of reform but has shown a widening trend since the mid-1980s. According to the survey conducted by the Project Team, the ratio of the actual income per capita of urban and rural residents was 2.36 in 1978, dropped to 2.14 in 1985, widened to 2.38 in 1987 (that is, returning to the level in the early stage of reform), and widened to 2.79 in 1995.

3 The inter-regional resident income gap, especially whether the relative gap has been widened, has always been a controversial issue in the academic community. However, according to the Project Team survey, the inter-regional income gap has widened to some extent, judging from each perspective. Specifically, the degree of widening of the rural inter-regional income gap was significantly higher than that of the urban inter-regional income gap.

4 The property income gap presents a new problem. As mentioned earlier, Chinese residents had hardly any property income except for a small amount of interest income of personal savings before the reform. Residents' property income, especially urban residents' property income, has been growing rapidly and distributed quite unequally since the reform. Specifically, inequality of income distribution resulting from inequality of financial assets and housing distribution became an eye-catching new problem all the more.

5 High-income class and rent-seeking activities pose a difficult problem. The issue regarding the high-income class has always aroused strong social responses. However, how to ascertain the real situation of the high-income class has always been a difficult problem. Our data in hand are made up of two types: various case surveys, and the sample surveys. The defect of the first type is that the national representativeness is unknown. The defect of the second type is that many high-income people cannot be covered by the sample surveys at all. Therefore, the studies in this regard have been unsatisfactory so far.[1]

Judging by the time sequence, I think the changes of the income distribution pattern over the past 20 years may be divided into the following three stages: Firstly, in the early stage of reform and opening-up, namely in the late 1970s and early and middle 1980s, the prevailing trend in income distribution was still equalitarianism left over by the planned economy period. Secondly, in the middle

94 *The income gap among Chinese residents*

and late stages of the 1980s and the early 1990s, income distribution was mainly featured by the coexistence of two phenomena due to the coexistence of and conflicts between the double systems (equalitarianism in the planning system, and the big income gap between people in the system and people outside the system). Such complaints as "surgeons are poorer than barbers" and "nuclear experts are poorer than egg sellers" are just a reflection of the conflicts in income distribution resulting from the coexistence of these systems. Thirdly, in the late 1990s, though equalitarianism still existed in certain departments and enterprises, the excessive income gap had become a prevailing trend throughout society. The income inflation that had nothing to do with the incentive mechanism (which helped increase efficiency), namely the so-called "sudden wealth", all the more provoked a public outcry.

What, then, is the most prominent problem in income distribution at present? In my opinion, except for those so-called "sudden wealth" problems that are not easy to ascertain through investigation, such as power-for-money deals and corruption, the following two problems are easy to ascertain through investigation:

1   The problem of the excessive urban and rural income gap. As the calculation calibers and methods are different, the estimation of the degree of the urban and rural income gap is often inconsistent. However, there is no disagreement on the judgment of the general trend of the urban and rural income gap that has been narrowed first and then widened since the reform and opening-up. In addition to the above research findings, relevant reports of the World Bank point out that in most countries in the world, the urban and rural income ratio is 1.5, and such ratios of more than 2 are extremely rare. However, this ratio already reached 2.5 in China in 1995. In addition, if the in-kind welfare of urban residents was added, the actual income of urban residents would increase by 72%.[2] Even if the factor that peasants go into cities to work and narrow the urban and rural income gap is taken into consideration, the ratio of the actual urban and rural income in 1995 was about 4. The report on the national economy operation in the first quarter of 2000, as released by the National Bureau of Statistics of China, points out that per capita disposable income of urban residents in the first quarter actually rose by 6.9% year by year, while the per capita cash income of rural residents rose by 1.3% year by year. Certainly, the data of one quarter or even a certain year do not necessarily represent a kind of trend, and the cash income and disposable income do not completely correspond to each other, either. However, this at least explains, from one side of the problem, how to reverse the trend of the widened income gap between urban and rural areas, which is still an urgent problem. China is about to join the WTO, and will be faced with bigger challenges in such issues as agriculture, peasants' income, and urban and rural income gap.

    Such a unique urban and rural income gap is not only an economic problem but also a social problem, and it also concerns realization of the four modernizations of the whole nation (not just in cities).

2   Inequality of income distribution resulting from inequality of property distribution. This is mainly reflected in two aspects. Firstly, it results from inequality of distribution of financial assets. The financial assets of China's urban residents have grown extremely rapidly since the beginning of the 1990s, and their distribution is quite unequal. According to the survey conducted by the National Bureau of Statistics of China, in five equant groups, the per household financial assets of the highest 20% of households were 12 times those of the lowest 20% of households by the end of June 1996. This gap is still widening at present. Secondly, it results from inequality of housing distribution. According to the study conducted by the Project Team, if the imputed rent of residents' owner-occupied housing after the housing reform is also regarded as a kind of property income, then the inequality coefficient of the imputed rent of owner-occupied housing (0.371 in 1995) has exceeded that (0.322 in 1995) of housing subsidies (invisible subsidies) formed in the planned economy era, while the inequality coefficient of housing subsidies has exceeded the overall inequality coefficient (0.286 in 1995) of urban residents. This indicates that if the housing reform, which visualizes the original inequality of invisible income (invisible subsidies), admits only the original inequality, then when the inequality of the imputed rent of owner-occupied housing exceeds the inequality of the original housing subsidies, we should see this as additional inequality during such visualization. We should also see that the situation has the risk of further deterioration if measures are not taken in a timely manner. At the crucial moment when housing distribution in kind transits from housing distribution in kind to monetary housing distribution, some departments and units are speeding up their pace of buying and building houses and are distributing big and good houses to their employees in an excessive way, so as to offer the "last supper" to their employees. People have found that the double-track price differences of houses are far greater than the double-track price differences of general merchandise. In cities such as Beijing, in particular, getting one more house means the value ranging from one hundred thousand yuan to hundreds of thousands of yuan. Therefore, "rent-setting" activities have also been produced in addition to "rent-seeking" activities. Departmental monopoly and trade monopoly are just the important conditions for such rent-setting activities. The uniformity of the planned economy era has collapsed, and the equal competition that should be available in the market economy has not been established. Rent-setting as a result of monopoly will not only hinder the process of housing reform, but also will cause new unequal distribution, which must arouse great attention.

III.   Outlook at the turn of the century

Concerning the changes and problems related to the income gap, there have been all kinds of discussions on their causes and effects in the academic community and in society. It is not my intention to discuss them here one by one. I just give some prospective thoughts from the perspective of policy implication.

96 *The income gap among Chinese residents*

In my opinion, at least three factors cause widening of the income distribution gap, namely economic growth or development, economic reform or economic system changes and economic policies and their changes. In terms of economic development, the factors are mainly the rapid development of the non-agricultural industries in rural areas and the rapid development of the non-state-owned economy in cities. Economic system changes may be divided into orderly changes and disorderly changes. Economic policies may be divided into the "policy inertia" left over by the planned economy era and the existing macroeconomic policy.

As we analyze the relationship between widening of the income gap and economic reform, two trends must be prevented. One trend simply attributes widening of the income gap and the problems that emerge to economic reform itself, while the other trend simply regards widening of the income gap as a price that economic reform should pay. In my opinion, widening of the income gap should be viewed from three different levels. The first level is the incentive part that helps increase efficiency. This part belongs to the achievements made in overcoming equalitarianism, and should be recognized. The second level is the price that economic reform must pay. For example, China's reform can be carried out only in a gradual way featuring double tracks, and such activities as "rent-seeking", which make use of double tracks, will definitely emerge. To some extent, this can be regarded as the price that the reform should pay. The third level belongs to the overhigh price, or the part that should not be paid, or that part that should be prevented and avoided. Certainly, it is not easy to identify, especially quantify, the boundary between the second level and third level. But theoretically, it is possible.

In terms of policy design, we should start with the following aspects:

1   We must focus on deepening reform. Only by deepening reform can we fundamentally solve the problem of income inequality caused by the disordered status in the transitional period. On the one hand, we must not deny the reform orientation or even require returning to the old system because of widening of the income gap. On the other hand, we must not slow down the reform step because China chooses gradual reform, thus increasing the reform cost or even solidifying some transient phenomena of the transitional period.

2   We must focus on development. Only once the economy develops and the "cake" is made bigger can we lay a solid material base for equitable distribution and poverty alleviation. Though the income gap has widened markedly, the poverty-stricken population has also dropped markedly over the past 20 years. According to official statistics, such population has dropped from 250 million in 1978 to about 30 million at present. This is mainly because the high economic growth has been achieved since the reform. Without economic development, it is difficult to alleviate poverty in a circumstance where the income gap has been widened. Judging by China's situations, we should attach particular importance to the development of the rural economy and speed up transformation from the dual economy to the modern economy. Only by speeding up this process can we create

The income gap among Chinese residents 97

the necessary conditions for narrowing the urban and rural income differences and regional income differences. We should attach importance to the development of the rural economy from a strategic perspective – we should not only provide food security and maintain social stability, but we should also narrow the urban and rural income differences, and realize nationwide modernization.

3   We should also improve a series of policies and measures. (a) The policy on personal income tax is an important policy and measure that narrows the income gap between the high-income class and ordinary people. In order to give play to this policy, firstly, we should increase income transparency; and secondly, we should ensure that people accept it with pleasure. (b) The social security policy is the most important policy and measure that solves disparity between the rich and the poor as a result of such factors as unemployment, disease and senility. (c) The labor flow policy provides a premise for narrowing the income gap – equal opportunity. It should be said that the degree of development of the labor market in China is still very low currently, and there seems to be much behind all this in the future. (d) With regard to educational policy, we should increase input in human capital, especially input in basic education. Only in this way can we increase the population quality, and provide another premise for narrowing the income gap – narrowing the gap in the educational background.

4   The government should give play to its function effectively in income redistribution. In a mature market economy, taxation and welfare (especially subsidies) are the important means for the government to redistribute income. In principle, regulation by means of taxation and welfare, namely redistribution of income, should be able to narrow the income gap. In the planned economy era, however, the net tax policy was implemented in rural areas, and the net welfare and net subsidy policy was implemented in cities. As a result of such "retro regulation" policy, as people call it, the income gap was widened. This situation has shown some improvement in the transitional period, but further efforts are still needed in order to enable these two means to get on the macroeconomic control track in the market economy. It must be particularly noted here that we must use these two means in combination and avoid attending to one thing and losing another. For example, if the progressive income tax is imposed on a certain high-income group in order to narrow the income gap, but the high welfare and high subsidies are also given to this group at the same time, then the income tax will be turned into a negative income tax and lose its meaning.

5   We should strengthen the study of the impact of macroeconomic policy on income distribution. Our study of the impact of macroeconomic policies, especially monetary and fiscal policies, on the resident income gap is still far from enough. According to the study conducted by James K. Galbraith, an American economist, the widening of the income gap in the United States from the late 1960s to the late 1990s is caused not by the non-human market forces, nor by the production factors, but mainly by the policy factor. The

98 *The income gap among Chinese residents*

so-called policy factor mainly means that the goal of full employment was given up, and the high interest rate policy was introduced to curb inflation. Such policy resulted in increased inequality, thus destroying the middle class in the United States and turning it into the victims of the anti-inflation policy. The decline of the middle class also impaired the democratic system of the United States. The United States has changed from a democratic society of the middle class to an authoritarian quasi-democratic society.[3] China's national conditions differ greatly from those of the United States. However, what kind of class or hierarchical structure should China's economic policies help build in order to achieve social stability and promote economic reform and development? This is indeed a question that calls for deep thought. It seems that a social structure that is small at both ends and big in the middle should be our long-term policy goal.

6   We should strengthen the study of the turning points of the income gap changes. We have not found the turning point between widening and stability or even narrowing for the urban and rural income gap so far. Is it possible for us to find a turning point between growth and stability or even slight decrease, just like the study of population problems? Therefore, in terms of income distribution, strengthening the study and prediction of such turning point is also an important task before us. We have a reason to hope that new breakthroughs will be made in this regard in the 21st century ahead.

(This paper was written at the invitation of Fan Chunping of Jilin People's Press, and was finished in July 2000. It was included into the book *100 Important Issues in Humanistic and Social Science Facing the 21st Century*, Shandong Education Press, 2005 edition. Its title was changed to read *Study of Chinese Residents' Income Gap* at the time of publication.)

Notes

1 For the summary of these five aspects and relevant data of the sample surveys by the Project Team of the Institute of Economics of Chinese Academy of Social Sciences, see Zhao Renwei and Li Shi. (1997). 中国居民收入差距的扩大及其原因 [Widening of Chinese Residents' Income Gap and Its Cause]. *Economic Research Journal*, 9; Zhao Renwei, Li Shi and Li Siqin (Eds.). (1999). 中国居民收入分配问题再研究 [Restudy of Income Distribution of Chinese Residents]. Beijing: China Financial & Economic Publishing.
2 See the World Bank. (1998). 共享增长的收入：中国收入分配问题研究 [Sharing the Increased Income: Study of Income Distribution in China] (pp. 14–17). Beijing: China Financial & Economic Publishing House.
3 James K. Galbraith. (1998). *Created Unequal: The Crisis in American Pay* (pp. 3–22). New York: The Free Press.

7 Building the taxation concept of "no progress means retrogression"

In his book *Economics*, Joseph Stiglitz, a winner of the Nobel Prize in Economics, wrote: "If the rich pay more taxes than the poor, but not in a proportionally incremental way, then such tax system is still considered as regressive."[1] He explained that tax equity should be focused on, and that in an attempt to define equity, economists follow two principles: horizontal equity, which means that people in the same or similar circumstances should pay the same or similar taxes; and vertical equity, which means that people who are better off should pay more taxes. The tax system where the rich pay a greater portion of their income than the poor is called the progressive system; otherwise, it is called the regressive system.

We may summarize such a tax concept as "no progress means retrogression" according to the habit of Chinese expressions. I think such concept of "no progress means retrogression" is of great significance in helping us to establish the scientific tax system and transfer payment system to make income redistribution, and to regulate the income gap between the poor and the rich. According to this concept, normally the progressive rate instead of the proportional tax rate is introduced for the personal income tax; that is, the tax rate imposed on high-income people is higher than that on low-income people. It can be said that China has just started in terms of regulating the income gap with the personal income tax. Due to various restrictions, it is still impossible to introduce the progressive system in all fields for collecting personal income tax. Take the interest tax as an example. As the deposit real-name system is not yet well-established, China can introduce only the proportional tax rate instead of the progressive rate currently; that is, an interest tax of 20% is imposed on the entire deposit. It should be said that this way of taxation is not perfect and is transitional. This is because it cannot narrow the gap between the rich and the poor, and it fails to comply with the principle of vertical equity. Imagine that A gets an interest income of 10,000 yuan and B gets an interest income of 1000 yuan in the same period. The pre-tax income ratio of the two is 10:1. After the interest tax of 20% is paid, the after-tax interest income is 8000 yuan for A and 800 yuan for B. The after-tax income ratio of the two is still 10:1. The interest income gap between them remains unchanged before and after tax. It is obvious that the proportional tax should develop into a graduated tax in order to regulate the income gap between the poor and the rich.

100 *"No progress means retrogression"*

Certainly, the tax concept of "no progress means retrogression" is valid in a relative sense. In an absolute sense, the proportional tax system is neither progressive nor regressive. It is regressive only with respect to the requirements of vertical equity. For example, in the previous example of the interest tax, the tax rate is 20% for everyone, which is neither progressive nor regressive.

As a result, it seems that we may classify the concept of "no progress means retrogression" into one in an absolute sense and one in a relative sense. Such classification is common in everyday life. Let's look at an illustrating example. When I was still a middle school student, my teacher often used the following proverb to encourage students to study hard: "Learning is like rowing upstream, not to advance is to drop back." In fact, both rowing and learning should be looked at from the absolute and relative perspectives.

Take rowing as an example. Let's assume that a river steamer goes against the current on the Yangtze River, with Shanghai as the starting point and Chongqing the destination. If the sailor stops going forward after the steamer reaches Wuhan, and lets the steamer flow freely backwards toward Shanghai along the river, that can be regarded as "no progress means retrogression" in an absolute sense. (Certainly, this is based on the relative relation between the steamer and the earth. If the earth's rotation, the revolution of the earth around the sun and other factors are also considered, the situation will be more complicated, which does not need to be discussed here and can be dealt with only by astronomers and philosophers.). Now suppose the sailor drops anchor and fixes the steamer in place after it reaches Wuhan, and the steamer neither moves forward to Chongqing nor moves back to Shanghai. In an absolute sense, this can be regarded as "neither progressive nor retrogressive"; however, compared to other vessels which keep going, this is still regarded as "no progress means retrogression".

As far as learning is concerned, if there is a very good theory, some people may study it very hard, make progress quickly and achieve good results, while others may study it in a perfunctory manner and achieve nothing. However, even among those who study well, if some people hold a dogmatic attitude towards such good theory, fail to develop it according to the progress of the time and changes of practices, or even hold a fundamentalist attitude, reject and crack down on any development and progress, then it is also a manifestation of "no progress means retrogression" in a relative sense.

Certainly, the problem is not that simple. A may say that B retrogresses, and B may say that A retrogresses. Therefore, as for what progresses and what retrogresses, we must first solve the positioning and orienting problems so as to avoid "regarding progress as retrogression" or "regarding retrogression as progress". We have given the income tax examples here to discuss the "progress and retrogression" issue. Before we discuss this issue further, let's review and summarize the debate on planning and market since the reform and opening-up in China.

There has been a great, heated debate on the relationship between planning and market in the economic circles in China from the end of the 1970s to the beginning of the 1990s. This is a debate of great significance that concerns the direction of the economic reform. There are mainly two kinds of opinions if the minor issues are put aside: One is that only gradually abandoning the planned economy and switching to the market economy is the general direction of the economic reform. The other is that only recognizing the supplementary and auxiliary role of the market mechanism or market regulation and adhering to the dominant role of the planned economy comply with the general direction of economic reform. Apparently, these two kinds of opinions have different concepts on progress and retrogression: the former regards itself as progress and the latter as retrogression, while the latter regards itself as progress and the former as retrogression. In 1992, after ten-plus years of discussions, Deng Xiaoping's Southern Tour speech and the 14th National Congress of the Communist Party of China finalized the reform direction from the planned economy to the market economy.

What's the significance of the summary of this huge debate and its achievements for us in building a correct progress and retrogression concept?

Firstly, we should not rigidly adhere to the superficial controversies over terms and concepts, but should focus on the nature of the problem. For example, the term "planned" in the planned economy is not a bad term. The reform does not mean that planning in any sense should be repudiated; rather, the planned economy in a specific sense should be sublated. Specifically, what should be sublated is the kind of planned economy which has been put into practice and proved to be unsustainable by the Soviet Union, Eastern Europe and such countries as China. Some western economists often call such an economy a "command economy", or even "mobilized command economy". I appreciate the summary of the planned economy made by Shigeru Ishikawa, a Japanese economist. He said that the original economic system in China, in a broad sense, may be defined as "a materialized planned resource allocation system under centralized management".[2] Professor Ishikawa's summary points out the following two characteristics of the planned economy in the traditional and specific sense. Firstly, overcentralization wipes out the diversity of decision makers and the diversity of interests. Secondly, materialization of resource allocation repudiates the role played by the market mechanism in resource allocation. Apparently, such a system is inefficient and unsustainable, and can only be replaced by the market economy. Therefore, whether an economic system progresses or retrogresses must be measured according to the efficiency standard or productivity standard in the end.

Secondly, we should also identify the "progress" in the reform from the "order restored" in the efforts to "put wrongs to rights" after the reform. In the early 1980s, there was a quite popular saying called "put wrongs to rights and restore order", "拨乱反正" in Chinese. According to the Modern Chinese Dictionary, this phrase means "bring order out of chaos, restore the normal order". What is the normal order? A popular explanation is "fight the disorders of the 'great-leap-forward movement', and restore the situation to the original state in 1956, and fight the disorders of the 'Great Cultural Revolution' and restore the situation to the original state in 1965". Admittedly, in the planned economy practice in China, 1956 and 1965 are the years with relatively normal orders. We may call them the relatively orderly planned economy periods. In the early 1980s, some comrades often described China's economy in the 1950s, especially the economy in these

102 *"No progress means retrogression"*

two periods, as the "golden age" of China's economy to foreign guests while giving an introduction to China's economic reform. No wonder some foreign friends asked such a question at that time: "Since you regard those periods as the golden age, all you do is just to restore the situation at that time. Why bother initiating the economic reform?" Obviously, reform means a kind of progress in its true sense, instead of simply returning to a relatively good state in the original system. To "put wrongs to rights and restore order" is by no means a reform in its true sense. However orderly a planned economy may be, a planned economy which is even supplemented by the market mechanism or market regulation is still a planned economy, instead of a market economy that allows the market mechanism to play its fundamental role in resource allocation.

In addition, it is also necessary to differentiate "advancing strategically" from "retreating in order to advance" tactically. As is known to all, the Soviet Union transformed from military communism to the New Economic Policy in the early 1920s, which was a tactical retreat that allowed the private economy to develop to some extent, and allowed a number of economic sectors to coexist, so that it could transform to the public-owned economy and planned economy when the time was ripe. And so it did. By the end of the 1920s, the Soviet Union began to advance towards the public-owned and planned economies in an all-around manner. Therefore, the Soviet Union's implementation of the New Economic Policy in those years was just a kind of tactical retreat, instead of a change in a strategic direction. However, we should not say that China's reform since the Third Plenary Session of the 11th Central Committee of the Chinese Communist Party at the end of 1978 is just a tactical retreat instead of a strategic progress. Ms. Xue Xiaohe, daughter of Mr. Xue Muqiao who was a famous Chinese economist, once said to me: "My father did participate in China's establishment of the planned economy in the 1950s. It was not easy to switch to the reform path that was market-economy-oriented in the 1980s after several decades of practice." I firmly believe that Mr. Xue held that the planned economy could create higher labor productivity when he participated in the establishment of the planned economy. However, after several decades of practice, he did realize that the planned economy was unsustainable, and that only the macro-control market economy could create higher labor productivity. Therefore, he resolutely gave up the planned economy and took the road of reform that aimed to transform to the market economy. Mr. Xue's change was typical among the communists and economists of the older generation. I think such change was sincere and valuable, because it followed the practice criterion instead of personal gain or loss. He did not hinder the transformation to the market economy just because he had participated in the establishment of the planned economy, which is quite admirable. I think Mr. Xue's activities, which ranged from participation in the establishment of the planned economy to flinging himself into the market economy reform, were all based on his belief and practice and "advanced with the times", and were not the opportunistic activities where he gave up his belief and deviated from practice. We should not blame them too much for their participation in the establishment of the planned economy in those years, because they established the planned economy as a great experiment.

They "knew their mistakes and corrected them" based on practice, which alone is praiseworthy. Therefore, measured from the perspectives of both practice and belief, their choice of the planned economy first and then of the market economy should both be regarded as progress instead of retrogression. Therefore, our only hope is that our choice of the market-economy-oriented reform today will not be regarded as the Soviet Union's New Economic Policy in those years, which was just a tactical retreat instead of a strategic progress. What we are reluctant to see is that after productivity is further developed, a highly centralized planned economy that allocates resources in kind comes again.

(Originally published in Volume 11 of *Teahouse for Economists*, Shandong People's Press, 2003 Edition.)

Notes

1 Joseph Stiglitz. (2000). *Economics* (Trans., Vol. 1, 2nd ed., p. 481). Beijing: China Renmin University Press.
2 Shigero Ishikawa. (1986). 社会主义经济和中国的经验－对经济改革的展望 [Socialist Economy and China's Experience: An Outlook on Economic Reform], *Science & Technology Review*, 2.

8 Study of property distribution of Chinese residents

I. Introduction

China's reform and opening-up have been going on for a quarter century. As China's economy grows rapidly and the resident income increases in this important historical period, the changes of the pattern of resident income distribution, especially widening of the income gap, have always been an important issue that people are concerned about. Income distribution is closely related to property distribution. In particular, the personal property of Chinese residents has undergone a period of rapid accumulation and prominent differentiation since the 1990s. Therefore, property distribution of Chinese residents naturally has become a new concern for people.

China has set the goal of building a well-off society in an all-around way. People's degree of well-being depends not only on income status but also on property status. In other words, well-being distribution depends not only on income distribution but also on property distribution (Michael Schneider, 2004). We are facilitating the construction of a harmonious socialist society. The construction of a harmonious society is closely related not only to such factors as employment, social security and income distribution, but also to property distribution. In the construction of a harmonious socialist society, not only the proportion of middle-income earners, but also the proportion of middle property owners should be increased. It seems that these are all important reasons why property distribution has aroused people's increasing attention.

Property mentioned here refers to wealth on the whole. However, when we divide such property or wealth into specific items (such as land, house property, and finance), we often call such items "assets". When we associate property with ownership, we will use the concept "property right". This paper uses such terms as wealth, property and assets as synonyms in terms of their meanings and uses them differently from different perspectives on different occasions only according to habits. This paper also uses the expression of "property distribution" while analyzing property allocation. Here, allocation and distribution are used as synonyms, and they are used differently on different occasions only according to habits.

As far as the general distinction between income and property is concerned, income refers to all the receipts of people (a person or family) within a given period, while wealth refers to the monetary net value of the assets possessed by people at a certain time point. Obviously, wealth is the stock at a time point, while income is the flow in unit time. Income and property interact with each other: the flow in the past definitely affects the stock today, while the stock today definitely affects the flow in the future. With the continuous expansion of the property scale and the change of the property distribution pattern, property distribution has an important impact not only on the stability of the entire macroeconomy, but also on the long-term change of income distribution in the future.

As there has been not much data and literature on the study of property distribution in China so far, this paper makes a general analysis of residents' personal property distribution in rural areas, in cities and across the country mainly according to the data in the household survey conducted by the Income Distribution Project Team of the Institute of Economics of the Chinese Academy of Social Sciences in 2002. If necessary, we will consult the findings of relevant surveys conducted by the Project Team in 1988 and 1995 (see Terry McKinley, 1993; Mark Brenner, 2001), refer to the findings of relevant surveys on urban household property conducted by the Urban Social-economic Survey Task Force (USSTF) of the National Bureau of Statistics of China (NBSC) in 2002 (see USSTF of NBSC, 2003), and make a comparative analysis. Within a limited range, we must also pay attention to the relationship between property distribution and income distribution.

The data cited in this paper, except for those whose sources are specifically indicated, all come from the survey data of the Income Distribution Project Team of the Institute of Economics of Chinese Academy of Social Sciences.

II.   Property distribution of rural residents

In order to analyze the property distribution of rural residents, first we need to take a brief look at the property level (scale) and composition. Statically, as shown in Table 8.1, the property of rural residents may be divided into six items, namely land, house property, financial assets, productive fixed assets, consumer durables and nonresidential debts. Specifically, the house property is calculated based on the value after the unsettled debts are deducted from the total value of the house

Table 8.1 Per Capita Property Level and Composition in Rural Areas in 2002

Property and composition items	Average value (yuan)	Percentage (%)
Total property (net value)	12,937.81	100
Including:		
Land value	3974.32	30.72
Net value of house property	5565.006	43.01
Financial assets	1592.615	12.31
Productive fixed assets	1181.616	9.13
Value of consumer durables	793.2804	6.13
Nonresidential debts	−169.0233	−1.31

106 *Property distribution of Chinese residents*

property, namely based on the net value of the house property. Nonresidential debts refer to all debts other than residential debts. The value of the total amount of all the property items minus nonresidential debts is the total value of property calculated based on the net value.[1]

Among the six property items, land and house property still take up the largest proportion, accounting for about 74%. Dynamically, there have been great changes since 1988: (1) The scale of the gross property has grown rapidly. The per capita total property was 2869.5 yuan in 1988, 10,560.6 yuan in 1995 and 12,937.81 yuan in 2002. On an inflation-adjusted basis, the real growth rate is 67% from 1988 to 1995, 13% from 1995 to 2002, and 89% from 1988 to 2002. (2) The changes in the land value are especially eye-catching. The per capita land value is 1698.3 yuan in 1988, 4944.6 yuan in 1995 and 3974.32 yuan in 2002. On an inflation-adjusted basis, it grows by 32% from 1988 to 1995, and drops by 26% from 1995 to 2002. Therefore, in composition, the proportion of the per capita land value in the gross property drops rapidly, while the proportion of the house property value and financial assets value rises rapidly. The proportion of the land value drops from 59% in 1988 to 47% in 1995, then to 31% in 2002, while the proportion of the house property net value and financial assets increase from 31% to 32% and 43% and from 3% to 10% and 12% respectively. The increased proportion of residential and financial assets reflects the accelerated market reform process in rural areas. However, it is abnormal for the importance of land, which is the scarcest resource in agricultural production, to drop so rapidly. We believe that a number of factors are behind this. Firstly, industrialization and transportation modernization have taken up too much farmland, causing the per capita land in rural areas to drop rapidly. Secondly, such factors as the low agricultural product prices result in the low profits of land. Throughout the 1990s, peasants have been almost gainless from cultivating land, and the yield and output value of the unit area of land have been hovering. The land value is calculated based on the total value of farm output; therefore, the role of land is underestimated.

The property distribution in rural areas in 2002 is analyzed as follows.

Firstly, the method of ten equant groups is used for analysis. We arrange the rural population based on the net output per capita and divide the population into ten equal parts, with each part containing one-tenth of the total population, then make a comparison. Table 8.2 shows that among the various kinds of property, the distribution of the financial assets is the least equal. The 20% population with the most per capita property possesses 55.25% of the financial assets, while the 20% population with the least per capita property possesses only 4.54% of the financial assets, with the ratio between the two being 12.17:1. House property comes second in terms of distribution inequality. The 20% population with the most per capita property possess 50.94% of the houses, and the ratio between such houses and the houses (4.71%) possessed by the 20% population with the least per capita property is 10.82:1. The degree of distribution inequality of consumer durables is very close to that of basic production assets, with the above ratios being 6.56:1 and 6.55:1 respectively. Of various kinds of property, land distribution is the most equal one. The 10% population with the most per capita property possess 30.51%

Property distribution of Chinese residents 107

Table 8.2 Proportion of Property Held by Each of Ten Equant Groups of Rural Population in 2002

Unit: %

Group (from low to high)	Total amount of property (net value)	Land value	Net value of house property	Financial assets	Productive fixed assets	Value of consumer durables	Non-residential debts
1 (lowest)	2.01	3.35	1.73	1.74	3.14	2.91	33.47
2	3.68	5.12	2.98	2.80	3.96	4.07	10.44
3	4.86	6.54	3.99	3.69	4.7	5.54	7.02
4	5.97	7.66	5.24	4.74	5.26	6.01	5.21
5	7.09	8.88	6.25	5.79	6.84	7.23	7.89
6	8.37	9.91	7.77	6.82	7.95	8.13	6.04
7	9.89	11.16	9.36	8.58	9.74	9.49	6.73
8	12.03	12.94	11.77	10.59	11.96	10.86	5.07
9	15.60	15.39	15.74	16.01	14.41	14.67	6.64
10 (highest)	30.51	19.05	35.20	39.24	32.07	31.10	11.49

of the gross property but only 19.05% of land. For the 20% population with the most per capita property and the 20% population with the least per capita property, the ratio of possessed land between them is 34.44/8.47 = 4.07:1. The distribution of nonresidential debts is different from that of other property items: Unlike other property items that rise or fall in a regular manner, the proportional change of each group in the ten equant groups often fluctuates, but on the whole, the poor owe more in debts than the rich. For the 20% population with the most per capita property and the 20% population with the least per capita property, the ratio of nonresidential debts owed is 2.42:1.

Dynamically, the gap of gross property (net value) distribution has expanded remarkably from 1988 to 2002. The ratio of the gross property owned by the 20% population with the most per capita property to the gross property owned by the 20% population with the least per capita property has expanded from 5.18:1 in 1988 to 5.33:1 in 1995, then to 8.10:1 in 2002. The ratio changes in these three years are different for different property items. The house property shows a trend of "narrowed first and then widened", and the ratios in these three years are 8.13:1, 7.15:1 and 10.82:1. The financial assets also show a trend of "narrowed first and then widened", with the ratios being 13.75:1, 9.34:1, and 12.17:1 respectively. The land changes are the smallest, with the ratios being 4.01:1, 4.30:1, and 4.07:1 respectively. However, the general trend over the past 14 years shows that for financial assets and house property that have grown rapidly and played a big role, their distribution gap has widened, while for land that has grown slowly and played a small role, their distribution gap is small and has not changed much.

108 *Property distribution of Chinese residents*

Secondly, we use such indexes as the Gini coefficient and concentration ratio to analyze the property distribution of rural residents.

Residents' property value is the result of the long-term accumulation of resident income. Therefore, generally speaking, the degree of inequality of property distribution exceeds that of income distribution, whether in developed countries or in developing countries. In other words, the Gini coefficient of property is higher than that of income (see details that follow). However, China's rural areas have been an exception for a long time. According to the survey conducted by the Project Team of the Institute of Economics, the Gini coefficient of income distribution was 0.338 and the Gini coefficient of property distribution was 0.311 in 1988, while the Gini coefficient of income distribution was 0.381 and the Gini coefficient of property distribution was 0.351 in 1995. The inequality degree of property distribution was lower than that of income distribution in both years. However, this situation changed fundamentally in 2002.

The Gini coefficient of rural property distribution was 0.399 in 2002, while the Gini coefficient of income distribution was 0.366 in the same year; that is, the inequality degree of property distribution exceeded that of income distribution. This indicates that in an era at the turn of the century, the inequality of rural property distribution and income distribution in China underwent a turning point – from greater inequality of income distribution to greater inequality of property distribution (see Table 8.3 and Figure 8.1). This situation is caused not by the increased proportion of land value in property or the greater inequality of land distribution, but by the increased proportion of other property items concerned and deepened inequality. However, the occurrence of this situation indicates, anyway, that the relationship between rural income distribution and property distribution in China is moving towards a usual direction. The highly equal distribution of rural land in China still restrains the increase of inequality of rural gross property, but it has stepped over a turning point after all and indicates the trend of the further expansion of inequality of property distribution and income distribution.

Table 8.4 shows that of all the property items, the land value is distributed most equally, with the Gini coefficient being 0.452. The financial assets are distributed least equally, with the Gini coefficient being 0.681. The pseudo-Gini coefficient (concentration ratio) of each property item, which is calculated based on sequencing of gross property, shows the distribution of all the property items and their relations

Table 8.3 Income Distribution and Property Distribution in Chinese Rural Areas (1988, 1995 and 2002)

	1988	*1995*	*2002*
Gini coefficient of income distribution	0.338	0.381	0.366
Gini coefficient of property distribution	0.311	0.351	0.399

Source of data: (Li Shi, Yue Ximing, 2004; Terry McKinley, 1993; Mark Brenner, 2001).

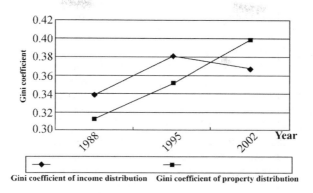

Figure 8.1 Changes of Income Distribution and Property Distribution in Rural Areas (1988, 1995 and 2002)

Table 8.4 Inequality of Per Capita Property Distribution in Rural Areas in 2002

Property	Mean value of property (yuan)	Proportion (%)	Gini coefficient	Concentration ratio	Contribution rate (%)
Total amount of property (net value)	12,937.81	100	0.399	0.399	100
Including:					
Land value	3974.32	30.72	0.452	0.260	20.02
Net value of house property	5565.006	43.01	0.538	0.456	49.15
Financial assets	1592.615	12.31	0.681	0.492	15.18
Productive fixed assets	1181.616	9.13	0.665	0.394	9.02
Value of consumer durables	793.8	6.13	0.659	0.377	5.79
Nonresidential debts	−169.0233	−1.31	0.95	−0.246	0.1

with the distribution of gross property. The concentration ratio of land is only 0.260 and is greatly lower than 0.399, the Gini coefficient of gross property, indicating that land distribution significantly reduces inequality for gross property distribution. The concentration ratio of basic production assets and consumer durables is slightly lower than the Gini coefficient of gross property, indicating that distribution of these two property items slightly reduces inequality for gross property distribution. The concentration ratio of financial assets and house property is far higher than the Gini coefficient of gross property, indicating that distribution of these two property items greatly increases inequality for gross property distribution. The concentration ratio of basic production assets is almost equal to the Gini coefficient of gross property,

110 *Property distribution of Chinese residents*

indicating that their distribution neither increases nor reduces inequality for gross property distribution. The distribution of basic production assets does not show a high degree of inequality, which is associated with the highly equal distribution of land. With the equal distribution of land and the limited scale of household-managed land, it is difficult to promote investment in agricultural fixed assets or to achieve a high degree of inequality for such investment. It is easy to understand the relatively equal distribution of consumer durables, because there are hardly any high-end consumer durables in Chinese rural areas at present, and general consumer durables, such as TV sets, are easy to popularize.

Because land distribution has a very low degree of inequality, it has the explanatory power or contribution rate of only 20.02% for the inequality of gross property, significantly lower than its proportion in gross property (30.72%). On the contrary, financial assets and house property have a high degree of inequality; therefore, their contribution rates for the inequality of gross property (15.18% and 49.15% respectively) are also higher than their proportions in gross property (12.31% and 43.01% respectively).

Dynamically, the Gini coefficient of gross property has significantly expanded from 1988 to 2002, namely from 0.311 in 1988 to 0.351 in 1995, then to 0.399 in 2002. Specifically, each property item changes differently. In these three years, the concentration ratios of land are 0.275, 0.285 and 0.260 respectively, the concentration ratios of house property are 0.41, 0.382 and 0.456 respectively, and the concentration ratios of financial assets are 0.578, 0.44 and 0.492 respectively.

On the whole, among all the property items in Chinese rural areas, the importance (proportion) and distribution inequality degree, as well as contributions to the gross property inequality of land, all have decreased over the past 14 years. On the contrary, the importance, distribution inequality degree (slightly exceptional for financial assets in certain years), and contributions to the gross property inequality of house property and financial assets have increased. For example, in gross property, land took the first place and house property came second in 1988 and 1995 in terms of importance; but in 2002, house property took first place and land slipped to second place.

In our opinion, we should make a dialectic analysis of such changes. On the one hand, it reflects the progress of economic development and economic reform. With the development of the rural economy, especially with the development of non-agricultural industries in rural areas and the increasing marketization of the rural economy, the development and importance of the financial industry and real estate industry will definitely be enhanced. However, land is the scarcest non-renewable resource, and its importance has decreased to such a low level that we have to find the deep cause from the defect of the land system itself. Nominally land is collective-owned at present and is contracted and used by households and individuals; but actually neither peasants nor local governments are responsible for cherishing and operating land. Some scholars hold that the existing rural land system in China is actually the quasi-national ownership (Zhu Qiuxia, 2004). Land has not been optimally allocated and rationally operated according to the law of the market economy so far. The frequent redistribution of land makes it impossible

Property distribution of Chinese residents 111

for peasants to use their own property for investment and operation, and the land expropriated by the state is neither compensated for properly nor used economically. Leaving the land uncultivated, a common phenomenon in the 1990s (which occurred in both rural and suburban areas), is just a vivid portrayal. This is a serious consequence of land's absence in the market so far. When peasants' investment and operation in land are restrained, they naturally shift their investment focus on house property and finance. Therefore, how to rationally allocate all the property items in rural areas so as to "make the best use of land" through the deepened reform of the land system is still an issue to be discussed.

III. Property distribution of urban residents

Like the analysis of the property distribution of rural residents, we also make a rough survey of the property level (scale) and composition of urban residents before we analyze the property distribution of urban residents.

As shown in Table 8.5, the property of rural residents may also divide into six items, namely land, house property, financial assets, basic production assets, consumer durables, other assets and nonresidential debts. Like rural areas, house property is calculated based on the net value, which is the result of deducting the outstanding debts in house purchase from the total value of house property. Nonresidential debts are the result of deducting outstanding residential debts from total debts. The value of the total amount of all the property items minus nonresidential debts is the total value of property (net value).

Judging by the property scale or level, the per capita total property was 46,133.5 yuan for urban residents and 12,937.81 yuan for rural residents in 2002, with the ratio between the two being 3.57:1. The income ratio of urban residents to rural residents, which was officially released in the same period, was 3.1:1. As the official data did not fully consider the differences between urban residents and rural residents in terms of subsidies (such as various subsidies in housing, medical treatment, old-age care, transport and education), many studies hold that the actual income differences between urban and rural residents far exceed the officially released

Table 8.5 Level and Composition of Per Capita Property in Cities and Towns in 2002

Property and composition items	Average value (yuan)	Percentage (%)
Total amount of property (net value)	46,133.5	100
Including:		
Financial assets	11,957.79	25.92
Net value of house property	29,703.13	64.39
Productive fixed assets	815.487	1.77
Value of consumer durables	3338.165	7.24
Estimated current value of other assets	619.6779	1.34
Nonresidential debts	−300.7456	−0.65

112 *Property distribution of Chinese residents*

differences (see Li Shi, Yue Ximing, 2004). We may also see from the bigger property distribution differences of urban residents than rural residents in 2002 that the differences as income subsidies will also precipitate year after year and become an important factor that leads to expansion of the property distribution gap.

In terms of the property composition, the biggest difference between urban residents and rural residents is that the former has land while the latter has no land. Among the six property items, land and house property take up the largest proportion for rural residents, accounting for 73.73%, and house property and financial assets take up the largest proportion for urban residents, accounting for 90.31%. This is mainly caused by urban residents' prominent proportion in terms of possession of the house property value. House property accounts for up to 64.39% of urban residents' property, and only 43.01% of rural residents' property, with the gap being 21.38%. Another difference is that the basic production assets account for 9.13% in rural areas, and only 1.77% in cities. On the whole, the property is made up of six items for both urban and rural residents, but the property of urban residents tend to be distributed among a small number of items.

As for the urban property distribution, we still use the method of ten equant groups for analysis first. Table 8.6 shows that for some urban residents, their debts have exceeded their total property amount. As a result, the 10% population with the least per capita property own so low a property proportion that it is almost negligible. For the 10% population with the most per capita property, their property accounts for up to 33.85% of the gross property in cities and towns. In addition, the 20% population with the least per capita property own only 2.75% of the property, while the 20% population with the most per capita property own up to

Table 8.6 Proportion of Property Held by Each of Ten Equant Groups of Urban Population in 2002

Unit: %

Group (from low to high)	Total amount of property (net value)	Financial assets	Net value of house property	Productive fixed assets	Value of consumer durables	Estimated current value of other assets	Non-residential debts
1 (lowest)	0.203	1.62	−0.54	0.376	4.25	2.18	32.32
2	2.55	3.14	2.06	4.03	4.84	3.98	10.31
3	3.98	4.17	3.80	4.76	5.34	4.44	11.89
4	5.25	4.89	5.22	5.36	6.56	6.12	4.28
5	6.54	6.37	6.50	3.84	7.95	6.23	2.98
6	8.01	7.78	8.02	7.07	8.60	9.25	7.75
7	9.92	9.78	9.96	8.56	9.74	13.11	8.80
8	12.55	12.22	12.70	16.13	11.33	10.69	6.33
9	17.22	18.17	17.15	14.24	14.28	15.87	4.09
10 (highest)	33.85	31.93	35.21	35.69	27.17	28.22	11.22

Property distribution of Chinese residents 113

51.07% of the property, with the latter being 18 times the former. Among all the property items, the distribution of house property is the least equal. For the 10% population with the least per capita property, the net value of their house property is a negative number; that is, the total value of their house property cannot repay their outstanding residential debts. The 20% population with the most per capita property possesses 52.36% of the house property, while the 20% population with the least per capita property possesses only 1.52% of the house property, with the ratio between the two being 34.45:1. The basic production assets rank the second in terms of distribution inequality, with a ratio of possession being 11.34:1 between the populations with the most and least property. Such ratio is 10.53:1 for financial assets, 7.15:1 for other assets, and 4.57:1 for consumer durables.

Why is the house property of urban residents so unequally distributed, and why does its degree of inequality far exceed that in rural areas? It seems that its cause should date back to the urban housing distribution system in the planned economy. As is known to all, in the shortage economy, grain, cotton and oil, etc. are distributed by head count (somewhat similar to land distribution in rural areas); while houses are distributed by position, which, to a great extent, is associated with power. Furthermore, the housing standard for people at different positions is set by people who are at the high power tiers. Therefore, housing distribution is highly unequal in the planned economy due to the intervention of power. The housing system reform in the market economy transformation, mainly the housing system reform since the 1990s, not only copies the inequality of housing distribution in the planned economy, but also further expands such inequality (Zhao Renwei, Li Shi, 1997). The reform of the urban housing system in the 1990s did not follow the basic principle of the market economy, so to speak. When the state sold the public houses to individuals, the selling prices that were formed considered not the houses' locations and quality, but mainly the area of those houses. Therefore, people whose houses had good locations and were of high quality in such sales could get a large sum of rental. In addition, in the housing reform, many cities and authorities also discretionarily increased the housing standard for employees at different positions, which helped some people receive another sum of rental from the expanded housing area. If we say that the market prices of urban houses are formed by the market, then the selling prices of private houses which are transformed from public houses are discretionarily set. Therefore, there was a huge difference between the selling prices of public houses and the market prices of commodity houses in the housing system reform. According to the studies by Wang Lina and Wei Zhong, the ratio of the market prices of commodity houses to the selling prices of public houses was 7.69:1 on average in 11 provinces and cities in 1995. The gap between the two was the largest in Hubei Province, with a ratio being up to 22.2:1 (see Table 8.7). Such rent-setting activities in the housing reform in the 1990s have greater accrual space than those in the commercial transactions in the double systems of the 1980s. Such inequality of house property distribution of urban residents not only stands out compared to the distribution inequality of other assets of urban residents (if the population with the most and least property is respectively 20% in the calculation, the ratio between the two is

114 *Property distribution of Chinese residents*

Table 8.7 Differences between Market Prices of Commodity Houses and Selling Prices of State-Owned Houses in 1995

Unit: yuan/square meter

Sample province or city	Market price of commodity house	Cost price in sale of state-owned house	Selling price ratio of commodity house to state-owned house
Beijing	3226.52	403.68	7.99:1
Shanxi	919.6	238.56	3.85:1
Liaoning	1491.45	272.85	5.47:1
Jiangsu	1247.26	191.28	6.52:1
Anhui	897.80	105.83	8.48:1
Henan	780.02	166.80	4.68:1
Hubei	2187.50	98.53	22.20:1
Sichuan	1050.20	87.04	12.50:1
Guangdong	3100.00	247.59	12.07:1
Yunnan	1276.34	201.01	6.35:1
Gansu	1169.87	241.53	4.84:1
Average selling price	1576.91	204.97	7.69:1

Source of data: Wang Lina, Wei Zhong (1999); Wang Lina (2001).

18.55:1 in terms of possession of the total property, and the ratio between the two is 34.45:1 in terms of possession of house property), but also appears to be high above that of the distribution inequality of house property of rural residents (the ratio is 34.45:1 for urban house property, and 10.82:1 for rural house property).

Why are the basic production assets of urban residents so unequally distributed, and why does their degree of inequality far exceed that of similar assets in rural areas? It seems that this is caused by the different industries or occupations that urban and rural residents are in. In cities, the basic production assets are mostly in the hands of a small number of self-employed persons and private enterprise owners (according to the above survey by the NBSC, only about 10% of all the urban residents invest in various kinds of business activities). In rural areas, the basic production assets are relatively scattered and are in the hands of many households.

Compared to the house property and basic production assets, the financial assets are not so unequally distributed as imagined, and as mentioned earlier, the degree of distribution inequality of financial assets in cities is lower than that in rural areas.[2] Of all the property items, consumer durables are most equally distributed, which seems to be easy to understand. This is because after more than 20 years of rapid economic development, and with people's living greatly improved, possession of such consumer goods as color TV sets and refrigerators is no problem at all for ordinary urban residents; and only a small number of households possess such consumer goods as cars, which therefore makes it impossible to substantially widen the gap. Among the aforementioned property items, the distribution of non-residential debts is the most intriguing. The 10% population with the least property holds 32.32% of the debts, while the 10% population with the most property

Property distribution of Chinese residents   115

Table 8.8 Inequality of Per Capita Property Distribution in Cities and Towns in 2002

Property	Mean value of property (yuan)	Proportion (%)	Gini coefficient	Concentration ratio	Contribution rate (%)
Total amount of property (net value)	46,133.5	100	0.4751	0.4751	100
Including:					
Financial assets	11,957.79	25.92	0.5961	0.4439	24.22
Net value of house property	29,703.13	64.39	0.5442	0.4989	67.62
Current value of consumer durables	3338.165	7.24	0.9839	0.323	4.92
Productive fixed assets	815.487	1.77	0.5018	0.4838	1.80
Other assets	619.6779	1.34	0.9148	0.3831	1.08
Nonresidential debts	300.7456	−0.65	0.9777	−0.2596	0.36

surprisingly holds 11.22% of the debts. Does it indicate that in Chinese cities, the poorest people have to borrow money, while the richest people dare to borrow money for consumption and investment?

Now we use such indexes as the Gini coefficient and concentration ratio to analyze the property distribution of urban residents.

As mentioned earlier, it was at the turn of the century not long ago that the inequality degree of property distribution exceeded the inequality degree of income distribution in Chinese rural areas. However, there has been no such turning point where two lines intersect in Chinese cities. The Gini coefficient of property distribution was 0.411 in 1995 (see Li Shi et al., 2000), and 0.4751 in 2002. The Gini coefficient of income distribution was 0.280 in 1995, and 0.319 in 2002 (see Li Shi, Yue Ximing, 2004). This indicates that the property distribution and income distribution have formed two parallel lines, with the former being higher than the latter, and with the gap between the two still being expanded.

Table 8.8 shows that among all the property items in cities, house property takes the lead in terms of each index. The net value of house property is 29,703.13 yuan, accounting for 64.39% of the total value of property. Its pseudo-Gini coefficient (concentration ratio) is 0.4989, which is higher than 0.4751, the Gini coefficient of the gross property, indicating that the house property distribution has expanded the degree of inequality of gross property distribution. As it accounts for a big proportion and has a high degree of distribution inequality, its explanatory power or contribution rate for the degree of inequality of the gross property is up to 67.62%, or even higher than its big proportion in the gross property by 3.23%. The concentration ratio of the basic production assets is 0.4838, which is higher than the Gini coefficient of gross property, and thus expands the degree of inequality of the gross property distribution. However, as it only accounts for 1.77% of gross property, its contribution rate for the degree of inequality of the gross property is only 1.8%, which is quite small. The concentration ratio of the financial assets is

116 *Property distribution of Chinese residents*

0.4439, which is lower than the Gini coefficient of the gross property, and thus narrows the degree of inequality of the gross property distribution. However, as it has a high proportion (25.92%) of gross property and ranks second only to house property, its contribution rate for the degree of inequality of the gross property, which is 24.22%, also ranks second. The concentration ratio of consumer durables is only 0.3230, apparently lower than the Gini coefficient of the total assets, which significantly narrows the degree of inequality of the gross property distribution. However, as it only accounts for 7.24% of gross property, its contribution rate for the degree of inequality of gross property is only 4.92%.

On the whole, among the six property items in cities, two items, namely house property and basic production assets, surpass the total assets in terms of the degree of inequality. Among the six property items in rural areas, the items of house property and financial assets surpass the total assets in terms of the degree of inequality. Therefore, in terms of the inequality of property distribution, house property plays a major role in both cities and rural areas.

As mentioned earlier, the total property owned by urban residents is 3.65 times that owned by rural residents in 2002. However, situations vary greatly if they are judged from the subitems. Specifically, the multiple is 7.51 times for financial assets, 5.34 times for house property and 4.20 times for consumer durables. This indicates that though the distribution of financial assets is more unequal in rural areas than in cities, urban residents have much more financial assets than rural residents. The distribution of house property is highly unequal in both cities and rural areas, but urban residents possess much higher house property value than rural residents. The distribution of consumer durables is relatively equal in both cities and rural areas, but urban residents possess much more valuable consumer durables than rural residents. Due to the factors mentioned previously, for the basic production assets owned by rural residents, not only their proportion of total assets (9.13% for rural residents, and 1.77% for urban residents), but also their absolute value exceed those in cities (1181.616 yuan for rural residents, 817.487 yuan for urban residents).

From the vertical perspective, the per capita total property is 12,385 yuan in 1995 (equivalent to 13,698 yuan based on 2002 prices), and the per capita total property is 46,134 yuan in 2002, with the actual growth rate being 236.8% and the average annual growth rate being 18.9% from 1995 to 2002. Specifically, the house property increases from 5412 yuan to 29,734 yuan in the same period (equivalent to 5985 yuan based on 2002 prices), with the actual growth rate being 396.3% and the average annual growth rate being 21.74% ($3.963^{(1/7)} - 1 = 0.2174$). The financial assets increase from 3427 yuan (equivalent to 3841 yuan based on 2002 prices) to 11,958 yuan in the same period, with the actual growth rate being 211.3%, and with the average annual growth rate being 17.6%. In the same period, the proportion in the gross property drops from 28% to 25.92% in terms of the financial assets value, and rises from 43.7% to 64.39% in terms of the net value of house property. The proportion, adding up both financial assets and net value of house property, rises from 71.7% to 90.31%. This indicates that in those years at the turn of the century, house property and financial assets play a major role for the property accumulation of Chinese urban residents. In particular, the growth of the house property value takes the lead, as judged from both the absolute value and the proportion.

Property distribution of Chinese residents   117

In the study of the property distribution of urban residents, it is quite significant to make a more detailed analysis of the specific composition and distribution of financial assets (and debts).

Table 8.9 shows that of the 10 subitems of the financial assets of urban residents, the fixed-term deposit in bank almost accounts for half (49.97%). The current deposit in bank (13.9%), stock (10.37%) and housing fund (8.65%) come next.

Table 8.9 Composition and Distribution of Per Capita Financial Assets (and Debts) in Cities and Towns in 2002

Assets (and debts)	Mean value (yuan)	Composition (%)	Gini coefficient	Concentration ratio	Contribution rate (%)
Financial assets	11957.79	100	0.5961	0.5961	100
Including:					
Fixed term deposit in bank	5975.307	49.97	0.6919	0.6023	50.49
Current deposit in bank	1662.306	13.90	0.7116	0.4732	11.03
Stock	1240.141	10.37	0.9302	0.7325	12.74
Various bonds	390.7546	3.27	0.9741	0.7732	4.24
Lendings	475.1597	3.974	0.953	0.6739	4.49
Own fund for family business activities	365.609	3.06	0.9816	0.6695	3.44
Investment in enterprises or other business activities (excluding stocks and bonds)	168.7289	1.41	0.9848	0.6406	1.52
Accumulated amount of housing fund	1034.852	8.65	0.7607	0.4381	6.36
Total amount of saving-type commercial insurance	469.0462	3.92	0.9340	0.6162	4.05
Estimated market value of collections	175.8827	1.47	0.9738	0.6623	1.63
Debts	1702.018	100	0.9517	0.9517	100
Including:					
Loans for house building and buying	1401.272	82.33	0.9664	0.9595	83.00
Business loans	141.1545	8.29	0.9944	0.9511	8.28
Loans for buying consumer durables	15.3532	0.90	0.997	0.8785	0.83
Debts for treating illnesses	55.7442	3.28	0.9932	0.895	3.08
Other debts caused by difficulties in life	29.1198	1.71	0.9948	0.8701	1.56
Educational loans	59.3738	3.49	0.9908	0.8803	3.23

Note: In the total of 20,632 urban individual samples, the number of samples with 0 per capita total financial assets is 1470 and accounts for 7.12% of the total samples. In addition, there are 2987 samples whose summation of per capita fixed-term deposit and current deposit is 0, accounting for 14.48% of the total samples.

118 *Property distribution of Chinese residents*

The total of the four items account for 82.89%. In terms of the distribution of the subitems of financial assets, the concentration ratio is 0.6023 for the fixed term deposit in bank and 0.4732 for the current deposit. The former is slightly higher while the latter is lower than the Gini coefficient of the total financial assets. This indicates that the fixed-term deposit has the effect of expanding the distribution gap of financial assets, while the current deposit can narrow the distribution gap of financial assets. Among the subitems of financial assets, eight subitems have a higher concentration ratio than the Gini coefficient of the total financial assets, and have the effect of expanding the distribution gap of financial assets. Only two subitems (current deposit and housing fund) have a lower concentration ratio than the Gini coefficient of the total financial assets, and narrow the distribution gap of financial assets. As most of the subitems take up a small proportion, only three items have a great impact on the distribution gap of total financial assets. Specifically, the fixed-term deposit and stock play the expanding role, with the contribution rates being 50.49% and 12.74% respectively, while the current deposit plays the narrowing role, with a contribution rate of 11.03%.

Now let's look at debts. In 2002, the total per capita debts in cities are 1702.018 yuan, accounting for 14.2% of the total assets. It shows that the debt ratio is not high for the urban residents in China. Of the six subitems of debts, only the subitem of loans for house building and house purchase comes out top. Accounting for 82.33% of debts, this subitem has a concentration ratio of 0.9595, which is slightly higher than 0.9517, the Gini coefficient of total debts. Its explanatory power or contribution rate for the inequality of total debts is 83%.

On the whole, the financial assets of Chinese urban residents are mostly bank deposits. If the aforementioned composition of assets of urban residents is also considered, we may seem to further find that: Not only the property of urban residents center on house property and financial assets, but also the debts of urban residents center on residential debts, with residential debts being 4.66 times of nonresidential debts.

What does such property composition of urban residents indicate, then? As some researchers point out, it indicates that for urban residents, "their property is still means of livelihood, their sense of investment is weak, and savings are still the most popular form of investment among urban families" (see the Urban Social-economic Survey Task Force of National Bureau of Statistics of China, 2003). In our opinion, the big proportion of savings is caused by a number of factors. Firstly, other investment channels are not smooth. For example, many residents flinch from the non-standard operations and unpredictable risks of the stock market and put their surplus money in banks. Secondly, the uncertain factors increase in the transitional period. For the expenses in old-age care, disease prevention, and children's education, etc., the part borne by individuals shows a widening trend, forcing people to put their money in banks against a rainy day. Thirdly, under the influence of the traditional culture, the Chinese people tend to suppress their propensity to spend and expand their propensity to save. Though such excessively deviated tendency is not favorable to the growth of the entire economy, it is not easy to change such "path dependence" in the cultural tradition.

IV. Property distribution of national residents

Based on the prior analysis of the property distribution of rural and urban residents, the property distribution of national residents is now analyzed in a general way.

Table 8.10 shows that the general level of national per capita property, level of each property item, and ratio of each property item are all between those of cities and rural areas. After being averaged by the national population (see the Appendix for calculation details), the total amount of the national per capita property is neither the rural per capita amount of 12,937.81 yuan, nor the urban per capita amount of 46,133.5 yuan, but 25,897.03 yuan. Of all the property subitems, the subitem of land is the most conspicuous.

As the urban population has no land, the land value, which is averaged by the national population, has dropped from the rural per capita amount of 3974.32 yuan to the national per capita amount of 2420.767, and its percentage has also dropped from 30.72% in the rural per capita property to 9.35% in the national per capita property. Other property items have smaller changes than land. The item with the smallest change is consumer durables, whose percentage is neither 6.13% of rural areas nor 7.24% of cities, but 6.89%. This indicates that the gap between cities and rural areas in terms of possession of consumer durables is small. Of the seven subitems of the national resident property, the most important items are house property, financial assets and land. The three items add up to 89.02% of the total resident property. Specifically, house property and financial assets are most prominent, which add up to 79.67% of the total property.

As for the national property distribution, we still use the method of ten equant groups and such indexes as the Gini coefficient for analysis. Judging by the gross property, the 20% population with the most per capita property possess 59.3% of the property, while the 20% population with the least per capita property possess only 2.80% of the property, with the ratio between the two being 21.18:1. This ratio is higher than that for rural areas or cities that is calculated respectively (8.1:1 for rural areas and 18.55:1 for cities). If the 10% population with the most property

Table 8.10 Level and Composition of National Per Capita Property in 2002

Property and composition items	Average value (yuan)	Percentage (%)
Total amount of property (net value)	25,897.03	100
Including:		
Land value	2420.767	9.35
Financial assets	5642.684	21.79
Net value of house property	14,989.26	57.88
Productive fixed assets	1037.309	4.01
Value of consumer durables	1784.31	6.89
Estimated current value of other assets	241.6361	0.93
Non-housing liabilities	−218.9326	−0.84

120 *Property distribution of Chinese residents*

is compared to the 10% population with the least property, then the property possession ratio between the two is 60.89:1. Apparently, such a huge gap in property distribution is inseparable from the huge differences between cities and rural areas. Among all the property items, the distribution of house property is the least equal. The 20% population with the most per capita property possesses 65.84% of the house property, while the 20% population with the least per capita property possesses only 1.05% of the house property, with the ratio between the two being 62.7:1. Furthermore, for the 10% population with the least per capita property, the net value of their house property is a negative number, which is similar to the situations of the above cities. That is, the total value of their house property cannot repay their outstanding residential debts. As for the distribution of other property items, the distribution inequality degree of financial assets is only second to that of house property, with the above ratio (the comparison between the 20% highest group and the 20% lowest group) being 29.13:1. The item with a low degree of distribution inequality is consumer durables, whose ratio is 9.556:1. As for the distribution of nonresidential debts, people in the highest group and lowest group have many debts, while people in the middle groups have fewer debts. Is such a situation similar to what we see in the analysis of urban property distribution – that is, the poor have to borrow money, while the rich dare to borrow more money for consumption and investment as they are backed by their existing property?

Table 8.12 shows that, the Gini coefficient of the distribution of national gross property in 2002 already reaches 0.550, which is not only higher than the Gini coefficient of income distribution in the same year (0.454), but also higher than

Table 8.11 Proportion of Property Held by Each of Ten Equant Groups of National Population in 2002

Unit: %

Group (from low to high)	Total amount of property (net value)	Land value	Financial assets	Net value of house property	Productive fixed assets	Value of consumer durables	Estimated current value of other assets	Non-housing liabilities
1 (lowest)	0.68	4.43	0.997	−0.18	2.82	2.84	0.96	30.39
2	2.12	8.67	1.31	1.23	4.52	2.81	0.78	8.65
3	2.95	11.03	1.80	1.93	5.40	3.49	0.63	5.97
4	3.81	13.86	2.12	2.59	8.07	3.88	1.11	5.78
5	4.84	15.01	3.16	3.62	8.90	4.94	1.55	6.94
6	6.3	15.76	4.41	5.09	11.80	6.08	3.04	6.82
7	8.32	14.05	7.16	7.63	10.74	8.96	6.64	8.64
8	11.76	8.34	11.87	12.15	10.12	13.02	12.35	5.07
9	17.89	5.84	19.40	19.30	13.92	18.22	24.16	10.95
10 (highest)	41.41	3.00	47.80	46.54	23.72	35.77	48.8	10.80

Property distribution of Chinese residents 121

Table 8.12 Inequality of Per Capita Property Distribution Nationwide in 2002

Property	Mean value of property (yuan)	Proportion (%)	Gini coefficient	Concentration ratio	Contribution rate (%)
Total amount of property (net value)	25897.03	100	0.550	0.550	100
Including:					
Land value	2420.767	9.35	0.6686	−0.0452	−0.77
Financial assets	5642.684	21.79	0.7404	0.6291	24.92
Net value of house property	14989.26	57.88	0.6736	0.6302	66.32
Productive fixed assets	1037.309	4.01	0.8373	0.2963	2.16
Value of consumer durables	1784.31	6.89	0.6431	0.48	6.01
Estimated current value of other assets	241.6361	0.93	0.9669	0.6885	1.16
Non-housing liabilities	−218.9326	−0.84	0.9674	−0.1749	0.27

the Gini coefficient of property distribution, which is calculated for cities and rural areas respectively (0.4751 for cities, and 0.399 for rural areas). This result is logical, so to speak: In a circumstance where the property distribution gap has exceeded the income distribution gap in both cities and rural areas, and where the urban and rural gap of property distribution is very huge, how can the Gini coefficient of national property distribution not be in the lead? Among the assets, the concentration ratios of the estimated current values of three items, namely house property, financial assets and other assets, have exceeded the Gini coefficient of gross property, which has thus expanded inequality of the gross property distribution. However, as other assets take up a tiny proportion (only 0.93%) in terms of the estimated current value, their explanatory power or contribution rate for the inequality of gross property is only 1.16%. House property and financial assets play key roles: for house property, the concentration ratio is 0.6302, and the contribution rate is 66.32%; for financial assets, the concentration ratio is 0.6291, and the contribution rate is 24.92%. Among all the property items, the role of land is the most thought-provoking. Its percentage in the gross property is only 9.35%, its concentration ratio is only −0.0452, and its explanatory power or contribution rate for the inequality of the gross property is −0.77. In terms of consumer durables, its concentration ratio is 0.408, and its contribution rate is 6.02%, which indicates that the distribution of consumer durables among national residents is relatively equal.

From the perspective of international comparison, it is a norm for the Gini coefficient of property distribution to be greater than the Gini coefficient of income distribution. The studies conducted by James B. Davies and Anthony F. Shorrocks show that the Gini coefficient of income distribution is 0.3–0.4, and the Gini coefficient of property distribution is 0.5–0.9 in developed countries. The

122 *Property distribution of Chinese residents*

1% population with the most property possess 15% to 35% of the gross property, while the 1% population with the most income possess less than 10% of the gross income (James B. Davies, Anthony F. Shorrocks, 1999). According to Smeeding's study, the Gini coefficient of income distribution of 21 developed countries was about 0.3 in the 1990s. However, the Gini coefficient of property distribution of these countries was 0.52–0.93 in the latter half of the 20th century, and was 0.52–0.83 if the Swedish who lived abroad were excluded (quoted from Michael Schneider, 2004). According to the international standard, the Gini coefficient of property distribution in China is not very high in the present stage. However, it still requires high attention if the following two aspects are considered: Firstly, personal property has accumulated for several hundred years in developed countries but has existed for only about 20 years in China if it is considered to start from the early 1980s. We may say that such speed and momentum of personal property accumulation in China are supernormal. Secondly, the Gini coefficient of income distribution in China has remarkably exceeded that in the above developed countries. As mentioned earlier, the differentiation of income distribution today will definitely affect the differentiation of property distribution in the future. Therefore, further expansion of the property distribution gap will be inevitable for a period of time in the future.

As for the relationship between property distribution and income distribution, this paper covers it only in an extremely limited range. Now let's make a simple comparison between the distribution of national per capita property and the distribution of per capita income by making use of the 2002 data. We divide all the urban and rural residents in the survey samples into ten equant groups by the level of per capita income and the level of per capita property. Table 8.13 lists the percentage of

Table 8.13 Percentage of Urban and Rural Residents in Ten Equant Groups by Income and Property

Unit: %

Sequence of ten equant groups	Per capita income		Per capita property	
	Percentage of rural residents	*Percentage of urban residents*	*Percentage of rural residents*	*Percentage of urban residents*
1 (lowest)	98.73	1.27	75.26	24.74
2	97.26	2.74	89.78	10.22
3	94.96	5.04	89.41	10.59
4	90.64	9.36	90.63	9.7
5	79.36	20.64	83.03	16.97
6	62.18	37.82	72.63	27.37
7	43.87	56.13	55.02	44.98
8	22.48	77.52	29.21	70.79
9	12.69	87.31	18.08	81.92
10 (highest)	6.91	93.09	5.99	94.01

Property distribution of Chinese residents 123

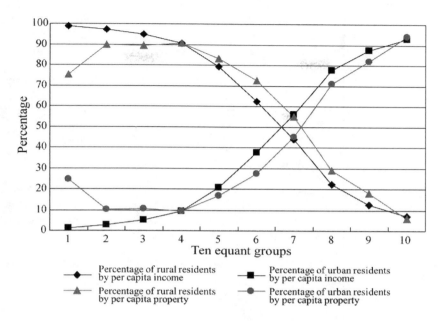

Figure 8.2 Distribution of Urban and Rural Residents by Income Level and Property Level

urban and rural residents in each of the ten equant groups by income and property. Figure 8.2 is the curve chart plotted based on Table 8.12.

The vertical axis in Figure 8.2 stands for the percentage of residents, and the horizontal axis stands for the equant groups of income and property from low to high. They show that rural residents are distributed mostly in the low-income group and low-property group, while urban residents are mostly distributed in the high-income group and high-property group, which indicates that the urban-rural gap is rather big, whether by income distribution or by property distribution. However, the situation becomes complicated if we further observe the property distribution gap and income distribution gap. In the low-income property group (Groups 1–4 in the figure), the property distribution gap is smaller than the income distribution gap. In the middle-income property group (Groups 4–7 in the figure), the property distribution gap is greater than the income distribution gap. In the high-income property group (Groups 7–9 in the figure), the property distribution gap is smaller than the income distribution gap. In the highest-income property group, namely Group 10, the distribution gap between the two is basically flat.

The situation of the low-income property group is easy to understand. This is because even the poorest rural residents have their own small pieces of land, especially in a circumstance where the land output and the income from land are humble, where it is quite natural for the income gap to exceed the property gap

124 *Property distribution of Chinese residents*

even if the land value is insufficiently estimated. In the middle-income property group, it is understandable for the property gap to exceed the income gap. This is because in the middle group, the role of land is relatively weakened, while the role of the house property and financial assets is relatively enhanced. As a result, the role of land is more than offset by house property and financial assets, and therefore the property gap exceeds the income gap. However, it is hard to explain why the income gap again exceeds the property gap after Group 7. Does it mean that the role played by housing-reform houses is declining in the high-income and high-property groups in cities? This seems to be a problem that must be further studied.

V. Epilogue – some policy advice

Chinese urban and rural residents have turned into a group of residents with property from a group of residents with hardly any property, or Chinese residents have transformed from the proletarian class to the propertied class since the reform and opening-up. Furthermore, Chinese residents have also undergone a not-so-long rapid property accumulation period since the 1990s. Though such process is unsatisfactory in many ways, it is highly praised as one of the important achievements of the reform and opening-up on the whole.

A comprehensive view of all the property items of the Chinese urban and rural residents shows that the most important three major items are land, house property and financial assets. As mentioned previously, these three items add up to 89.2% of the total assets. We can seize the gist so long as we can properly handle these three items and their distribution. The analysis here shows that these three items of assets and their distribution have their own respective features as well as problems.

There seems to be a paradox in terms of land: land is so important and scarce, but the land value is so underestimated, and the use of land is so extensive. As mentioned earlier, the unclear property right is still a big problem that puzzles us and has become a big obstacle in increasing land use efficiency. In addition, various defects in land management have become the important reasons that result in inefficient use and waste of land in China at present. Therefore, deepening the reform of the land management system and strengthening land management have become a top priority. (Wen Jiabao, 2004)

The urban-rural house building climax since in the 1980s and the reform of the urban housing system since the 1990s have indeed realized people's house dreams to a large extent, achieving the ideal of "home ownership" to some extent. However, the urban housing reform is conducted under the special circumstance of economic transformation. For many residents, acquisition of houses is the result not of the long-term accumulation of income, but of what turns them from house-less people to house owners overnight. The existence of the aforementioned rent-setting activities has also made housing distribution quite unequal. Therefore, the main problem with house property is the too unequal distribution. If we say that the existing inequality is an established fact, then the future countermeasures can only be the following two measures: Firstly, prevent the reoccurrence of rent-setting activities. Secondly, narrow the property distribution gap by such measures as

Property distribution of Chinese residents   125

collecting property taxes and inheritance taxes. Admittedly, collecting these new taxes is no easy in countries such as China. However, a journey of a thousand li begins with a single step. Why can't we introduce the property tax and inheritance tax that help narrow the property gap (which should be the progressive tax that helps narrow the property gap), instead of just introduce the interest tax (which is the proportional tax called "the regressive tax" implemented at present) that does not help narrow the income gap?

The high-speed accumulation of financial assets among the urban and rural residents in China is a good thing, but it has problems. The main problem is the irrational structure in addition to the unequal distribution. Due to too many uncertain factors, bank deposits account for 64% of the composition of residents' financial assets. Such over-strong propensity to save helps neither stimulate consumption and domestic demand nor facilitate the healthy growth of the entire economy. Apparently, this problem can be solved not through one single measure, but only through deepening reform and rationalizing various kinds of economic relations.

In a historic stage not so long ago, China underwent a period when the resident property accumulated rapidly and was divided, and when the property distribution gap between urban and rural residents had exceeded the income distribution gap. More than 20 years ago, the World Bank held that Chinese residents at that time had hardly any property income except for a small amount of negligible interest income (see the World Bank, 1981). However, the current situation and future situation cannot be mentioned in the same breath. In the long run, property income will become increasingly important in residents' income source composition. For example, more residents will get income from house property, namely the housing rent, in cities. Therefore, expansion of the property distribution gap will definitely become an important factor that affects expansion of the income gap. This situation sets higher requirements for the redistribution policy in China's macro-control policy; that is, the tax policy and transfer payment policy should be made to help narrow the income gap and property gap, so as to facilitate stabilize stability.

In order to correctly apply the redistribution policy, we must first solve the problem of "reverse redistribution" which has been left over by history. The so-called "reverse redistribution" goes against the original purpose of income redistribution – redistribution does not narrow the income and property gap, it expands the gap. Simply put, it did not "take from the fat to pad the lean" but "took from the lean to pad the fat". In the planned economy era, the net tax policy was implemented in rural areas, and the net welfare and net subsidy policy was implemented in cities. As a result of such "retro regulation" policy, as people call it, the income and property gap between cities and rural areas was widened. This situation has changed to some extent since the reform and opening-up, but it still exists. It should be pointed out that the huge income gap and property gap between the cities and rural areas in China are closely associated with "reverse redistribution". The reform of taxation expenses that has been implemented in rural areas in recent years is definitely an effective measure to change this situation, but it takes time to fundamentally change this situation.

126 *Property distribution of Chinese residents*

When the government uses taxes as an important means of redistribution, special attention should be paid to whether a tax is progressive or regressive. In order to give play to the positive role of taxes in redistribution, normally the progressive rate is used, with the tax threshold set. However, this should be based on the premise of highly transparent income and property. For example, as the deposit real-name system is not yet well-established and the interest income is not transparent enough, only the proportional rate instead of the progressive rate can be implemented for collection of the interest tax, that is, an interest tax of 20% is imposed on all the deposit interest. It should be said that such measure is not perfect, and is transitional, because it cannot help narrow the income gap. Joseph Stiglitz holds that "if the rich pay more taxes than the poor, but not on a proportionally incremental basis, then such tax system is still considered as regressive" (Joseph Stiglitz, 2000). Obviously, such a taxation concept featuring "no progress means retrogression" indicates that we should develop towards the progressive system based on more transparent income and property in order to give play to the regulatory function of taxes. The property tax and inheritance tax in our suggestions above apparently should develop towards the progressive tax instead of the proportional tax.

In national macroeconomic policy, taxation and transfer payment definitely have direct impacts on narrowing the gap between property distribution and income distribution. However, we cannot ignore the roles of other macroeconomic policies in narrowing this gap – some policies are not as immediately effective as taxation and transfer payment, but fundamentally they are favorable to long-term peace and order. For example:

1   The educational policy. Nowadays, the role played by labor, which is a production factor, in income and property distribution no longer purely depends on the labor quantity, but more importantly depends on the labor quality. Improvement of the labor quality depends on education to a great extent. Therefore, improving education for low-income and low-property people becomes an important precondition for narrowing the income and property gap. In other words, improvement of education can help narrow the human capital gap among people and thus help create a relatively equal starting point for people to get relatively equal income and property.

2   The labor flow policy. Gradually removing obstacles in the labor flow can help create relatively equal opportunities for people in their participation in income and property distribution. The facts since the reform and opening-up have proved that the labor flow, especially the labor flow between cities and rural areas, has played a significant role in narrowing the income and property gap. Certainly, we should also see that the situation resulting from the stringent restrictions on the labor flow in the planned economy era cannot be changed within a short time. The systematic obstacles that hinder the labor flow, such as the household registration system, benefit system, housing system and employment system, have been considerably removed in the reform but are still far from the requirements of the market economy.

Therefore, cultivating and perfecting the labor market, especially the labor market that can freely flow between cities and rural areas, is still an important aspect in future macroeconomic policies.

3 The policy on industrial structure transformation. The macroeconomic policies should also improve income and property distribution by promoting transformation of the industrial structure. Narrowing the income and property gap between cities and rural areas is a historical task before us. In a long period in the future, the fundamental ways to increase peasants' income and narrow the income and property gap between cities and rural areas are to speed up transformation of the industrial structure, actively develop the secondary and tertiary industries and strive to push labor transfer from the primary industry to the secondary industry, and especially to the tertiary industry.

References

James B. Davies, Shorrocks, A. F. (1999). The Distribution of Wealth. *Handbook of Income Distribution*, 1, 605–675.

Li Shi, Wei Zhong, Björn Gustafson. (2000). 中国城镇居民财产的分配 [Property Distribution of Chinese Urban Residents]. *Economic Research Journal*, 3.

Li Shi, Yue Ximing. (2004). 中国城乡收入差距调查 [Survey on the Urban and Rural Income Gap in China]. *Finance*, 3–4.

Mark Brenner. (2001). Chapter 11: Reexamining the Distribution of Wealth in Rural China. In Carl Riskin, Zhao Renwei, Li Shi. (Eds.), *China's Retreat From Equality: Income Distribution and Economic Transformation*. Armonk, New York: M.E. Sharpe.

Michael Schneider. (2004). *The Distribution of Wealth*. Northampton, USA: Edward Elgar Publishing, Inc.

Stiglitz, J. (2000). 经济学 [Economics]. Volume One. Beijing: China Renmin University Press.

Terry McKinley. (1993). The Distribution of Wealth in Rural China. In *The Distribution of Income in China* (pp. 116–134). London: Palgrave Macmillan.

Urban Social-Economic Survey Task Force of the National Bureau of Statistics of China. (2003). 财富：小康社会的坚实基础 [Wealth: Solid Foundation of an Affluent Society]. Taiyuan: Shanxi Economics Press.

Wang Lina. (2001). Urban Housing Welfare and Income Distribution. In Zhao Renwei, Li Shi, Carl Riskin. (Eds.), *China's Retreat from Inequality: Income Distribution and Economic Transition*. Armonk, NY: ME Sharpe.

Wang Lina, Wei Zhong. (1999). 城市住宅福利与收入分配 [Urban Housing Welfare and Income Distribution]. In Zhao Renwei, Li Shi, Carl Riskin. (Eds.), *China's Retreat from Inequality: Income Distribution and Economic Transition*. Beijing: China Financial & Economic Publishing House.

Wen Jiabao. (December 15, 2004). 深化土地管理制度改革依法切实加强土地管理 [Deepen the Reform of the Land Management System and Effectively Strengthen Land Management According to Law]. *People's Daily*.

The World Bank. (1981). 中国：社会主义经济的发展 – 世界银行经济考察团对中国经济的考察报告 [China: Development of the Socialist Economy: Investigation Report by Economic Investigation Group of the World Bank]. Beijing: China Financial & Economic Publishing House.

Zhao Renwei, Li Shi. (1997). 中国居民收入差距的扩大及其原因 [Expansion of Chinese Residents' Income Gap and Its Cause]. *Economic Research Journal*, 9.

Zhu Qiuxia. (November 12, 2004). 论现行农村土地制度的准国家所有制特征及改革的必要性 [On the Features of the Quasi-Government Ownership of the Existing Rural Land System and Reform Necessity]. Nanjing University of Finance and Economics, *Working Paper*.

Appendix

A. Description of calculation methods for various items of per capita property in rural areas

The total number of rural individual samples was 37,969.

1 Calculation of land value

Firstly, in terms of the land area, adjustment was made based on the assumption that one mu of irrigable land is equal to two mu of dry land. Secondly, the net income of agricultural operations of each household was calculated (gross income – operating cost). Finally, it was believed that 25% of the net income of agricultural operations came from land according to the calculation methods in 1988 and 1995, and the rate of return of land was 8%. In this way, the land value of each household was obtained. In the questionnaire, some households did not respond to the questions concerning the gross income of agricultural operations and operating costs but did respond to the questions concerning the land area. Therefore, the average net income of agricultural operations of the local county was used instead to calculate the household land value. Then such value was equally divided to each person in the household to get the per capita land value.

2 Calculation of house property

For the questions concerning house property in the questionnaire, the house property value was regarded as 0 if the house property was not self-owned by the responder. In the questionnaire, some households who owned the house property answered the questions concerning the living area, but did not respond to the questions concerning the house property value. The countermeasure was to calculate the house property value per square meter of the local county, multiply it by the living area of the household to get the value of the household property, and then equally divide it to each person in the household.

3 Value of basic production assets

The questionnaire contained questions concerning the value of the basic production assets and specific subitems. First the subitems were summed up, and then the total values and the summation of the subitems were compared.

130   *Property distribution of Chinese residents*

The summation of the subitems was used in lieu of those total values that were not equal to it to get the value of the household basic production assets, and then this value was equally divided to each person in the household.

4   Value of consumer durables

The questionnaire contained the questions concerning the value of consumer durables. If some households did not provide the specific values but described their possession of TV sets, bicycles, washing machines, etc., then a function was first made for all the samples:

Value of consumer durables = a1 × color TV set + a2 × black and white TV set + a3 × bicycles + a4 × motorcycle + a5 × refrigerator + a6 × washing machine + a7 × (sound equipment/radio cassette) + a8 × (video recorder/video disc player) + a9 × air conditioner + a10 × family car

The regression method was used to estimate each coefficient. Secondly, for those households that described their possession but did not provide the specific values, the coefficient was multiplied by the possessed quantity of each item respectively to get the value of the household consumer durables, and then such value was equally divided for each person in the household.

5   Financial assets

Firstly, the sampling inspection was conducted over the total rural samples, and the input errors were corrected. Secondly, the subitems of financial assets were summed up and compared to the total values in the questionnaire, and then they were used to replace those total values that were inconsistent with the subitem summation. Thus the value of household financial assets was obtained and then equally divided to each person in the household.

6   Debts

The total values and subitem values of the debts were compared. The subitem values were used to replace those total values that were inconsistent with them to get the household debts, and such debts were equally divided to each person in the household.

7   The per capita debts were subtracted from the summation of the per capita land value, per capita house property, per capita basic production assets, per capita value of consumer durables and per capita financial assets, so as to get the per capita gross property.

B.   Description of calculation methods for various items of per capita property in cities

The total number of individual urban samples was 20,632.

1   Calculation of house property

For the questions concerning house property in the questionnaire, the house property value was regarded as 0 if the house property was not the private

Property distribution of Chinese residents   131

house, commodity house or housing-reform house. There were three questions concerning house property in the questionnaire, and the maximum value was chosen. In the questionnaire, some households who owned the house property answered the questions concerning the living area but did not respond to the questions concerning the house property value. The countermeasure was to calculate the house property value per square meter of the local city, multiply it by the living area of the household to get the value of the household property and then equally divide it to each person in the household.

2   Value of basic production assets and estimated current value of other assets

The answered values in the questionnaire were directly used.

3   Value of consumer durables

The questionnaire contained the questions concerning the value of consumer durables. If some households did not provide the specific values, but described their possession of TV sets, bicycles, and washing machines, etc., then a function was first made for all the samples:

Value of consumer durables = a1 × color TV set + a2 × black-and-white TV set + a3 × bicycles + a4 × motorcycle + a5 × refrigerator + a6 × washing machine + a7 × (sound equipment/radio cassette) + a8 × (video recorder/ video disc player) + a9 × air conditioner + a10 × family car

The regression method was used to estimate each coefficient. Secondly, for those households that described their possession but did not provide the specific values, the coefficient was multiplied by the possessed quantity of each item respectively to get the value of the household consumer durables, and then this value was equally divided to each person in the household.

5   Financial assets

Firstly, the sampling inspection was conducted over the total urban samples, and the input errors were corrected. Secondly, the subitems of financial assets were summed up and compared to the total values in the questionnaire, and they were used to replace those total values that were inconsistent with the subitem summation. Thus the value of household financial assets was obtained and then equally divided to each person in the household.

6   Debts

The total values and subitem values of the debts were compared. The subitem values were used to replace those total values that were inconsistent with them to get the household debts, and such debts were equally divided to each person in the household.

7   The per capita debts were subtracted from the summation of the per capita house property, per capita basic production assets, per capita value of consumer durables, per capita estimated current value of other assets and per capita financial assets, so as to get the per capita gross property.

132 *Property distribution of Chinese residents*

C. Calculation description of national per capita property

The total number of urban samples was 20,632, and the total number of rural samples was 37,969. The ratio of the two failed to comply with the rural and urban population ratio provided by the National Bureau of Statistics of China (NBSC), and therefore needed to be adjusted accordingly. The method used in this paper was to randomly increase the urban samples to 24,367, and to make the ratio between them and the rural samples comply with that provided by the NBSC. Then the urban and rural samples were combined into one database, which contained 62,336 samples. Specifically, the per capita land value of the urban samples was regarded as 0, and the per capita estimated current value of other assets of the rural samples was regarded as 0. Then the per capita house property, per capita financial assets, per capita value of consumer durables, per capita basic production assets, per capita land value, per capita estimated current value of other assets and per capita debts were summed up to get the per capita property.

(This paper was written by Zhao Renwei. Li Shi participated in the design, and Ding Sai was responsible for calculation. It was originally published in the *Research Report of Xinzhi Research Institute*, Southwestern University of Finance and Economics Press, 2006 Edition.)

Appendix End Here

Notes

1 For the calculation of the property items in this paper, see the Appendix.
2 In the questionnaire survey by the Project Team of the Institute of Economics in 2002, 14.48% of the urban residents refused to provide the amount of their bank deposits, which was not the case among rural residents. It seems that the total financial assets of urban residents have been underestimated, and the degree of distribution inequality has also been underestimated.

9 Income distribution, property distribution and gradual reform – in commemoration of the 20th anniversary of the publication *Comparative Economic & Social Systems*

I. On income distribution

Income distribution is a very important subsystem in the entire social and economic system. The status of income distribution affects not only production efficiency, but also people's vital interests, and thus affects social harmony and stability. I have studied the issue of income distribution of Chinese residents with some domestic and foreign peers since 1988, and I have published such books as *Study of Income Distribution of Chinese Residents* and *Restudy of Income Distribution of Chinese Residents*. Through the systematic and empirical analysis, I believe that we should look at the changes of the income distribution pattern during China's economic reform and economic development in an objective and all-around way. Among these changes, three issues are especially worthy of attention.

A. *How to measure and regard the income gap nationwide*

As is known to all, the income gap is normally measured with the Gini coefficient. In terms of the national Gini coefficient, various kinds of estimates at present may be summed up into the following three kinds: about 0.4 for low estimate, about 0.45 for moderate estimate and about 0.5 for high estimate. If the differences in the calculation methods are not taken into consideration, then the differences of these three kinds of estimates are as follows: the first estimate mainly considers monetary income and hardly considers income in kind, especially subsidy income. The second estimate gives more considerations to the income in kind. The third estimate considers not only monetary income and income in kind, but also illegal income and abnormal income.

People have given various opinions on the increasing expansion of the Gini coefficient. Specifically, two kinds of opinions are worth discussing. The first opinion is that because internationally some people regard 0.4 as the warning line for an excessive gap, the Gini coefficient should be controlled to be below 0.4 in order to control the income gap in China within a reasonable range. However, China is a country with a vast territory, a huge population, and a very low degree of homogeneity, which objectively allows a high Gini coefficient and does not need to stick to 0.4 rigidly. However, how further should we go after we stride over this line needs to be carefully studied. The other opinion is that China is a

134   Income/property distribution, gradual reform

dual economy society, and great income differences between cities and rural areas are inevitable. Therefore, the urban and rural Gini coefficients can only be calculated respectively, instead of jointly. Otherwise, the income gap in China will be exaggerated. In my opinion, the national Gini coefficient, urban Gini coefficient, rural Gini coefficient or even provincial Gini coefficient can all indicate different problems respectively, and there is no need to treat them with partiality. In fact, many developing countries that belong to dual economies calculate the urban, rural and national Gini coefficient respectively, and there seems to be no need for China to seek an exception in this regard.

B.   How to measure and regard the urban and rural income gap

As the calculation calibers and methods are different, the estimation of the degree of the urban and rural income gap is often inconsistent. However, there is no disagreement on the judgment of the general trend of the urban and rural income gap: namely, this gap has been narrowed first and then widened since the reform and opening-up. Relevant reports of the World Bank point out that in most countries in the world, the urban and rural income ratio is 1.5, and such ratios of more than 2 are extremely rare. However, such ratio already reached 2.5 in 1995 in China even according to the official estimate. In addition, if the in-kind welfare of urban residents was added, the actual income of urban residents would increase by 72%. Even if the factor that peasants go into cities to work and thus narrow the urban and rural income gap is taken into consideration, the ratio of the actual urban and rural income in 1995 was about 4. According to official data, the urban and rural income ratio in China already reached 3.2 or 3.2:1 in 2003. Various nongovernmental estimates show that the urban and rural income ratio is 4:1, 5:1 or even 6:1 in China at present. Furthermore, it is worth noting that the more underdeveloped a region is, the bigger the urban and rural income gap is. The urban and rural income gap is not only an economic problem but also a social problem, and it must arouse the attention of the whole nation.

C.   How to regard the income gap caused by inequality of housing distribution

According to the study conducted by the Project Team of the Institute of Economics of Chinese Academy of Social Sciences, if the imputed rent of residents' owner-occupied housing after the housing reform is also regarded as a kind of property income, then the inequality coefficient of the imputed rent of owner-occupied housing (0.371 in 1995) has exceeded that (0.322 in 1995) of the housing subsidies (invisible subsidies) formed in the planned economy era, while the inequality coefficient of housing subsidies has exceeded the overall inequality coefficient (0.286 in 1995) of urban residents. This indicates that if the housing reform, which visualizes the original inequality of invisible income (invisible subsidies), admits only the original inequality, then when the inequality of the imputed rent of owner-occupied housing exceeds the inequality of the original housing subsidies, we should see this as the additional inequality during such visualization. Furthermore, we should also

Income/property distribution, gradual reform   135

see that this situation has deteriorated in the housing reform since the middle-late stages of the 1990s. At the crucial moment when housing distribution in kind transits into monetary housing distribution, some departments and units are speeding up their pace of buying and building houses and are distributing big and good houses to their employees in an excessive way, so as to offer the "last supper" to their employees. People have found that the double-track price differences of houses are far bigger than the double-track price differences of general merchandise. In cities like Beijing, in particular, getting one more house means the value ranging from 100,000 yuan to hundreds of thousands of yuan. If we say that the "rent-seeking" activities that were prevalent in the late 1980s seek profits by making use of the existing price differences, then the "rent-setting" activities that were prevalent in the late 1990s seek profits by setting price differences. This is because the market price and planned price in "rent-seeking" are given – the planned price is left over by the planned economy era, while the market price is formed in the market during system transformation. However, "rent-setting" is just another story. If we say that the market price in "rent-setting" is also given, then the planned price in "rent-setting" is greatly subjective and arbitrary – it often depends on the subjective will and profit drive of the power holders and monopolists. Such new unequal distribution caused by power and monopoly must arouse great attention.

For the above widening of the income gap, people have probed into the reason one after another, especially its relationship with the economic reform. In my opinion, two trends must be prevented while we analyze the relationship between widening of the income gap and the economic reform. One trend simply attributes widening of the income gap and the problems that emerge to the economic reform itself; the other trend simply regards widening of the income gap as a price that the economic reform should pay. In my opinion, widening of the income gap should be viewed from three different levels. The first level is the incentive part that helps increase efficiency. The incentive part helps overcome equalitarianism and promotes economic development, is the result of the economic reform, and should be recognized. The second level is the price that the economic reform must pay. For example, China's reform can be carried out only in a gradual way, featuring double tracks, and such activities as "rent-seeking" which make use of double tracks will definitely emerge. To some extent, this can be regarded as the price that the reform should pay. The third level belongs to the overhigh price, or the part that should not be paid, or that part that should be prevented and avoided. Certainly, it is not easy to identify, especially quantify, the boundary between the second and third levels, but I think theoretically it is possible. Furthermore, some "rent-setting" activities, especially the "rent-setting" activities that emerge in the real estate development and housing reform, are avoidable to a great extent, so to speak.

II.   On property distribution

The changes of the pattern of resident income distribution, especially widening of the income gap, have caused a high degree of concern. However, studies of property distribution or property allocation are still in the starting stage nowadays.

136 *Income/property distribution, gradual reform*

Income distribution is closely related to property distribution. In particular, the personal property of Chinese residents has undergone a period of rapid accumulation and prominent differentiation since the 1990s. It is foreseeable that property distribution of Chinese residents will become a new concern for people.

China has set the goal of building a well-off society in an all-around way. People's degree of well-being depends not only on the income status, but also on the property status. In other words, well-being distribution depends not only on income distribution, but also on property distribution. It seems that this is also one of the reasons that property distribution has aroused people's increasing attention.

As far as the general distinction between income and property is concerned, income refers to all the receipts of people (a person or family) within a given period (normally one year), while wealth refers to the monetary net value of the assets possessed by people at a certain time point. Obviously, property is the stock at a time point, while income is the flow in unit time. Income and property interact with each other: the flow in the past definitely affects the stock today, while the stock today definitely affects the flow in the future. With the continuous expansion of the property scale and the change of the property distribution pattern, property distribution has an important impact not only on the stability of the entire macroeconomy, but also on the long-term change of income distribution in the future.

According to the survey conducted by the Project Team of the Institute of Economics of the Chinese Academy of Social Sciences, the most important three items of property for Chinese residents are house property, financial assets and land. The three items add up to 89.02% of the total resident property. Specifically, house property and financial assets are most prominent, which add up to 79.67% of the total property.

As for the national property distribution, it is quite unequal, whether the method of ten equant groups or the Gini coefficient is used for analysis. Take the method of ten equant groups as an example. Judging by the gross property, the 20% population with the most per capita property possesses 59.3% of the property, while the 20% population with the least per capita property possesses only 2.80% of the property, with the ratio between the two being 21.18:1. This ratio is higher than that for rural areas or cities that is calculated respectively (8.1:1 for rural areas and 18.55:1 for cities). If the 10% population with the most property is compared to the 10% population with the least property, then the property possession ratio between the two is 60.89:1. Apparently, such a huge gap in property distribution is inseparable from the huge differences between cities and rural areas. Among all the property items, the distribution of house property is the least equal. The 20% population with the most per capita property possesses 65.84% of the house property, while the 20% population with the least per capita property possesses only 1.05% of the house property, with the ratio between the two being 62.7:1. Furthermore, for the 10% population with the least per capita property, the net value of their house property is a negative number; that is, the total value of their house property cannot repay their outstanding residential debts. As for the distribution of other property items, the distribution inequality degree of financial assets is second

Income/property distribution, gradual reform 137

only to that of house property, with the above ratio (the comparison between 20% highest group and 20% lowest group) being 29.13:1.

Let's look at the Gini coefficient. In 2002, the Gini coefficient of the distribution of national gross property already reached 0.550, which is not only higher than the Gini coefficient of income distribution in the same year (0.454), but also higher than the Gini coefficient of property distribution calculated for cities and rural areas respectively (0.4751 for cities, and 0.399 for rural areas). This result is logical, so to speak: In a circumstance where the property distribution gap has exceeded the income distribution gap in both cities and rural areas, and where the urban and rural gap of property distribution is very huge, how can the Gini coefficient of national property distribution not be in the lead? Among the assets, the concentration ratios of the estimated current values of three items, namely house property, financial assets and other assets, have exceeded the Gini coefficient of gross property, which has thus expanded inequality of the gross property distribution. However, as other assets take up a tiny proportion (only 0.93%) in terms of the estimated current value, their explanatory power or contribution rate for the inequality of gross property is only 1.16%. House property and financial assets play key roles: for house property, the concentration ratio is 0.6302, and the contribution rate is 66.32%; for financial assets, the concentration ratio is 0.6291, and the contribution rate is 24.92%.

From the perspective of international comparison, it is a norm for the Gini coefficient of property distribution to be greater than the Gini coefficient of income distribution. In developed countries, the Gini coefficient of income distribution is between 0.3 and 0.4, while the Gini coefficient of property distribution is between 0.5 and 0.9. The 1% population with the most property possesses 15% to 35% of the gross property, while the 1% population with the most income possesses less than 10% of the gross income. The Gini coefficient of income distribution was about 0.3 in 21 developed countries in the 1990s, but the Gini coefficient of property distribution was 0.52 to 0.93 in these countries in the latter half of the 20th century. According to the international standard, the Gini coefficient of property distribution in China is not very high in the present stage. However, it still requires high attention if the following two aspects are considered: Firstly, personal property has accumulated for several hundred years in developed countries, but has existed for only about 20 years in China if it is considered to start from the early 1980s. We may say that such speed and momentum of personal property accumulation in China are supernormal. Secondly, the Gini coefficient of income distribution in China has remarkably exceeded that in developed countries. As mentioned earlier, the differentiation of income distribution today will definitely affect the differentiation of property distribution in the future. Therefore, further expansion of the property distribution gap will be inevitable for a period of time in the future.

The Chinese urban and rural residents have turned into a group of residents with property from a group of residents with hardly any property, or Chinese residents have transformed from the proletarian class to the propertied class since the reform and opening-up. More than 20 years ago, the World Bank held that Chinese residents at that time had hardly any property income except for a small

138 *Income/property distribution, gradual reform*

amount of negligible interest income. However, the current situation and future situation cannot be mentioned in the same breath. In the long run, property income will become increasingly important in residents' income source composition. For example, more residents will get income from house property, namely housing rent, in cities. Therefore, expansion of the property distribution gap will definitely become an important factor that affects expansion of the income gap. This situation sets higher requirements for the redistribution policy in China's macro-control policy; that is, the tax policy and transfer payment policy should be made to help narrow the income gap and property gap, so as to facilitate stability.

III. On new challenges ahead for gradual reform

As early as the end of the 1970s and the early 1980s, the economic circles in China held heated discussions on whether the radical or gradual approach should be adopted for the economic reform. In practice, China's reform has been carried out in a gradual way on the whole, except that the reform of the household contract responsibility system in rural areas in the early 1980s carried some radical factors. Furthermore, this transition approach is basically successful based on China's national conditions. Not only many Chinese scholars, but also some foreign scholars who advocate radical reform on the whole believe that China's gradual reform approach is successful. For example, Professor J. Sachs with Harvard University (United States) is a prominent scholar who promoted the radical reform approach (so-called "shock therapy") in the Soviet Union and some Eastern European countries, but he made positive comments on China's gradual reform while giving lectures in China in the early 1990s. Another example is Professor W. Brus with the University of Oxford (UK), who proposed that the "one-package" approach, namely the radical approach, should be adopted for China's reform, so as to avoid conflicts resulting from the double-track prices which are regarded as "chaotic traffic rules". However, he also held that China's gradual reform approach is suitable for China's national conditions when he revisited China in the early 1990s.

Challenges are still ahead despite success.

Firstly, it should be pointed out that the gradual reform itself is faced with challenges. This is because the differentiation between gradual reform and radical reform is not absolute; neither is the true benefit of one approach versus another. In the initial period of the reform, we did make great achievements with small risks and low costs in a gradual way, but China's gradual reform approach itself had the connotation of "from easy to difficult" and "from periphery to strong fortress". Therefore, we must be soberly aware that the most difficult problems have not been solved yet, and we must put forth efforts to overcome difficulties in the future.

In addition, the original intent of the gradual reform is to reduce the reform cost, but the risk of increasing reform costs also exists. The gradual reform is often called the "incremental reform"; that is, the stock part of wealth still stays in the old system, while the incremental part enters the new system and operates according to the market rules. In practice, however, new wealth enters the old system. A typical example is the use of government vehicles. A large number of

Income/property distribution, gradual reform   139

new government vehicles have increased since the reform and opening-up, but almost all of these new vehicles have entered the old system. The waste of operating according to the old system is a fact known to all. Such phenomenon of waste does not meet the requirements for building a conservation-minded society, nor meet the requirements for building a harmonious society. Furthermore, the scheme on the monetization reform for the use of government vehicles was also drawn up in 1998. However, seven years have passed, and such reform has still been slow and halting. Is new wealth's entry into the old system a kind of price or cost? Is such price or cost inevitable? Isn't the long-term existence of such phenomenon a challenge for the gradual reform?

Another challenge for the gradual reform is how to prevent and overcome power-for-money deals (some people even regard power-for-money deals as the power capital). The aforementioned rent-setting activities, which emerged during the real estate development and housing reform, are actually the activities where power is utilized to get economic interests. The rent-setting activities that emerged in China in the 1990s have caused us to pay a high price. If we say that the accrual space of the rent-seeking activities in the 1980s are 50 percent more to double, then the accrual space of the rent-setting activities in the 1990s will often be many times or even dozens of times. Apparently, not all of these costs are inevitable in the reform process. Therefore, the task before us is to prevent us from paying undesirable prices.

The examples presented here show that we must supervise and counterbalance power if we want to push forward the economic reform. With the lack of the checks and balance of power, the public ownership is very likely to be turned into the private ownership for people with power. In order to prevent people from turning the public ownership into private ownership by using their power, checks and balances are necessary. The political reform also needs to be pushed forward while the economic reform is promoted in order to strengthen checks and balances.

Here I also want to talk about the requirements set by the social and economic transformation for economics. The economic transformation promotes the transformation of economics. The economics transformation is reflected not only as the transformation of the research content and methods of economics, but also as the transformation of economists.

The studies of economics in China must be rooted in China's actual national conditions. Our experience shows that we should not only carry out empirical studies and get as much firsthand original data as possible, but we should also always understand the general economic background of China in the present stage – the system transformation from planned economy to market economy, and the development transformation from dual economy to modern economy.

In the studies of economics in China, some advanced theories and methods that are suitable for China's national conditions should be introduced from foreign countries. Learning from foreign countries may help improve the academic ability of Chinese scholars and increase the scientificity of economics within a short period.

140 *Income/property distribution, gradual reform*

Apparently, as long as we focus on the above two aspects, we can not only promote internationalization and modernization of the studies of economics in China, but we can also make greater international contributions with our own national characteristics, and help the studies of economics in China go to the world.

Accomplishing the above tasks requires the combined and constant actions of several generations. We are acutely aware that it was after several decades of seclusion that China took the road of reform and opening-up. China's economy is in the process of transformation, and so are China's economists. Such transformation is tough for the economists of the old generation. However, if they can realize their transitional roles in such hardship, then it is only natural to put efforts into the growth of the economists of the new generation. From the studies which have been conducted by the Income Distribution Project Team of the Institute of Economics of the Chinese Academy of Social Sciences over the past ten-plus years, we not only see the results of the combined actions of several generations, but also gladly see the rapid growth of the new generation, and may look to the effects of the constant efforts of several generations.

(Originally published in *Comparative Economic & Social Systems*, Issue 5, 2005.)

10 Significance of attaching importance to residents' property and their income

The report at the 17th National Congress of the Communist Party of China, held in October 2007, mentioned the issue of residents or families' property and property income several times. For example, the report said, in Part I, that "the income of urban and rural residents has greatly increased, and most of families have increased their property" while talking about the achievements made in the past years; and said, in Part VIII, that "we should create conditions to allow more people to possess property income" while talking about social construction centering on improvement of people's livelihood. It was the first time that a report of the National Congress of the Communist Party of China has attached so much importance to residents' property, so to speak, which is quite creative as well.

My personal perception after study is that the report of the 17th National Congress, by attaching so much importance to residents' possession of personal (family) property and property income, is of extremely important significance.

I. It points out the importance of residents' possession of personal property and reflects the philosophy of possession of wealth among the people, as well as the spirit of building a well-off society in an all-around way

My understanding is that the premise of recognizing residents' possession of property income is to recognize residents' possession of personal property. The report of the 17th National Congress not only pointed out the fact that residents' personal property has increased in a general sense, but also pointed out the importance of residents' possession of personal property from the perspective of residents' possession of property income.

In the early 1980s, the World Bank sent a delegation to China for inspection, and the experts of this delegation wrote a report. The report specifically mentioned: Chinese residents deposit a little money from their low salaries, and get a minute quantity of interest from the small amount of deposits in the banks, which can be considered as property income. They have no other property income at all other than this. Therefore, the property income of Chinese residents in those years was so little that it could be ignored. The situation today is totally different after about 30 years of reform. Now we finally realize that socialism is by no means a society

142　*Attaching importance to residents' property*

where the nation is prosperous but its people are poor, but a society where the nation is prosperous and its people are rich. After the National People's Congress passed the property law, the Congress of the Communist Party of China further recognized the importance of residents' possession of personal property, which, so to speak, is an important achievement of the reform and opening-up, as well as an embodiment of reform deepening.

The real meaning of "create conditions to allow more people to possess property income" is to attach importance not only to the increase of resident income, but also to the increase of resident property. Income is the flow in a given period, while property is the stock at a certain time point, just like the water flowing out of a river in a certain period is the flow, while the water stored in the reservoir at a certain time point is the stock. A resident's or family's level of wealth depends not only on the monthly and yearly income, but also on the property accumulated at a certain time point.

II.　It clearly specifies property income in addition to labor income for residents, which not only helps increase the efficiency of allocation of human, material and financial resources, but also helps expand channels for residents to increase income, reflecting the diversified sources of resident income

According to the law of the market, the income of various production factors is closely related to the price of various production factors. If the law of the market is interference-free, then the rationality of the income of various factors can show the rationality of the price of various factors. The rationality of the factor price reflects the scarcity of various factors, and thus rationally allocates various factors. In our words, it rationally allocates human, material and financial resources and thus increases the efficiency of resource allocation. Otherwise, the irrational factor income and factor price will cause signal confusion and thus cause the waste of resources. The waste phenomenon in land development, which was caused by the irrational income and price of land in previous years, is just a clear example.

Attaching importance to both labor income and property income also helps expand channels for residents to increase income, which reflects the diversified sources of resident income and helps to build a harmonious and stable society. Even in western developed countries, workers may have property income in addition to labor income, which is also significant for a stable life. For example, during my stay in the United Kingdom as a visiting scholar, I saw some unemployed workers rent out part of their personal houses to get some rental income so as to make a living, as they had no salary income other than unemployment relief during unemployment. Obviously, diversified income sources help maintain family and social stability.

Certainly, attaching importance to the increase of property income does not mean ignoring the increase of labor income. However, the proportion of the remuneration of Chinese laborers in the GDP has shown a downtrend over the past

Attaching importance to residents' property 143

ten-plus years. According to the bluebook of the 2007 "Report on Competitiveness of China's Enterprises", which was released by the Institute of Industrial Economics of the Chinese Academy of Social Sciences, the proportion of laborers' remuneration in the GDP has dropped from 53.4% to 41.4% from 1990 to 2005, down by 12%. People worried that "salaries would erode profits" in the 1980s, but they worry that "profits would erode salaries" today. It seems that "increasing the proportion of the labor remuneration in the primary distribution", as pointed out in the report of the 17th National Congress, is on a targeted basis. This indicates that we should never ignore the proportionate increase of labor income while the GDP grows rapidly and corporate profits and state revenue have greatly increased. Only in this way can the majority of laboring people share the achievements of reform and opening-up. Further, increasing corporate profits by holding down employees' salaries or laborers' income does not help stimulate laborers' enthusiasm or increase economic efficiency. Only once a balanced relationship between the corporate profit growth and laborers' income growth is established can the requirements for building a people-oriented harmonious society be met.

III. It points out the interaction relationship between income and property

The report of the 17th National Congress not only attaches importance to the increase of resident income and property but also points out the interaction between income and property. With residents' income increasing, the beyond-consumption part may be turned into property. When residents use beyond-consumption income to buy stocks or deposit it into banks, income is turned into financial assets. Income is turned into house property that belongs to material property when residents use beyond-consumption income to buy houses. On the contrary, property may be turned into income when residents' property increases. Like the rental gained from house renting and the interest gained from bank deposits, the dividend gained from stocks is also property income.

To handle the interaction relationship between income and property, we need to prevent a vicious circle between the excessive income gap and excessive property gap, and we should create a virtuous cycle between the proper income gap and proper property gap. Certainly, this is no easy task. We should first suppress the trend of an ever-expanding gap, strive to reach a turning point from expansion to narrowing, and then seek a proper gap that is in line with the national conditions of China.

IV. We should prevent an excessive gap between property and income

My understanding is that the expression "allow more people to have property income" itself, as used in the report of the 17th National Congress, has contained the meaning of preventing an excessive gap between property and income and realizing common prosperity. As mentioned earlier, Chinese residents' property

144 *Attaching importance to residents' property*

and income were so little that they could be ignored 30 years ago. However, Chinese residents' property has accumulated rapidly and differentiated remarkably within about 20 years. The preliminary study of the Project Team of the Institute of Economics of the Chinese Academy of Social Sciences shows that the property of Chinese residents is composed of six to seven subitems. Specifically, the most important three items are house property, financial assets and land. Land mainly refers to rural areas. House property accounts for about 60%, financial assets account for 21%, land accounts for about 10%, and the total of the three items accounts for about 90% of the resident property. In 2002, the Gini coefficient of the resident income gap in China was about 0.45, the Gini coefficient of property income was about 0.55, and the inequality degree of property distribution was higher than that of income distribution by about 10%. Specifically, the inequality degree of distribution of house property and financial assets is still higher and reaches 0.6 and above.

From the perspective of international comparison, the Gini coefficient of income distribution in China has significantly exceeded that in the developed countries. Though the Gini coefficient of property distribution in China has not exceeded that in the developed countries, the trend of rapid accumulation and prominent differentiation of property is significant. Obviously, how to prevent the further expansion of the income distribution gap and property distribution gap is indeed an important task before us. Certainly, this is no easy task. We should first suppress the trend of an ever-expanding gap, strive to reach a turning point from expansion to narrowing, and then seek a proper gap that is in line with the national conditions of China.

As for how to create conditions to prevent the excessive gap between the rich and the poor, I think that, firstly, we should deepen reform. Many problems resulting in the excessive income gap and property gap are related to power-for-money deals, and rent-seeking and rent-setting activities, etc.; in other words, related to the lack of checks and balances. In order to prevent people from turning public ownership into private ownership by using their power, checks and balances are necessary. The political reform also needs to be pushed forward while the economic reform is promoted in order to strengthen checks and balances. China's reform has been going on for about 30 years, but we should be soberly aware that the reform is not finished yet. Both market competition factors and monopoly factors exist in the economic life in China. As is known to all, the market competition cannot solve the problem concerning fair distribution and the gap between the rich and the poor, and government intervention is required. Various kinds of monopoly, including departmental monopoly and regional blockade, cannot solve the problems concerning fair distribution of income and property. Instead, they can only widen the gap between the rich and the poor. These problems can be solved only through deepening reform.

Secondly, we should give play to the government's redistribution function. Simply put, to redistribute is to "take from the fat to pad the lean". Specifically, it means that the government transfers income and property from the rich to the poor by means of taxation and transfer payment (including subsidies), so as to realize social equity and harmony under the premise that the incentive mechanism is safeguarded. However, situations against the original intention of redistribution often occur in real life. That is, the government's redistribution function does not achieve the goal of "taking from the fat to pad the lean"; instead, the situation of "taking from the lean to pad the fat", namely the "reverse redistribution", occurs. In order to correctly apply the redistribution policy, we must first solve the problem of "reverse redistribution" which has been left over by history. In the planned economy era, the net tax policy was implemented in rural areas, and the net welfare and net subsidy policy was implemented in cities. As a result of such "retro regulation" policy, as people call it, the income and property gap between cities and rural areas was widened. This situation has changed to some extent since the reform and opening-up, but it still exists. It should be pointed out that the huge income gap and property gap between the cities and rural areas in China are closely associated with the above "reverse redistribution". The reform of taxation expenses that has been implemented in rural areas in recent years is definitely an effective measure to change this situation, but it takes time to fundamentally change this situation.

In terms of how to prevent an excessive property and income gap, I think two questions need to be raised for study and discussion.

Firstly, how can peasants get due income or profits from land, which is an important property (or even from the contract and management right)? This is a major issue that is worth studying. As is known to all, peasants have received few profits from land circulation over the past 20-plus years. Is this situation one of the factors that causes the gap between the rich and the poor? How can we change this situation? The solution is to follow the spirit of the 17th National Congress.

Secondly, do we need to gradually create conditions to introduce the property tax and inheritance tax into the tax system in order to prevent the excessive property distribution gap? Some people in the academic community (including myself) have raised this question. Certainly there are different opinions, and many problems concerning technologies and interests need to be solved. Though we must be prudent in making decisions on such important issues, it is absolutely necessary to strengthen surveys on such issues.

(This paper was published in Issue 1 of the 2008 Edition of *China Reform*. Its title was changed to "Correctly Handle the Relationship between Property Income and Labor Income" at the time of publication. It was previously published in the December 2007 issue of the journal *BIZBUZZ* in Shanghai.)

11 Focusing on vertical imbalance in income distribution

I. Vertical imbalance – a field worth expanding in the study of income distribution

All the studies of income distribution in China have focused on the horizontal imbalance or horizontal inequality of resident income distribution so far,[1] which is definitely correct. In terms of resident income distribution, China has transferred from a country with prevailing equalitarianism to one that is highly unequal since the reform and opening-up more than 30 years ago. The academic communities at home and abroad have estimated the inequality degree of resident income distribution in China differently. However, the inequality degree, which is measured with the Gini coefficient, has greatly exceeded the international warning line, which is 0.4, or has even approached the level of 0.5. Therefore, China has been rated as one of the most unequal countries in terms of income distribution. That is why income distribution has time and again become a focus of attention. People have studied the urban-rural income gap, income gap within cities, income gap within rural areas, and inter-department income gap (especially the income gap between monopolistic departments and competition departments) extensively for a long time. These studies have all focused on horizontal inequality, so to speak. The studies in this field have expanded to some extent in recent years. For example, concerning the constant decrease of the proportion of labor income in the national income of China since the 1990s, the economic circles in China have carried out many studies on the national income's distribution among the state, enterprises and individuals, especially on how to increase the proportion of resident income in the national income. The studies in this regard have apparently expanded the earlier studies of resident income distribution. To put it in plain language, the small distribution relations (income distribution relations among residents) have expanded to the big distribution relations (income distribution relations among the state, enterprises and residents). For another example, the economic circles in China have conducted some studies of property distribution in view of the interaction between income distribution and property distribution, as well as the fact that Chinese residents have developed from possession of hardly any personal property to the rapid accumulation and prominent differentiation of personal property. These studies have shown that the inequality degree of personal property distribution has greatly exceeded that of income distribution in China. The studies

Vertical imbalance in income distribution 147

of the relationship between property distribution and income distribution have apparently expanded the previous studies of resident income distribution. However, in terms of expansion in these two aspects, the focus of people's attention is still on horizontal inequality. Specifically, they observe the income and property distribution relations among residents, as well as the income distribution relations among the state, enterprises and residents. Even if sometimes there is observation at different time points in different periods, the focus of observation is still on horizontal inequality and rarely involves income distribution inequality among people of different generations. In real life, however, the inequality of income distribution or the vertical imbalance of income distribution between people of different generations, or the inter-generational imbalance, objectively exists. Here we see the income distribution imbalance between people of different generations as the vertical imbalance of income distribution, or the "inter-generational imbalance". Certainly, we should not judge imbalance from the equalitarian perspective. The so-called imbalance here means that the income gap has exceeded the rational range. In this short thesis, I provide some cases and thoughts on this issue solely based on my knowledge, and analyze the causes to some extent, so as to serve as a modest spur to my peers in the academic community.

II. Some examples of vertical imbalance of income distribution

A. *Intergenerational imbalance resulting from long-term salary freezing*

China implemented the policy of basic freezing of salaries after the salary reform in 1956 and before the salary adjustment in 1977. In 1963, during this period, the policy on minor salary adjustment for some people was implemented. Long-term freezing of salaries resulted in an unfavorable income distribution situation for the young generation. Superficially, long-term freezing of salaries seems to have the same impact on everyone; in other words, everyone is equal before salary freezing. Actually, this is not so. This is because the changes of the labor contribution curve are different in different stages of a person's life cycle. On the whole, the curve of a laborer's labor contributions in his/her lifetime is in the parabolic shape;, that is, the contributions are small at the starting point of work, reach the peak in the mature stage, and fall in old age. Therefore, the labor remuneration of a laborer in his/her lifetime should also be in a parabolic shape; that is, the labor remuneration is low when he/she begins to work, reaches the peak in the mature stage, and falls afterwards. However, salary freezing means that the labor remuneration curve is turned into an unchangeable straight line. Such income distribution situations, which resulted from the long-term freezing of salaries and were unfavorable to the young generation, were similar in those days, whether in the state organs, public institutions (including schools) or state-owned enterprises. Recently, I recollected and investigated relevant situations of the Institute of Economics of the Chinese Academy of Sciences (renamed "Institute of Economics of Chinese

148   *Vertical imbalance in income distribution*

Academy of Social Sciences" after 1977) where I worked. I chose two groups of people who had been working in the Institute of Economics from around 1957 to around 1977: One group was made up of the research fellows and the senior cadres above Administrative Level 11 ("Senior Researcher Group") who worked in or around 1957. The other group was made up of the junior researchers who worked in or around 1957, and whose professional titles were mostly research apprentices ("Junior Researcher Group"). According to my recollection and relevant data, the average age was about 45 years in the Senior Researcher Group, and about 25 in the Junior Researcher Group; the average monthly salary was 227 yuan in the Senior Researcher Group, and 64 yuan in the Junior Researcher Group. In 1963, the state made a minor adjustment of salaries for some people in the Junior Researcher Group. However, the average monthly salary of the Junior Researcher Group rose by only 8 yuan after the minor adjustment, and was only 72 yuan in 1977. The salary of the Senior Researcher Group was not adjusted, but was still far higher than that of the Junior Researcher Group in 1977. In 1977, people in the above two groups were all 20 years older. In other words, after 20 years of change, people in the Junior Researcher Group were as old as those in the Senior Researcher Group 20 years before. However, their salary was still less than one-third of that of people in the Senior Researcher Group 20 years before. Such a situation had never occurred, even in the Soviet Union and Eastern European countries where the planned economy was implemented. This lesson with strong Chinese characteristics is worth our review and reflection. The inter-generational imbalance and its consequences caused repercussions in society in the 1980s. In the academic community, what caused strong repercussions were reports on some middle-aged scientific workers who died young in Zhongguancun, Beijing. In the circle of literature and art, what caused strong repercussions was an embarrassing situation for Doctor Lu Wenting, a role (played by Pan Hong) in a film called *At Middle Age*, where her rewards were far lower than her efforts, and she was looked down upon because her social status was as low as her income.

B.   *Imbalance between in-service employees and retirees*

Here we take colleges and universities (research institutions are in line with colleges and universities) as an example. As is known to all, the positions (or professional titles) differed from the salary grades in the salary reform in 1956. The positions or professional titles were divided into four levels, namely full professor, associate professor, lecturer and teaching assistant; but the salary was divided into 12 levels (expanded to 13 levels in 1957). The salary level was Level 1, Level 2, Level 3 and Level 4 for full professors, Level 4, Level 5, Level 6 and Level 7 for associate professors, Level 7, Level 8, Level 9 and Level 10 for lecturers and Level 10, Level 11, Level 12 and Level 13 for teaching assistants. However, the 1985 salary reform implemented the position-based salary system and cancelled the different salary levels under the same position or professional title. After this system had been implemented for about 20 years, the original system of several salary levels under a position or professional title was gradually restored. For

Vertical imbalance in income distribution 149

example, as before, the salary levels for full professors were made up of Level 1, Level 2, Level 3 and Level 4. Therefore, the positions or professional titles that had been formed since 1985 had to enter corresponding salary levels again. Take full professors as an example. They had to enter Level 1, Level 2, Level 3 and Level 4 respectively, and the starting point for them could be only Level 4. However, such restoration only applied to in-service employees. Therefore, there was one problem: what about people who had retired over the past about 20 years since 1985? As they had retired, they could not enter the salary levels reset. If their retirement pension could only match the lowest level of the corresponding professional titles (for example, the lowest level for full professors was Level 4), then how can it reflect the differences of the labor contributions they had made over these 20 years? Apparently such a system and policy changes resulted in an income distribution situation which was unfavorable to retirees. In other words, the inter-generational imbalance between in-service employees and retirees was caused in terms of income distribution.

C. *Imbalance within retirees*

During the salary reform in 2006, I wrote an article at the invitation of the parties concerned. I received many letters from readers after the article was published, which talked about the imbalance of internal income distribution among retirees. For example, the cadres of the same official rank, who retired 20 years ago, 10 years ago and recently, might have greatly different incomes. There were two reasons: firstly, the retirement pension was calculated based on a certain substitution rate before retirement. Due to the rapid economic development of China, even the cadres of the same official rank had different before-retirement salary levels in different periods of time. In other words, the later a person retired, the higher before-retirement salary level he or she had. This therefore led to such a consequence: the generation who had made contributions to the reform and opening-up and the economic development failed to enjoy corresponding achievements. Secondly, the subsidies for in-service employees were increasing but were not regarded as the base number in the calculation of the retirement pension. Therefore, even if the nominal substitution rate of the retirement pension in China reached up to 90% or even 100%, the actual substitution rate was often below 50%. In contrast, western countries often had a higher actual substitution rate than that of China, even if their substitution rate was only about 60%.

D. *Imbalance between retired cadres and ordinary retirees*

There is only the retirement system for old people in foreign countries. In China, however, there are two different institutional arrangements for ordinary retirees and retired cadres; that is, people who began to work before October 1, 1949, are treated as retired cadres, while people who began to work afterwards are treated as ordinary retirees. Such institutional arrangements may give greater care to people who began to work before the People's Republic of China was founded, and have

150 *Vertical imbalance in income distribution*

certain positive significance; but they have also brought the vertical imbalance of income and economic benefits between retired cadres and ordinary retirees. The most prominent imbalance is the imbalance between people who began to work during the war to resist US aggression and aid Korea and people who began to work before October 1, 1949. I saw such examples in a survey conducted in a state-owned enterprise in 2002: Some cadres made contributions with their blood in the war to resist US aggression and aid Korea, but they were not allowed to stay in hospital when they were ill as their reimbursement amount was too low. Those retired cadres who began to work just about one year before, however, might stay in hospital and enjoy free medical care.

E. Intergenerational imbalance caused by rapid change of house prices

Houses are the stock as property, and the flow as income. The stock and the flow interact with each other. The imbalance of stock distribution will definitely aggravate the imbalance of flow distribution. House prices have soared since 2005, resulting in the serious inter-generational imbalance in income and property distribution. As some scholars have pointed out, actually people in China have been divided into two major groups: people aged over 35 and people aged under 35 as the result of the rapid changes of house prices. People aged over 35 either already obtained the welfare-oriented houses, or bought houses when they got married at the age of about 30. However, people aged under 35 failed to catch up with the welfare-oriented public housing distribution due to their age, but the house prices rose by several times when they got married and wanted to buy houses, which made them powerless and frustrated. Obviously, the soaring house prices in recent years have resulted in an unfavorable distribution pattern to the generation who were born after the middle 1970s.

The preceding items listed are just some cases of the vertical imbalance in income distribution. Speaking of the vertical imbalance, the issue exists not only in China, but also in foreign countries.

The studies concerning the vertical imbalance in foreign countries focus on the social welfare fields, such as old-age care, medical treatment and education. For example, with regard to old-age security, if laborers of the younger generation pay heavy taxes to aid those retired people who get the public pension, and perhaps can never get the compensation which is equivalent to what they pay, then the inter-generational imbalance problem between payment and compensation will emerge. For another example, medical services are often offered for a certain special stage of a person's life cycle. Most medical services are used in the early stage and terminal stage of a person's life cycle, especially in the terminal stage. As a result, there is separation between the providers (bearers) and receivers of medical services, and the inter-generational imbalance emerges. Education services are mainly offered to the younger generation, which also have the inter-generational problem. Therefore, the inter-generational problem has become an important perspective in the study of income distribution. Some scholars in foreign countries

Vertical imbalance in income distribution 151

propose that attention should be paid to inter-generational harmony. I believe that so-called inter-generational harmony does not mean opposing inter-generational mutual aid. With human civilization evolving to where it is today, inter-generational mutual aid in each field, including the inter-generational mutual aid in income distribution, is absolutely necessary. The point is to properly control the degree, so that inter-generational mutual aid will not turn into an inter-generational imbalance. Certainly, it is not easy to control such degree. It is said that President Eisenhower of the United States, while in office, raised funds by issuing national debts to build interstate expressways. At the end of his presidency, he on the one hand felt proud to have supported the construction of the interstate highway system; on the other hand, however, he felt sorry about the national debts he had left. Obviously, President Eisenhower was also puzzled about how to find a balance between "proud" and "sorry" and between "benefiting future generations" and "getting benefits from future generations".

If we say that the inter-generational imbalance in foreign countries is mainly manifested in the public service domain, then the inter-generational imbalance in China is manifested more extensively, which results from China's special development background and policy background. Now let's analyze the cause of the vertical imbalance, or inter-generational imbalance, in income distribution under the special background in China.

III. Analysis of cause of vertical imbalance of income distribution

A. *Radical changes during development*

The aforementioned vertical imbalance, to a great extent, is caused by the radical changes during development. The 20-year-long basic freezing of salaries is apparently associated with historical reasons. Obviously, the economic difficulties are the root causes for the distorted income distribution relations resulting from the basic freezing of salaries.

The soaring house prices apparently reflect the economic development imbalance in the price fluctuations. It is impossible for the economic development to be a straight line, but how to prevent drastic fluctuations, namely the so-called radical changes, is still an issue worth studying. The above inter-generational imbalance in income distribution and property distribution resulting from the soaring house prices is just at the primary level in the causation chain, namely the relation between distribution imbalance and house prices. The deeper level in this chain is, why do house prices soar? People would say that there are many reasons. One such reason is undeniably the too-high land grant cost. However, such a high land grant cost is inseparable from the land finance of the local government. Therefore, some international experts believe that China's local governments rely too much on land grant and regard it as the income sources, which deprive residents of their income from land assets in the future, and hold that this is a "time bomb" which should be defused as soon as possible. If this remark is advisable, then another

152 *Vertical imbalance in income distribution*

problem of inter-generational imbalance emerges, as today's land finance deprives the next generation of income. In terms of housing alone, we have been faced with the problem of double inter-generational imbalance. How should we untie the knot of double inter-generational imbalance? It seems that we should have not only the strategic insight but also the tactical measures.

B.   *Continuity and coordination during policy evolution*

People often say that various reform measures and policies should support each other. In English, the words "consistent" and "harmonious" are often used to express this concept. However, people often look at such harmony from a horizontal perspective. In fact, such harmony between policies and measures are manifested not only horizontally but also vertically. Specifically, it means that policy development and changes should be consistent to some extent. Apparently, there is the lack of vertical harmony and consistency between the salary reform in 1985, the previous salary reform (the salary reform in 1956 created the basic framework of the salary system before the reform and opening-up) and the subsequent salary reform (the salary reform in 2006). Whether the salary formation mechanism should continue to follow that of the planning system or be transformed into one that is based on the market mechanism is indeed a system reform issue (special attention should be paid to labor flows and whether the labor market is created). However, some issues concerning salary grading, such as whether professors' salary should be divided into four grades, has nothing to do with planning or market, not to mention socialism or capitalism. In the system reform, there is no need to make such frequent changes on such purely technical issues.

The housing reform also concerns policy consistency. As is known to all, under the guidance of Deng Xiaoping's Southern Tour speech and the 14th National Congress of the Communist Party of China, there was a great upsurge in further promotion of the market-oriented reform in China in the 1990s. However, some oversimplified thinking and policies emerged in the reform, probably due to the lack of deep understanding of the different roles played by the market and government in the market economy. For example, such a slogan at that time goes: "Seek solutions from the market instead of the mayor if you have any problems." In the policy practice, some quasi-public products (such as education, medical treatment, houses for low-income earners) that should not have been launched into the market were excessively launched into the market. Therefore, insufficient marketization (those that should be marketized were not marketized) and excessive marketization (those that should not be marketized were launched into the market) coexisted in society. It can be said that the policy of excessive marketization was implemented in the housing reform in the 1990s. When we further understood the nature of these quasi-public products in the 21st century, we had to turn around for the further development of security housing.

The imbalance between retired cadres and ordinary retirees does not involve policy consistency, but involves the "rigid uniformity" problem of the policy. Differentiating different groups by when they began to work is an easy and quick way,

Vertical imbalance in income distribution   153

but it will lead to the disadvantage of "rigid uniformity". It seems that this policy should be adjusted based on the actual situations during implementation, so as to dilute such inter-generational imbalance.

C. *Multi-player game among different interest groups during the decision-making process*

The multi-player game must be available during the decision-making process, so that the interests of all parties concerned can be relatively balanced in the game, and that excessive interest to a certain one or some groups, which impair the interests of other groups, can be avoided. As mentioned earlier, the policy on the long-term basic freezing of salaries is certainly closely related to the economic difficulty resulting from the radical changes of economic development, but the choice of policies before the economic difficulty is associated with the availability of the game among different interest groups during the decision-making process. From the perspective of summing up experience and lessons, the choice of the freezing policy in those years is apparently associated with the fact that the vulnerable groups had no right to participate in the game. The policy, which was chosen by the vested interest groups unilaterally, could only be favorable to such vested interest groups. As a result, the economic losses resulting from the economic difficulty was mainly borne by the younger generation. We must learn from experience and lessons, and listen to the opinions of different interest groups, especially the opinions of the vulnerable groups, in the decision-making concerning the reform of income distribution in the future, and encourage the multi-player game among different interest groups. Only in this way can we realize the balance of interests among all parties concerned, and avoid the imbalance of interests, including the vertical or inter-generational imbalance.

(Originally published in *Exploration and Free Views*, Issue 5, 2012.)

Note

1 This paper regards the horizontal imbalance and horizontal inequality as synonyms, and the vertical imbalance and vertical inequality as synonyms. The vertical imbalance in this paper refers to the inter-generational imbalance.

Index

absoluteness of distribution according to work 1–2, 3–4
age, and income determination 50–51
agricultural sector 30; development 81
assets 104, 105

benefits 21
Brus, W. 138
bus drivers, income 20

calculation methods: basic production assets 129–130, 131; consumer durables 131; debts 129–130, 131; financial assets 129–130, 131; house property 130–131; house property value 129; land value 129
capitalist countries, Gini coefficient 6
challenges of China's economic reform 138–140
characteristics: of China before the reform 90–92; of income distribution before reform 67–68, 69, 70; of planned economies 101
China: agricultural sector 30; challenges of gradual reform 138–140; "Cultural Revolution" xii; development 67; economic reform 24, 25, 39, 67; "gang of four" xii; home phones 13, 15; household registration system 30, 34–35; housing 14–15; income distribution before the reform 67, 68, 69, 70; income gap 3–4; industry sector 30; insider control 84; inter-regional income gap 43; intra-provincial income distribution 43; land management reform 124; legacy left by the planned economy 90–92; macroeconomic policies 126–127; medical services 150; modernization 140; normal order 101–102; old system

138–139; outlook at the turn of the century 95–98; political reform 139, 144; property ownership 137–138, 142, 144; redistribution policy 125, 126, 144–145; well-being of society in 104, 136; *see also* economic reform; political reform; report of the 17th National Congress of the Communist Party of China
commodities: inflation 21; pricing 22
consumer goods distribution 91–92; commodity-money relationship 13; free supply based on position 12–13, 14–15; rationing based on head count 12; shortages 15
converse-u hypothesis 7, 50–51, 63, 64, 81, 92
"Cultural Revolution" xii

Davies, J. B. 121
debts, calculating 129–130, 131
decline of the middle class 97–98
Deng, X. 101, 152
departmental monopoly 84
development 41, 43, 67, 81, 87, 96–97; economic policies and their changes 84–86; inter-regional and intra-regional income gap 58, 59–60; multi-variate regression analysis of income determination in rural areas 53–55; and rural income distribution 51–52; and vertical imbalance 151–152
disorderly change 20, 22, 84
disparities in income distribution, causes of: disorderly change 20; double systems 19; inflation 21; opportunity inequality 19–20; solutions 21–23
distribution according to needs 4–5
distribution according to work xvi, 1, 4–5, 13; and equalitarianism 18; trends

Index   155

in income by age group 8, 9, 10–11;
  see also distribution according to needs
distribution in kind 70, 91
dual economy 19, 25, 83; and income
  inequality 94; unplanned system
  25, 26

economic laws 2; retrogression 101
economic policies and their changes
  84–86
economic reform 39, 40, 41, 86–87,
  90, 104, 144; challenges 138–140;
  characteristics of income distribution
  before 67–68, 69, 70; deepening 144;
  disorderly change 20, 84; and double
  systems 83; economic policies and
  their changes 84–86; housing 134–
  135; impact in rural areas 110–111;
  incentives 96, 135; income distribution
  after 81, 92–93; and insider control 84;
  market economy 101; policy inertia 96;
  and progress 101–102, 103; resident
  income distribution after 70–71; and risk
  of rising costs xiv–xv; "shock therapy"
  138; *see also* political reform
education 59–60, 150–151; developing
  excellence in xx–xxii; developing
  the science of economics xxii–
  xxiv; "income misplacement
  between intellectual and manual
  workers" hypothesis 46–47; policy
  recommendations 97, 126
entrepreneurs, high-income earners and
  rent-seeking 79, 80, 81
equalitarianism 17, 18, 20, 24, 71, 91;
  among small producers 4–5; and the
  double systems 94; and the income gap
  25; "new" 18; before the reform 68,
  69; and salary freezing 92; in Taiwan
  81; in taxes 99; *see also* disparities in
  income distribution, causes of; income
  distribution
extra-salary income, in urban areas 35, 36,
  37, 39

fairness 69, 91
Fan, C. 98
financial assets 125, 137; calculating
  129–130, 131; inequality of distribution
  95; in rural areas 106; in urban areas
  114, 116, 117, 118
free supply, based on position 12–13,
  14–15

Galbraith, J. K. 97
"gang of four" xii
Gini coefficient 5–6, 7, 18, 23n1, 26, 32,
  33; measuring inequality 86
gradual reform, challenges of 138–140
gross property, in rural areas 106

high-income earners 49–50, 75, 93; and
  rent-seeking activities 79, 80–81;
  taxation 99
home phones 13, 15
horizontal inequality 146, 147
house property value, calculating 129,
  130–131
household registration system 30, 34–35,
  69
housing 14–15, 105, 106; commercialization
  77, 78; double-track price differences 95,
  135; inequality of distribution 134–135;
  property income gap 76, 77, 78; public
  77, 83, 84; reform 83, 95; rent-seeking
  135; rent-setting 135; subsidies 84, 95

income 15; and property 136, 143;
  report of the 17th National Congress
  of the Communist Party of China on
  142–143
income distribution 3–4, 17, 42, 104, 133,
  147; after the reform 70–71, 81, 92–93;
  and age 50–51; benefits 21; causes of
  disparities in 18–21; characteristics
  of before the reform 67–68, 69, 70;
  converse-u hypothesis 7, 63, 64; during
  development 51–52; and the double
  systems 94; economic policies and their
  changes 84–86; equalitarianism 17–18;
  extra-salary income in urban areas 35,
  36, 37, 39; gap between rural and urban
  areas, measuring 134; Gini coefficient
  18; high-income earners 49–50;
  horizontal inequality 146; and housing
  distribution 134–135; imbalance
  between in-service employees and
  retirees 148–149; inequality between
  private and state-owned enterprise
  employees 45–46; intergenerational
  income inequality 147–148; inter-
  regional 43; intra-provincial 62–65;
  materialization 22; micro aspects
  64; outlook at the turn of the century
  95–98; in the planned system 26, 27;
  poverty 57–58; Project Team survey on
  24–25, 26, 27, 28, 29–30; and property

156 *Index*

distribution 136; recommendations for improving 86–88; redistribution policy 125, 144–145; "small-big-small" trend 5; solutions for disparities in 21–23; trends 4–8; trends by age group 8, 9, 10–11; in the unplanned system 25, 26; between urban and rural areas 24, 30, 31–32, 33, 34–35, 69, 72, 74, 75, 91; urban areas, internal income gaps in sectors of different ownership 45–46; wealth 104–105; *see also* disparities in income distribution, causes of; resident income distribution; unfair income distribution

income gap: causes of xvii–xix; measuring nationwide 133–134; preventing 143–145

"income misplacement between intellectual and manual workers" hypothesis 46–47

"incremental reform" 138–139

industrialization 85

industry sector 30; policy recommendations 127

inequality: after the reform, reasons for 91–92; horizontal 146, 147; measuring 86; policy factor 97–98; in urban housing 113, 114

inflation 21, 22

insider control 84

intellectual workers, income gap with manual workers 46–47

interest groups 153

interest tax 99

intergenerational income inequality 147–148

inter-provincial income gap: in rural areas 60–61; in urban areas 61–62

inter-regional income gap 43, 59–60, 93; controversial issues 75, 76

intra-provincial income distribution 43, 62–65

Ishikawa, S. 101

joint ventures 17

Kornai, J. 13

Kuznets, S. 7, 63, 92

labor flow policy recommendations 126–127

land management reform 124

land property 76; income gap 77, 78

land value: calculating 129; in rural areas 106

law of distribution according to work 2

law of value 2

"leftism" 9

legacy left by the planned economy 90–92

Li, Shi xvii, 65, 132

Li, Siqin 70

Liu, G. "On the Relationship between Planning and Market in the Socialist Economy" xiii

loading capacity 10–11

Lorenz curve 5–6, 7

macroeconomic policies 126–127

manual workers, income gap with intellectual workers 46–47

market economy 13, 19–20, 100–101, 101; leveraging the functions of xv–xvi

materialization 22, 25

material supply 19

measuring: income gap between rural and urban areas 134; inequality 86; nationwide income gap 133–134

middle class, decline of 97–98

middle-aged laborers, salary 9

modernization 96–97, 140; in rural areas 106

monopolistic behavior 84

multi-player game 153

multi-variate regression analysis of income determination, in rural areas 53–55

national residents: national per capita property 132; property distribution 119, 120, 121, 122, 123, 124, 136–137

New Economic Policy 102

"new equalitarianism" 18

nonresidential debts 106; in rural areas 107

normal order 101–102

opportunities, inequality in 19–20, 22–23

over-expenditure families 12

peasants: analysis of property distribution 55, 56; multi-variate regression analysis of income determination 53–55; per capita income 55; sources of income 52, 53; subsidies 91

personal income tax 87

physical allocation 12; *see also* rationing

planned economy xiv, 26, 27, 100–101; income gap with unplanned system

27–28, 29–30; and the normal order
101–102; production 19, 24, 25; in the
Soviet Union 102, 103; *see also* market
economy; unplanned system
policies 87; continuity and coordination
during evolution 152–153; interest
groups 153; macroeconomic
126–127; recommendations 96–98;
recommendations for the industrial
sector 127; "retro regulation" 97;
taxation 97
political reform 139, 144
poverty 66n12, 69, 80; in rural areas 57–58
power-for-money deals 139
price fixing 14
private enterprises 17, 20, 22, 26;
comparing employee income gap
with state-owned enterprises 45–46;
high-income earners and rent-seeking
79, 80, 81; *see also* state-owned
enterprises
production assets, calculating 129–130
progressive income tax 87, 126
Project Team survey on income
distribution 24–25, 26, 27, 28, 29–30,
41, 67, 71, 80, 85, 93, 95, 105, 134, 136,
140, 144
property, and income 136, 143
property distribution 104, 135–138,
147; house property 105, 106; and
income distribution 136; of national
residents 119, 120, 121, 122, 123, 124;
nonresidential debts 106; in rural areas
55, 56, 105, 106, 107, 108, 109, 110,
111; in urban areas 111, 112, 113, 114,
115, 116, 117, 118; wealth 104
property income gap 76, 77, 78, 93, 95
proportional tax system 99, 100
pseudo-Gini coefficient 42, 48, 49, 65n4
public housing 83, 84
public ownership 90

rationing 14; based on head count 12
reassessing the function of subsidies
47–48, 49
recommendations: for education policy
126; for improving the income
distribution status 86–88; for labor flow
policy 126–127; for policy design 96–98
reform *see* economic reform
regression analysis, of income
determination in rural areas 53–55
regressive taxation 99

relativity of distribution according to work
1–2, 3–4
remuneration 2, 3; benefits 21; extra-salary
income 35, 36, 37, 39; salary freezing
9, 10; trends in income by age group
8, 9, 10–11; trends in the income gap
between laborers 4–8
rent-seeking 29, 49–50, 65n8, 93, 95, 96,
135; and high-income earners 79, 80, 81
rent-setting 95, 113, 124, 135, 139
rent subsidies 13
report of the 17th National Congress of
the Communist Party of China 141; on
the importance of income and property
143; on preventing an excessive
property and income gap 143–145; and
property income 142–143; and property
ownership 141–142
resident income distribution 24, 41, 43,
64–65, 67, 90; after the reform 70–71;
inter-regional 75, 76; inter-regional
income gap 59–60; and poverty 57–58;
reassessing the function of subsidies 47–
48, 49; recommendations for improving
86–88; urban areas 43, 44, 45
retirees, income distribution among
149–150
"retro regulation" policies 97
"reverse redistribution" 125, 145
rural areas: concentration ratio of
basic production assets 109–110;
concentration ratio of land 109;
development 81, 96–97; distribution
of consumer durables 110; economic
policies and their changes 84–86;
financial assets 106, 125; gross property
106; gross property distribution
107; impact of economic reform in
110–111; income distribution 18;
income distribution during development
51–52; income distribution inequality
in 42–43; income gap with urban
areas 24, 30, 31–32, 33, 34–35, 42,
59–60, 69, 72, 74, 75, 91, 94; income
gap with urban areas, measuring 134;
increased income in 32; inter-provincial
income gap 60–61; inter-regional
income gap 93; land property 106; land
value 106; modernization 106; multi-
variate regression analysis of income
determination 53–55; nonresidential
debts 107; over-expenditure families
12; per capita income 32; poverty

158 *Index*

57–58; property distribution 55, 56, 105, 106, 107, 108, 109, 110, 111; property income gap 76, 77, 78; reassessing the function of subsidies 47–48, 49; sources of income 52, 53; tax collection 125

Sachs, J. 138
salary: and benefits 21; imbalance between in-service employees and retirees 148–149; imbalance within retirees 149; "income misplacement between intellectual and manual workers" hypothesis 46–47; of middle-aged laborers 9; reform 20; in rural areas 54; and seniority 51; and vertical imbalance 147–148
salary freezing 9, 10, 70, 92
Shorrocks, A. F. 121
shortages 15
skewness 3
"small-big-small" trend 4, 5
socialism 90–91, 141–142
socialist countries, Gini coefficient 7–8
social security 87; policy recommendations 97
sources of income, in rural areas 52, 53
Soviet Union: New Economic Policy 102; planned economy 102, 103; "shock therapy" 138
state-owned enterprises 20, 22; comparing employee income gap with private enterprises 45–46
Stiglitz, J. 126; *Economics* 99
stockpiling 15
subsidies 13, 20, 57, 85, 91; distribution in kind 70; housing 84, 95; reassessing the function of 47–48, 49
Sun, Y. xii, xxii

Taiwan, equalitarianism in 81
taxation 22, 87, 99, 125; "no progress means retrogression" 99, 100; policy recommendations 97; proportional 99, 100; redistribution policy 125, 126, 144–145; regressive 99
taxi drivers, income 17, 18, 20
teachers 100; benefits 21–22; income gap between 18; "income misplacement between intellectual and manual workers" hypothesis 46–47
trade monopoly 84
trends: of commodity approach in consumer goods distribution 12–13,

14–15; in the income gap between laborers 4–8; in laborers' income by age group 8, 9, 10–11; "small-big-small" 4, 5; widening of the income gap 71, 72

unfair income distribution 24, 25
universities, "income misplacement between intellectual and manual workers" hypothesis 46–47
unplanned production 19, 24, 25, 26
unplanned system 25, 26; income gap with planned system 27–28, 29–30
urban areas: composition and distribution of income of residents 43, 44, 45; concentration ratio of consumer durables 116; concentration ratio of financial assets 115–116; economic policies and their changes 84–86; financial assets 114, 117, 118, 125; high-income earners 49–50, 75; house property 111, 116; housing reform 124; income distribution inequality in 42; income gap with rural areas 24, 30, 31–32, 33, 34–35, 42, 59–60, 69, 72, 74, 75, 91, 94; income gap with rural areas, measuring 134; inequalities in production assets 114; internal income gaps in sectors of different ownership 45–46; inter-provincial income gap 61–62; inter-regional income gap 59–60, 93; nonresidential debts 114, 115; per capita debts 118; per capita income 32; per capita total property 111, 116; property composition 112; property distribution in 111, 112, 113, 114, 115, 116, 117, 118; property income gap 76, 77, 78; reassessing the function of subsidies 47–48, 49; rent-setting 113; salary and extra-salary income 35, 36, 37, 39; tax collection 125; unequal distribution of house property 113, 114
Urban Social-economic Survey Task Force (USSTF) 105

vertical inequality 99; continuity and coordination during policy evolution 152–153; and development 151–152; imbalance between in-service employees and retirees 148–149; imbalance between retired cadres and ordinary retirees 149–150; imbalance within retirees 149; intergenerational imbalance caused by house prices 150–151; and the multi-player game 153; from salary freezing 147–148

Wang, L. 113
Wang, Y. 4
waste 15; and China's old system 138–139
wealth 104, 105; distribution of xix–xx
Wei, Z. 113
welfare 87, 91, 150–151; policy recommendations 97
well-being of China's population 104, 136
widening of the income gap 71, 72, 93, 94, 96

World Bank 25, 30, 65n2, 80, 91, 125, 137; report following China's inspection 141–142
World Trade Organization (WTO) 94

Xue, M. 36, 102
Xue, X. 102
Xuezeng, Z. 6

Yang, X. 6

Zhao, R. 132; "A Number of Variation Trends in Personal Income Distribution of Laborers" xvi–xvii; "On the Relationship between Planning and Market in the Socialist Economy" xiii

Taylor & Francis eBooks

www.taylorfrancis.com

A single destination for eBooks from Taylor & Francis with increased functionality and an improved user experience to meet the needs of our customers.

90,000+ eBooks of award-winning academic content in Humanities, Social Science, Science, Technology, Engineering, and Medical written by a global network of editors and authors.

TAYLOR & FRANCIS EBOOKS OFFERS:

- A streamlined experience for our library customers
- A single point of discovery for all of our eBook content
- Improved search and discovery of content at both book and chapter level

REQUEST A FREE TRIAL
support@taylorfrancis.com